# Good Kids, Bad City

# Good Kids, Bad City

A STORY OF RACE AND
WRONGFUL CONVICTION IN AMERICA

KYLE SWENSON

PICADOR  NEW YORK

picadorusa.com • instagram.com/picador
twitter.com/picadorusa • facebook.com/picadorusa

Picador® is a U.S. registered trademark and is used by Macmillan Publishing Group, LLC, under license from Pan Books Limited.

For book club information, please visit facebook.com/picadorbookclub or email marketing@picadorusa.com.

Library of Congress Cataloging-in-Publication Data

Names: Swenson, Kyle, author.
Title: Good kids, bad city : a story of race and wrongful conviction in America / Kyle Swenson.
Description: New York : Picador, 2019.
Identifiers: LCCN 2018022982 | ISBN 9781250120236 (hardcover) | ISBN 9781250120243 (ebook)
Subjects: LCSH: Ajamu, Kwame—Trials, litigation, etc. | Jackson, Ricky, 1957—Trials, litigation, etc. | Bridgeman, Wiley—Trials, litigation, etc. | Trials (Murder)—Ohio—Cleveland. | Judicial error—Ohio.
Classification: LCC KF224.A38 S94 2019 | DDC 345.771/02523—dc23
LC record available at https://lccn.loc.gov/2018022982

Our books may be purchased in bulk for promotional, educational, or business use. Please contact your local bookseller or the Macmillan Corporate and Premium Sales Department at 1-800-221-7945, extension 5442, or by email at MacmillanSpecialMarkets@macmillan.com.

First Edition: February 2019

10  9  8  7  6  5  4  3  2  1

To Kim

Seem like the whole city go against me

—KENDRICK LAMAR, "M.A.A.D CITY"

To know a place, like a friend or lover, is for it to become familiar; to know it better is for it to become strange again. Not novel in the easy way of the new, but strange in a deep, disturbing way that does not dissipate, an unsettling revelation of what should have always been known, a revelation that implicates its belated discoverers.

—REBECCA SOLNIT, *SAVAGE DREAMS*

# Contents

# Author's Note

Rickey, Wiley, and Kwame were incarcerated for a total of 106 years, one of the longest wrongful imprisonment cases—if not the longest—in American history. Many carry the blame for that injustice. And many were integral in righting that wrong. At certain points over four decades, people made choices and took actions that would lead to the exonerations. Carrie Wood decided to keep Rickey Jackson's OIP file open. Anthony Singleton asked Ed Vernon a hard question in a hospital room. Terry Gilbert sent me an email. Each of us carried the ball down the field as far as we could. Passing the finish line was a collective effort. This book aims to string those moments and contributions together.

This is a work of nonfiction. The book is based on hours of interviews with Rickey, Wiley, Kwame, and other subjects. Scenes, dialogue, and interior thoughts attributed to subjects were all mined from these interviews, as well as cross referenced with accounts from other sources.

When possible, these accounts were backed up by documentation. The paper trail on this case is significant; the original court transcripts, crime scene photos, police files, prison records, psychological reports, and depositions from civil litigation all helped fill in the picture. My own reporting notes and recordings from 2011 and 2014 were also key.

In instances where police misconduct is alleged, the accounts are pulled from legal documents, depositions, and interviews.

A number of sources were critical in forming the historical accounts in this book, as well as some of the legal theory sitting behind the narrative. Few texts do a better job of sketching the city's backstory than Kenneth Kusmer's *A Ghetto Takes Shape: Black Cleveland, 1870–1930*. Elizabeth Hinton's *From the War on Poverty to the War on Crime: The Making of Mass Incarceration in America* deeply shaped my understanding of the federal government's impact in black urban areas. My thoughts on the legal system were heavily influenced by William J. Stuntz and James Q. Whitman. Jane Leovy's essential *Ghettoside* completely rearranged how I thought about the mechanics of the American law and order. Robert J. Norris's recent history of the Innocence Movement, *Exonerated*, was also essential.

# Prologue
# BUSTED PAVEMENT

*START IN CLOSE WITH THE PAVEMENT. THIS IS A CLEVELAND STORY,* so there will be some abused infrastructure in the mix. Asphalt chopped and diced by winters past, roadways split like bad fruit—eyesore miles in all directions. There are places in the city where winter and neglect and budget priorities have knifed open the street, revealing the old brick or cobblestones below, history riding under the modern routes. In Cleveland—and in a Cleveland story—the past is always near and persistent.

This particular no-account chunk of municipal pour was just a bent elbow of sidewalk on the city's eastern lip. Midmorning traffic floated by steadily, spinning off the streets to the north coiling around University Circle, a prim collection of hospitals, college greens, and museums. The money there—the new money reaching up in abstract glass medical buildings, the old money anchored in beaux arts marble and stone—was a one-eighty contrast from the surrounding neighborhoods, among the poorest in the country. The drivers slinging past us like pinballs in the chute likely had stopped paying attention to the blight long ago. I had. I'd probably driven past this street corner hundreds of times without ever eyeballing the spot where we were now standing.

We were an odd pair, a mixed-race Laurel and Hardy with twenty-odd years stacked between us. Me: skinny, twenty-five, white, shivering in a parka, fingers wrapped around a spiral notebook, sneakers knocking rocks into the gutter. Kwame: fifty-four, black, athletically built from head to toe, meaty hands stuffed into his hoodie pocket. He usually gave off a friendly vibe, his cheeks tending to wander up his face into a half smile. But today his mouth was a tight nervous dash, his eyes clocking the surrounding street.

Perhaps he was placing his memories up against what he was seeing now. Weeds and grass where the Cut-Rate store had once stood. A quiet mosque in place of the flower shop. What had once been a tight line of two-story houses filling the streets to the south now was a battered run of gutted lots. Even the name of the thoroughfare pouring traffic into the nearby suburbs had changed in the last thirty years— no longer Fairhill Boulevard, now Carl Stokes Boulevard.

If he couldn't place the old neighborhood, the old neighborhood probably couldn't place him. The last time he'd stood on this pavement, he'd been seventeen, his name had been Ronnie Bridgeman, and he was on his way to catching a murder charge.

It was now March. This was the overcast time of the year in Northeast Ohio when the days look like they've been rubbed over with charcoal. After a few minutes of silence, Kwame nodded north to a stoplight where another street, Cedar Avenue, crossed Stokes. "The bus will be coming from there."

In 1975, a white man was robbed and gunned down outside the Cut-Rate store where we now stood. Kwame was arrested, tried, and convicted of the crime. His older brother, Wiley, and best friend, Rickey Jackson, were also found guilty. No physical evidence tied the three young black men to the killing. The prosecution's only witness was a twelve-year-old neighborhood kid named Ed Vernon. The boy testified that he'd seen the three commit the homicide. On this alone, they were sentenced to death, only missing the electric chair thanks to a U.S. Supreme Court ruling. Kwame was paroled in 2003. At the time we were standing together, his brother and best friend were still locked away, all due to lies.

"We weren't guilty," Kwame had explained to me six weeks earlier, when we first met. "My mother, who was very religious, told me, 'Trouble is easy to get into but hard to get out of, but if you're not guilty of anything, the truth will set you free.' But that won't work in politics and the law."

This was not something Kwame had broadcast loudly since his release. He only trusted me now because he wanted help. As a reporter for a local weekly paper, I'd agreed to dig around his case. Yet as we stood on the corner, I wasn't sure whether or not I believed him. I'd only been a journalist for three years, but I already knew belief was tricky terrain in journalism. From white-lie shading to outright prevarications, reporting, I learned early, largely involves unknotting bullshit.

There was also the drawer. Back at my desk downtown at the newspaper, my cubicle's left bottom drawer was filled with letters. The metal space was overflowing on my first day of work, and I imagine every newsroom in the world has a similar dumping ground. Some were written on prison library typewriters, others in careful, neat lettering, many in kindergarten-blackboard scrawls. They all told the same story: *I didn't do it. I'm innocent.* These jailhouse pleas were often trapdoors: you read one, fall into the case, spend untold hours reporting out the nooks and crannies of what happened, only to find, well, the guy *was* in the house that night robbing the place when the old lady was murdered; or, hey, even though she *says* she didn't shoot him, she *did* get arrested with his drugs. It's easy to say guilt and innocence are rarely black and white; it's harder to reconcile, both professionally and personally. "Nobody," a journalist friend once said to me, "is completely innocent." That cynicism was taking root in me: Some complicity must tie most offenders to their convictions, I reasoned; the criminal justice system had the proper safety nets installed to catch the truly innocent. So the letters piled up.

It turns out experts on wrongful conviction have the same problem. Despite the legal organizations devoted to the issue, hard numbers on innocent men and women in prison remain difficult to come by. We can pin down actual exonerations—by 2011 the National Registry of Exonerations counted nearly nine hundred.[1] But this tally only started in 1989. What about cases experts have missed? Have we missed them? One team has estimated that as many as two thousand to four thousand wrongful conviction cases slip into the legal system each year. Another theory puts the number of innocent inmates between 1 and 5 percent of all convictions.[2] What frustrates a determination of the size of the actual problem is the avalanche of frivolous claims—those stuffed drawers at the newsroom. One legal expert has written that finding a truly innocent inmate is like looking for a "meritorious needle in the meritless haystack."[3]

Kwame, however, didn't remind me of those letter writers. He had a booming voice, keyed in a bebop mix of prison-yard slang, legal-speak, and touches of Arabic. He radiated calm, wisdom, and a been-there, seen-it-all attitude. He delivered his story simply, not with the heat of someone desperate to convince me but as if he was just relating the facts of his case. This, his calm delivery seemed to say, was just how it all went down.

"At seventeen, I didn't know a whole lot about nothing, let alone the law," Kwame told me. "There was no DNA or evidence. It was all who said what, and how strong who said what could be supported. But there were so many things that just didn't jive. Just check out the bus route."

The bus. In court, Ed Vernon, the state's only eyewitness, had laid out a simple story for the jury: On the day of the crime, he'd left his middle school early, catching a city bus home. While the bus was waiting at the light at Cedar, a car pulled up to the driver's side. The boy recognized three older guys from the neighborhood—Ronnie, Wiley, and Rickey. He waved. They waved back. Side by side, the bus and car made the left-hand turn. The boy got out. As he walked up the street, he saw the same young men attack the victim.

As I was replaying that testimony in my head, standing on that very same street corner, I spotted a city bus, its sides graffitied with streaks of road salt, huff to a stop at the Cedar light. Left-hand turn signals blinked. Kwame swung around to make sure I was watching, the air between us foggy with frozen breath. The bus swung left and drove off. Despite the traffic piled up behind the bus to make a similar turn, nobody moved alongside the bus. There was only one turn lane. If a car had been riding close to the bus, it would have banged into the curb.

"Edward Vernon said that he saw us in the car while we were turning," Kwame said, his voice jumping with excitement. "But you can't make that turn at the same time."

What the witness had described was physically impossible, I realized. "And if you're going to commit a crime," Kwame said, "what the hell are you doing waving at somebody on the street for?"

Like loops on an elaborate signature, the Cuyahoga River splits Cleveland and the surrounding suburbs into east and west. It's less a natural divide than a marker for social division—between economic status, ethnicity, and race. Much of your life in this city is rooted in where your days play out in relation to this zigzagging waterway garlanded overhead with elegant steel bridges and navigated by barges and container ships off the Great Lakes. They say even your accent—whether you murder your vowels with the sharp end of that characteristic midwestern nasal or not—depends on whether you're an East or West Sider.

Public Square is the middle ground, the original municipal center plotted by the town founders in 1796. Stand here and you see all the downtown architectural touchstones: the Old Stone Church; the Civil War Memorial; and, shadowing the green space, the city's most iconic building, Terminal Tower, fifty-two stories of Jazz Age elegance that until 1964 held the bragging rights as the tallest building in North America outside New York City. Turn west, toward the river, and you're facing white working-class neighborhoods—Tremont, Ohio City, West Park, the Detroit Shoreway, Old Brooklyn. Swing east, and you're looking at a long run of African American areas—Central, Hough,

Fairfax, or "down the way," in the local-speak. These black neighborhoods run more than a hundred blocks to the eastern edge of the city line, where the terrain itself climbs up to a shelf of land holding some of the most exclusive and wealthy—and white—suburbs in the country: Cleveland Heights, Shaker Heights, University Heights.

The town I knew growing up was hard edged but bighearted. No one would argue it was an easy place to live, and this seemed to stamp resilience onto the natives. The winters were endlessly Siberian. The sports franchises were heartbreaking laughingstocks, bereft of championship trophies since 1964. The river was so choked with toxins, it had burst into flames numerous times. But the circumstances also fed a fierce sense of hometown pride. It might be a mess, but it was ours. Philip Wiley Porter, a longtime Cleveland newspaperman, put it well in 1976: "A comfortable place to live and work, but a great place to complain about," he wrote. "Volatile, emotional, gung-ho for winners, merciless toward losers, torn by the two-bit view point and a suicidal yen toward disunity. . . . Unhappy about the status quo, but sensitive to criticism, and quarrelsome about how to change."[4] Around the same time those words went to press, a T-shirt was popular around town: CLEVELAND: YOU'VE GOT TO BE TOUGH.

But by 2011, Cleveland's civic struggles seemed to be in overdrive. The Cleveland stories were all ugly. We were poster-child postindustrial. The numbers were all bad.

In 2010, Cleveland's population was sitting near 390,000 residents, a significant downgrade from the 478,000 people counted in the city a decade earlier.[5] The poverty rate was the second highest in the country, with 35 percent of Clevelanders below the poverty line—a figure that had increased significantly in just two years.[6] Around half of Cleveland's children were living in poverty.[7] A rising murder count regularly slotted the town in rankings of America's most dangerous cities.[8] In 2010, *Forbes* crowned Cleveland "America's Most Miserable City"; the French government even issued a travel advisory warning citizens to stay clear.[9] And in one final kill shot to our collective pride and ego, LeBron James—NBA supernova and beloved son of Northeast Ohio—exited the Cleveland Cavaliers' organization to splash around the waves in South Beach.

Cleveland wasn't the only city sinking. The 2008 Great Recession seemed to kick off a parade of grim forecasts for similar heartland metros, places that had apparently spent all their capitalistic mojo in the first giddy-up decades of the last century and now were struggling to segue to the next. Milwaukee, Flint, Toledo, Youngstown, Erie, Buffalo—the familiar steel, iron, and auto hubs that hang from the Great Lakes like a necklace. But you could argue that Cleveland's case was worse because we'd lost the most. In 1950, Cleveland was the seventh-largest city in the country, widely known for its booster motto as "the best location in the nation." The only city that had suffered a comparable fall was Detroit, regularly put in the spotlight by the national media as the main crash site of American industry. But behind the doomsday headlines on Motor City, Detroit was celebrated as a test lab for any and all long-shot ideas about the future of American urban spaces. No such optimism framed Cleveland's deepening woe.

As 2010 rolled into 2011, in Cleveland we weren't really sure whether we'd hit the bottom or were still in free fall. It could get worse. The only fact we had was that the basic mechanics of the civic apparatus seemed completely busted. The city had stopped working. Urban melodrama here bounced between slapstick and operatic tragedy.

Consider local politics. In 2008, the FBI launched a massive public corruption probe on the government of Cuyahoga County, the region including Cleveland. The main target of the investigation was a former sanitation worker turned county commissioner named Jimmy Dimora. Three-hundred-plus pounds stuffed in cheap suits and tacky ties, Dimora was the undisputed kingfish of the local Democratic Party. By the time of his arrest in 2010, federal prosecutions had uncovered a vast system of payoffs and bribes. Court documents showed Dimora would trade county business and votes for money, steak dinners, nights with high-end call girls, discounted Rolexes, even a tiki hut for his backyard pool. Phone taps caught Dimora salivating over payoffs or demanding sex from women in return for county gigs.[10]

The investigation turned up hundreds of names: the entire local political elite was implicated, from the county sheriff and state senators to Cleveland's city council president and a future gubernatorial candidate.[11] Such was the scope of the corruption—eventually forty individuals served jail sentences—that it was clear Dimora had not rigged this system himself but merely inherited it. The backroom chutes and ladders of graft and sex were apparently how the city and county had been run for more than thirty years. Reeling in disgust from this, county residents voted to tear the whole damn thing down, passing a referendum ushering in a new style of countywide government based on an elected executive and sixteen-person council.

This political storm also made landfall at the Justice Center downtown. Two judges were eventually charged with steering court decisions based on political favors. It also threatened the reputation of the region's top lawman, Cuyahoga County Prosecutor Bill Mason. Along with Dimora, Mason was the top man in the local party. In fact, Mason openly used his office as a farm system for future Democratic candidates, urging his attorneys and employees to run for office. The countywide scandal singed the office with reports that Mason had ignored complaints of payoffs at the county building years before the FBI hit pay dirt there. While the prosecutor boasted one of the highest felony conviction rates in the state, there was also an apparent indifference to the quality of cases brought to trial. A 2010 investigation by the *Plain Dealer* dug into the numbers, finding the office regularly jammed cases through the system with little merit that were eventually thrown out by a judge mid-trial.

"Almost anyone arrested in Cuyahoga County can be indicted, jailed and taken to trial whether guilty or not because Mason runs the prosecutor's office like a factory," the newspaper wrote.[12] "Prosecutors pump out hundreds of cases for trial every year without always considering their flaws."

Consider the neighborhoods. Cleveland's African Americans who sought bank loans had been historically blackballed; subprime mortgage slingers, however, hit African American neighborhoods hard with their low interest rates and no-money-down paper. When the housing crisis arrived, pink slips started papering over low-income areas of the town. Between 1995 and 2007, foreclosures countywide quadrupled. From 2007 to 2010 alone the county court was catching between thirteen thousand and fifteen thousand foreclosures each year.[13] Besides further hurting a tax base already kneecapped by years of steady suburban flight and factory closures, the crisis turned whole neighborhoods into ghost towns. Officially, the city put the number of vacant addresses at around eight thousand.[14]

Consider the schools. By 2010, the Cleveland Municipal School District was dwelling in the cellar in Ohio, with a 52 percent high school graduation rate. The system—with about forty-five thousand students—was staring at a seventy-four-million-dollar projected budget deficit.[15] But the dirtiest stat attached to the education system was the blatant gulf between its success rate compared to suburban—and largely white—districts. A national study found that only 38 percent of Cleveland's freshmen went on to graduate in four years. In the surrounding districts, on both the East and West Sides, 80 percent of freshman did.[16] The disparity was the largest in the country.

Consider the police. Already operating under a 2002 consent decree with the Department of Justice over excessive-force complaints, by 2011 the Cleveland Police Department—understaffed, underpaid, undertrained—had turned Keystone Kop fumbling into a continuous urban grotesque. In October 2009, police, following up on a report of an attempted rape, discovered a hell house belonging to a fifty-year-old ex-con named Anthony Sowell. The raped and murdered bodies of women were found all over the address on the East Side's Imperial Avenue—in the living room, basement, crawl spaces, shallow graves in the backyard. Sowell was eventually tied to eleven dead women going back to 2006. Later it developed that Cleveland cops had ignored reports on Sowell going back years, writing off the pleas of family and victims as "unfounded." Then there was the smell. Imperial Avenue stank of decaying bodies. But for years Cleveland police had blamed the odor on a nearby meat store.[17]

The knocks continued for the department: Less than a year later, two officers responded to a call about a dead body lying on the side of a highway interchange south of downtown. The cops drove past the site without stopping, reporting back to dispatch that what they saw was just a dead deer. It was actually the strangled, nude body of a mother of three. After missing the body, the officers drove to a nearby cemetery, where they sat for two hours waiting out the end of their shift.[18]

It was hard to tally the net effect all this institutional calamity had on your average Clevelander. I remember this distinct feeling soaking through headlines and nightly newscasts that we'd moved beyond the standard-issue Cleveland jokes. When the basics of your city—catching killers or putting diplomas in kids' hands or stabilizing a tax base—don't work anymore, there's a sense of being edged out of the American mainstream. Wherever the country was going, whatever the twenty-first century would look like, you started to wonder if Cleveland would get there in one piece. Or at all.


Back on the street corner, a lightbulb had popped in my head and wouldn't go dark again. "So basically what Ed testified to couldn't have happened," I said, less as a question than just to keep the thought rolling.

"Exactly," Kwame said.

This was a tiny fragment of the testimony that had landed three men in prison. But it was like pulling a thread on a cheap sweater—everything began coming apart. The bus was like a starter pistol that sent thoughts sprinting through me. Leading the charge, and shifting everything, was that Wiley was innocent. Rickey was innocent. Kwame, the man standing here with me on a Cleveland street in 2011, was innocent. For a moment I felt like all the air had suddenly fled my lungs. A man whose life was ruined before it started—how do you look him in the eye? I suddenly felt like I couldn't. I felt like I didn't deserve to.

City life begs heavy questions, real Political Science 101 head-scratchers. I'm not talking about 911 response times or trash pickup. But what's the best way to govern? What do the citizens owe a city? How do you balance the interests of the few against the many? What deal must be struck between ideals and compromise, facts and aspirations? And finally, the most basic: What does a city owe the people who call it home?

The region's current low position in the nation was all the more tragic considering the history. For a good chunk of the nation's life, the Midwest—or Middle West, in the old rusty jargon—was the country's best self in action, and its success or failure in reconciling the tensions within the modern American state was the measuring stick for the whole experiment conceived by the Founders.

From the street level this might seem grandiose. But consider that the establishment of the states beyond the original thirteen colonies was originally seen as a radical experiment in representative democracy, test cases to see if the benchmarks of such a government—representative assemblies, common law, broad voting—could actually sprout without the influence of a colonial power. During the decades bridging the Civil War and World War I, the central part of the country between the Allegheny Mountains and the Mississippi River produced thirteen presidents, the most of any region; nurtured towering new metropolises like Chicago, St. Louis, Indianapolis, and Cleveland; and served as the springboard for rock-star industrialists like Rockefeller, Carnegie, and Westinghouse, the figures who would gild the age.

This was no accident, according to the prevailing historical thought of the day. "The Midwest was seen as the valley of democracy and the homeland of the greatest American democrat, Abraham Lincoln," historian Jon C. Teaford wrote. "As opposed to the effete, aristocratic East and decadent, caste-ridden South, the Midwest was the true embodiment of the American political dream, a region where a rail-splitter could become president and where government was actually supposed to be of the people, by the people, and for the people."[19]

This idea found its fullest contemporary voice in Frederick Jackson Turner, a Wisconsin-born historian at Harvard University whose entire output was essentially a valentine to the possibilities of the region. Now out of fashion and largely forgotten, Turner published his "Frontier Thesis" in 1893; the theory proposed that the roughshod experience of settling the open spaces of the Midwest, an enterprise of constant invention and all-hands-in opportunity, fostered the ingredients necessary for the political dreamland that had sprung out from the pens of Jefferson, Madison, Hamilton, and Monroe. "The ideals of equality, freedom of opportunity, faith in the common man are deep rooted in all the Middle West," Turner wrote.[20] Cleveland, like similar cities, gulped this down in the early twentieth century, an influence you can spot in the dramatic public building program that drew heavily on Washington, D.C.'s neoclassical architecture, or in the reformist political agendas that buzzed then through city halls.

But the architect of the Midwest's national image was also sharp to the region's challenges, particularly as its industrial strength ballooned. "The task of the Middle West is that of adapting democracy to the vast economic organization of the present," Turner wrote. "This region which has so often needed the reminder that bigness is not greatness, may yet show that its training has produced the power to reconcile popular government and culture with the huge industrial society of the modern world." The stakes couldn't have been higher, Turner felt. "It is important that the Middle West should accomplish this; the future of the Republic is with her."

From the altitude of these high-minded aspirations, it was hard not to recognize that the Rust Belt I knew was grappling with more than regional decline but also the failure of this reconciliation Turner warned of between lofty American ideals and gangbuster capitalism. It dropped a sadder note on the city, recast its problems in headier terms. Cleveland in 2011, then, was a product of unfulfilled potential as much as anything else, and the city's own failures weren't just embarrassing headlines, but broken promises.

Kwame's story seemed at home in that larger failure. If we'd hit the point where we no longer expected our police officers to stop serial killers before body counts reached the double digits, or even know the difference between a dead animal and a black woman, or if we could no longer rely on the public schools to graduate the majority of students, or for the locals to negotiate new contracts, much less slow the flow of work overseas or protect pensions, if whole neighborhoods could disappear now under fine-print mortgages while the county government simply watched a tax base drain away, and if we could no longer expect the basic business of government to get done without a motel-room quickie—was it so hard then to believe the criminal justice system had put the wrong men in jail for a murder?

As I began digging into Kwame's case, I realized this was a story that highlighted all the major issues marking Cleveland's history, the same mix of politics, race, and law that has stained and steered every American city in the last seventy years. Yet for all the historical and personal pain his story contained, there were also lights leading forward. This story is about more than three lives unjustly stolen; it's also about how a city can finally face down—and fix—its ugly past.

# Part I

*DOWN THE WAY*

# 1

## A SPARK PLUS A SPARK PLUS A SPARK

Cleveland, July 23, 1968

THE CITY IN SUMMER, BRIGHT AFTERNOON DIMMING IN THE SKY. THE narrow jigsaw streets of Glenville tangle along the hills on Cleveland's edge, brick double- and triple-deckers slotted tight on modest lawns fizzy with bugs. Windows were wide open to the heat. Porch radios murmured. Ronnie Bridgeman, a peewee-sized ten-year-old with nothing heavier sitting on his mind than his sister's birthday party the next day, scuttled carefree down the alley next to his house. He was looking for his friend Kenneth. Together, they were going to do some garage hopping, jumping from one tin roof to the next. But when he popped out on Auburndale Avenue, he saw the men with guns.[1]

They looked like movie bandits, young heavies with bandoliers strung over their dashikis. Two hefted long M1 carbines. The third gripped a .45 caliber submachine gun. Ronnie recognized all three from two houses down. The man he knew as Ahmed—an ex-army grunt and felon born Fred Evans—was the guy on the block if you wanted to get into heavy talk about cosmic law or astrological signs or UFOs. Maybe a notch or two stranger than the rest, but Ahmed wasn't much different than the half dozen other young black men in the neighborhood, guys preaching Afro-pride, community betterment, and black nationalism. But the guns were new.

"Hey," Evans said. He nodded to the porch of Ronnie's house, where the boy's mother was yammering into the phone. "Tell the seniors to go in. There's fitting to be some trouble up here on the corner."

The police had been there all day. Ronnie knew that. Impossible to miss—a car full of white guys just sitting in Glenville, binoculars steady on Evans's house. What neither Ronnie nor Evans and his followers knew then was that it was really a botched surveillance job. The FBI had alerted the Cleveland police about possible violent plans being hatched by Evans's group. The police higher-ups ordered rolling surveillance—black officers only. Somehow the message was hacked up in translation, and now these cops—some of them legally drunk—were just sitting in the open.

"Mom!" Ronnie told his mother, pulling on her arm. "Mom!" Bessie Bridgeman swatted her son away. Then suddenly the Tuesday afternoon split with sound.

Thunderclaps of gunfire rolled in from down the street, where Auburndale crossed East 124th Street. More ripped out from Beulah. Mrs. Bridgeman dropped the phone and shouted for her children to come inside. Ronnie fell to the ground, crawling on his stomach for the house like a soldier bellying up a Normandy beach. Safe inside, he crept up to the front windows. He wanted to see.

Somewhere close to 8:20 P.M., gunshots pelted the two unmarked cars assigned to watch the militants. The vehicles roared off, bullets giving chase. Within a minute, a city tow-truck driver hauling an abandoned Cadillac around the corner on Beulah was blasted in the back with a shotgun.[2]

An "all units" distress call blurted on the police radio at 8:30 P.M. Across Cleveland, patrol cars left their assignments and headed into what had suddenly become an urban war zone. The police had been waiting for this. They abandoned their patrol cars on the Glenville curbs, some engines still puttering, and blitzed the scene with no plan other than pouring rounds into every twitching shadow in the hazy twilight.

After an hour of shooting, twenty-two people were dead or wounded. Three officers and three black nationalists died in the street. A high-powered rifle round punched into the motor of a police car, blowing the cruiser into a fireball. One cop had to wrench a shotgun from his bleeding partner's hand in order to cut down a sniper firing from the bushes. Evans's men shot from alleys and apartment balconies. Tear gas clouds soured the air. Homes on Lakeview began to burn.

The chaos seemed to give off a contact high, reignite familiar feelings. Two years earlier and less than a ten-minute drive away, black Clevelanders in the Hough neighborhood had rioted for six nights in July. Now it seemed that whatever outrage propelled that earlier violence had not been dispelled but only suspended, momentarily unplugged. A block north from the shooting in Glenville, where a group of black residents had gathered, police and rioters picked up where they had left off two summers earlier. Arriving emergency vehicles were pelted with rocks. A Molotov cocktail wrapped flames around a police cruiser, while a crowd pulled another officer from his car and beat him bloody. A panel truck driven by a white man plowed into pedestrians; the driver was wrenched from the cab and attacked while the vehicle was flipped and burned. Looters busted into the storefronts on Superior Avenue. Arriving Cleveland police officers removed their badges so no one would be able to identify them. A group of cops marched into a Glenville bar, firing into the ceiling and pistol-whipping the clientele. When two local black men tried to carry a wounded black nationalist out on a stretcher, they were attacked by Cleveland police. "Leave that nigger here to die," the cops reportedly said.

Gunshots stopped, but the looting and fires picked up. By 11:00 P.M., the militant leader Evans emerged from a nearby house to surrender. "You police have bothered us too long," he told the cops when asked why they'd attacked. Later, however, the black nationalist acknowledged that whatever forces were loose in the city now were beyond his control or planning. "I had come to be the leader," Evans would say. "But the night of the twenty-third, there was no leader. After we got our guns, it was every man for himself."

Nose to the windowsill, Ronnie Bridgeman watched it all play out. The window frame might as well have been a television screen—it was like *The High Chaparral*, but live action, real time, more vivid than Technicolor. The little boy was dazed and enthralled. It was cops against robbers. Good guys versus bad. Ronnie watched, even though he didn't completely understand everything happening as the guns jumped and the night shadows stretched and pooled.

A little over a century before race hate split the city open for the second time in as many years, Cleveland bowed its head for John Brown.

The radical abolitionist who led the failed slave revolt at Harpers Ferry swung from the gallows in Charlestown, Virginia, on December 2, 1859. When the news hit the settlement lapped by the fresh waters of Lake Erie three hundred miles to the northwest, Cleveland went dark with mourning. Shops closed. Flags lowered. Church bells echoed through the city. Brown's own words—*I do not think I can better honor the cause I love than to die for it*—were draped in a banner over a main road. At night, fourteen hundred Clevelanders—about one adult for every fifteen on the census roll—gathered to honor Brown and his cause. It was the largest public event in the community's short history.[3]

The town was shifting gears then, pushing off from an early start as a young frontier outpost stuck on a foul swamp. Cleveland was founded as a business hustle. Early colonial surveyors dubbed the flat land rolling off the hills of Pennsylvania the Western Reserve. The area was claimed by the Connecticut Land Company; but after first planting the flag in 1796 where the Cuyahoga River met Lake Erie, the absentee landowners had little interest in structural improvement or community building. They just wanted to sell deeds. Picture the giddy New Englander, land purchase agreement in his pocket, trekking hundreds of rough miles west, only to find a muddy, malarial nub of land frequented by, in the words of one early visitor, "itinerant Vaga-bonds" and "a phalanx of Desperadoes . . . setting all Laws at defiance."[4] In 1800, Cleveland boasted one permanent resident. Two years later, a visiting churchman was shocked by what he found. "There were five families here, but no apparent piety," he wrote home. "They seemed to glory in their infidelity."[5]

But when canal and lake traffic gave Ohio and other lakeside set-tlements a straight shot to the East Coast, Cleveland's significance as a trade port greatly increased. The swamps were cleared, waterways im-proved. In 1840, the town tallied six thousand residents; a decade later seventeen thousand people called Cleveland home.

Most of these new arrivals were from New England—early-model WASPs. They set the social tone. Still fevered by the religious and social energies behind the abolitionist movement, the expat East Coasters remade Cleveland as a progressive place on the question of race. With Canada across the lake, the city was a natural stop for the Underground Railroad. But the city's moral stance was consis-tent aboveground as well. As Kenneth L. Kusmer noted in his book *A Ghetto Takes Shape: Black Cleveland, 1870–1930*, southerners seek-ing fugitive slaves in Cleveland were arrested, tried, and convicted of kidnapping as early as 1819.[6] The Cuyahoga County Anti-Slavery Society pressured local public officials to come out against the practice throughout the 1830s. In 1859, an effort to build an all-black school was drowned out in public outcry over segregation. The local courts were also exceptionally favorable to early civil rights actions. A lawsuit in 1864 triggered by an effort to segregate streetcars led to court-ordered integration. Four years later, when a black Clevelander was turned away from a skating rink, he successfully sued for three hun-dred dollars in damages.

This moral high ground set Cleveland apart from the rest of the Buckeye State. "Whites in southern and central Ohio, where hostility to blacks was widespread and growing during the 1850s, often ex-pressed incredulity over the egalitarian or antislavery sentiments of many Clevelanders," Kusmer wrote.[7] Clevelanders, however, seemed to embrace that distinction. "An indication of the civilized spirit of the city of Cleveland," one newspaper editorial boasted in the 1860s, "is found in the fact that colored children attend our schools, colored people are permitted to attend all public lectures and public affairs where the fashion and culture of the city congregates, and nobody is offended."[8]

But some tectonic shifts were coming. Post–Civil War, southern blacks, pulled in by reports of the city's equality, arrived at a steady clip. In 1870, thirteen hundred African Americans lived in Cleveland.[9] Two decades later, the number was three thousand, and that figure doubled over the next ten years. This pipeline ran parallel to another: European immigrants. Beginning in the 1870s, Cleveland received a steady flow of German and Irish arrivals, followed by Hungarians, Russians, Romanians, Poles, and Slavs. Each group bedded down in a distinct part of the city, pockets that became synonymous with specific ethnicities. Slavic Village. Little Italy. Little Bohemia. These encampments created a city that was less a civic whole than "essentially a group of juxtaposed tribes more or less at war with one another," a contributor to *Forum Magazine* wrote in the 1920s. "She is a melting pot that never melted but continues to boil."[10]

Cleveland's blacks also followed the demographic realignment, mostly collecting along Central Avenue, just southeast of downtown. After enjoying an integrated city for so long, local blacks weren't prepared for this new social isolation: thanks to the liberal spirit of the city before the Civil War, Cleveland had no tradition of all-black schools or businesses or hospitals. Kusmer also pointed out that as the century slid toward its close, the upper-class WASPs, traditionally in the corner for blacks, moved out to the new suburbs carved out of the land east of the city. This sliced the "paternalistic" cord that had connected the two groups for so long.

It may have been that new isolation. Or the lack of all-black institutions. Or the new ethnic arrivals—many crossing the Atlantic to escape political chaos—bent on grabbing their own prosperity and holding tight. But chasing close behind the geographic segregation were systemic, policy-bound stabs at discrimination—the kind that would have shocked Cleveland's proud progressives of the 1850s.

In 1910, Luna Park, a popular amusement park, began allowing blacks in only on special "Jim Crow Days." Five years later, the Women's Hospital implemented a new policy of taking black patients only on Saturday. White-linen restaurants and hotels downtown stopped hiring black waiters. The most significant exclusion, however, was the ban on blacks in unions affiliated with the American Federation of Labor. This block kept Cleveland's African Americans out of factory work, the route many whites and immigrants were taking to the new middle class across the Midwest.

As the other ethnic groups spread from their original neighborhoods to new parts of the city, Cleveland's blacks stayed put. By the 1920s, 90 percent of local African Americans lived in a single patch of the East Side, bounded by Euclid Avenue on the north, East 105th Street on the east, and Woodland Avenue to the south. This was living "down the way." And these demarcations would largely pen in black Cleveland for the rest of the century.

This isolation was, in Kusmer's analysis, partly due to a tension hardening between black Clevelanders and European arrivals. "It seems likely that these [European] ethnic communities were composed of individuals highly prone to what social scientists have called 'status anxieties,'" he wrote. "Having raised themselves above poverty, acquired a small home . . . and attained a modest level of income, they were fearful of association with any group bearing the stigma of low status. They naturally resisted the encroachment of a racial group that American society had designated as inferior. In so doing, they unthinkingly helped create a black ghetto."

Yet Cleveland's black neighborhoods continued to bulge to capacity as more black southerners fled Jim Crow during the Great Migration. Between 1910 and 1920, Cleveland's black population jumped 308 percent; by 1930, the population would again double, to seventy-two thousand. Confined to a small space, Cleveland's blacks were subject to the classic slate of American slum troubles: high rent, terrible living conditions, flaring racial tensions, and police harassment. "The majority live in drab, middle or low class houses, none too well kept up," one contemporary wrote in 1930. "While the poor live in dilapidated, rack-rented shacks, sometimes a whole family in one or two rooms, as a rule paying higher rents than white tenants for the same space." Another black newspaperman at the time noted, "There has been a growing tendency upon the part of the police, both public and private, to kill members of the race sought for committing crimes and misdemeanors."

Meanwhile, Cleveland's own place in the national economy was on a rocket trajectory. By the end of the Second World War, the region's choice rail and port position made the city an industrial powerhouse. In 1945, Cleveland ranked fifth in the country in industrial-output dollars, and in 1949 Cleveland was one of the largest cities in the nation, with a population of 914,800. Still, the city center was leaking population—and tax base—to the new suburbs cupping Cleveland on all sides like a human palm. Of the 170,000 jobs created in the region after the war, 100,000 were outside Cleveland in the greater county.[11]

Black demographics also grew. Between 1940 and 1960, Cleveland's black share of the population jumped to 251,000—more than 30 percent. However, in 1960 blacks were only 10 percent of the workforce, and in the same year reviewers found that 28.2 percent of black-occupied housing was dilapidated.

City hall was not providing any solutions. At the time, the U.S. Department of Housing and Urban Development had earmarked significant funds for Cleveland to redevelop the blasted areas. Cleveland in turn offered six thousand acres for new housing, a whole one-eighth of the city and twice as much as any other municipality in the country. When the bulldozers went into action, the federal projects uprooted many residents in the older Central Avenue ghetto. But Cleveland then failed to move ahead with planned construction, forcing the residents to cram into Hough and Glenville. Between 1957 and 1962, the city destroyed 460 residences along Woodland and East Fifty-fifth, home to nine hundred families—yet no new housing was ever constructed for the displaced. Ninety percent of these demolished homes were in good condition. In 1966, Cleveland's head of urban renewal admitted before a congressional committee that the department's policy was to allow property marked for urban renewal—property inhabited by black families—to deteriorate as much as possible so the city could pick it up on the cheap. HUD eventually cut all funding to the city. One federal official at the time referred to Cleveland as "this office's Vietnam."[12]

The city's thin infrastructure couldn't field the demands of the growing population. The issues flared first with schooling. The school board didn't have enough elementary schools to handle the East Side. Teachers were placing children in libraries and storerooms to accommodate the numbers. Throughout the 1950s, thousands of East Side children couldn't enter kindergarten for lack of space. On the whitewashed West Side, schools were half-empty.

By the early 1960s, local black activists had begun tuning into the social frequencies beaming out of the southern civil rights protests. Recognizing the education situation in Cleveland as wink-wink segregation, and that the school board's unwillingness to bus black students west was tied to fears of outraging working-class whites, black activists launched a campaign of protests and sit-ins in 1963. They organized under the banner of the United Freedom Movement (UFM), and the early action seemed to get results—the board agreed to bus. But reports came back to parents that the transplanted East Siders were locked down in all-black classrooms. The UFM decided to take the fight directly to the white neighborhoods digging in against integration.

On January 26, 1964, the UFM marched in Collinwood, an East Side neighborhood filled with working-class Italians. White hecklers showed up. Slurs—"dirty niggers!"—were reportedly tossed at picketers. Four days later, the group planned a similar demonstration in Murray Hill. A tight web of streets crawling up a hill on the city's eastern line, the neighborhood—known as Little Italy—was the heartbeat of white Cleveland, not to mention the local Mafia. As such, it was a no-go zone for blacks. But on a Thursday morning, UFM marchers showed—to find fourteen hundred whites standing outside Memorial Elementary School. They were clutching clubs, baseball bats, guns. A brutal riot ensued. Bullets hit the cars of fleeing blacks. The Cleveland police just watched. A black reporter on the scene begged an officer to do something. "You went in there and started something," the cop replied. "You incited a riot." No one was arrested. Cleveland's mayor, Ralph Locher, refused the UFM's request to step into the situation.

The school desegregation crisis continued to careen on a violent course. In April, as the UFM demonstrated outside the construction site of a new East Side elementary school, a twenty-seven-year-old white minister and activist named Bruce Klunder was accidentally killed by a bulldozer. That night, angry young blacks took to the street, wearing their arms out throwing rocks at police and smashing up stores.

Whether the words were rolling through the looters' heads or not, Cleveland's larger black community was suddenly weighing the real-world value of what Malcolm X had said at a Cleveland rally only days earlier, words that would pin themselves to the next decade of conflict: *the ballot or the bullet.*

For the next year, racial skirmishes broke out regularly in the city, mostly along Superior Avenue, the northern border between black and white enclaves. Black youths assaulted a white man and his son. A white man shot a ten-year-old black boy. White motorists had their cars pelted with rocks. From porches, white adults lobbed words like "savages" and other slurs at black children heading to school. Black and white gangs routinely battled in local parks. "If you are going to beat up those niggers," a police officer is reported to have told white teens, "take them down to the park where we can't see it."[13]

The city's blood pressure climbed. On July 18, 1966, in Hough—sagging, overcrowded houses; boarded storefronts; food stores that jacked up their prices on days when the welfare checks came in—a white bar owner hung a sign on his door at Seventy-ninth and Hough: NO WATER FOR NIGGERS. The angry crowd that circled the bar only grew as the white owner and his son paraded before the door with guns. They grew louder and angrier when the police arrived to disperse them. By dusk, glass showered the pavement from shop windows and streetlamps, and fires ate through abandoned houses. The National Guard and Cleveland police stormed the area. Crowds fled on foot in packs. Cops busted into houses, dragging out everyone they found inside—teenagers and old folks included—and holding them overnight. More than 275 people were arrested. Police opened fire on one black couple as they were driving on their street; the sixteen-year-old young woman lost an eye.

Six nights later, Cleveland's first major race riot was over—four dead, 240 fires, and two million dollars in damage. A grand jury, headed by prominent local businessmen and newspaper publishers, was tasked with sniffing out the origins of the violence. The group claimed a small number of communist agitators had incited the black community to revolt. The report—a tone-deaf Eisenhower-era antique piece in the post-Selma world—so angered the black community that they held their own hearings on the riots; the event became a public grievance forum for a part of Cleveland that felt it had been ignored and abused for far too long.

"You don't need anything to incite people when they know they're being mistreated," one witness told the packed audience. "I have seen police brutality," another reported. "*This* was outrageous."

"A spark was all you need and then you had your riot," a third witness told the committee.[14] "A spark plus a spark plus a spark, what you get? You have a war."

Any mother would squeeze her children close while gunfire screamed outside her home. But Bessie Bridgeman was a step ahead. While Glenville became a combat zone in July 1968, she put Ronnie and his sister in the bathtub, placing a few inches of porcelain between the children and the bullets winging around outside.[15]

Her own people were originally from South Carolina. Although the family didn't regularly share the details, the legend was that Bessie's grandfather had been a sharecropper who fled north to escape a murder charge. When he and his wife, who everyone called Smoke, settled in Cleveland, they opened up a laundry. It was still in business as Bessie grew up, Smoke doing the linens in the way her own mother had learned on the plantation down south.

Bessie graduated from John Marshall High School on the East Side. Her children would never know for sure, but it seemed like she had even taken some college classes. It was clear she was a thinker; when a problem got before her, she'd burn down the candle, as they liked to say, working out a solution. She was also a killer on the chessboard. And she was always trying to pad the schooling her children were receiving. Classrooms might teach education, Bessie felt, but they didn't teach knowledge. So she would press her kids with big words—*anti-establishment*, *materialism*—and address them in the stiff elocution of an English gentry grande dame—*excuse me, sir. Pardon me.* Ronnie would sometimes put a hand under his pillow to find a letter his mother had written to him. It was Bessie's way of encouraging her youngest to read.

They all had nicknames. The oldest was Hawiatha, born in 1950. Everyone called him *Kitch*. Beatrice came eighteen months later; she went by *Bebe*, but by the time Ronnie came around he couldn't pronounce his *B*s, instead mangling the name into *Gege*. It stuck. Wiley, arriving in 1954, was called *Buddy*. And Ronnie, three years later, because he was so small, was *Bitzie*, as in *itsy-bitsy*. Bessie had her own names for the kids as well. Her own thoughtfulness showed up in Wiley, so she dubbed him *the Professor*. She called Ronnie *Skipper*, which seemed to match his easygoing attitude. Ronnie, by some random calculus of the little boy's mind, always called his mother *Dot*.

As warm and close as the Bridgeman kids were with their mother, their father was a different story. Hawiatha Bridgeman Sr. was a towering slab of a man, a doorway-filling six-foot-six with a voice as deep and rolling as a plucked upright bass, just like Melvin Franklin from the Temptations. A few syllables alone were enough to freeze his kids still as statuary.

But you wouldn't catch that voice in the house now, and that was the family's trouble. Back in 1961, Hawiatha Sr. had been in a car accident he didn't walk away from. A neck injury left him paralyzed. By '68 he was living in a treatment facility two hours outside Cleveland. That left all the parenting and bill paying on Bessie. She juggled shifts at the phone company with time at the family laundry, all the while raising four children on her own. The pressure wore her own health down. Not that she showed it. After long days pulling two jobs to keep her family fed, Bessie was still home every night to put her youngest children to bed, her sweet voice lullabying "Silent Night" as Ronnie, her little Skipper, closed his eyelids.

And now, like every other parent across Cleveland as the night of July 23 ended, the gunshots gone but the fires still going, Bessie Bridgeman had to tuck her kids in bed wondering what was coming with the next morning.

You could have hung a sign on the door: NO WHITES ALLOWED.

Cleveland's city hall is an imposing copper-topped four stories of marble and stone squatting near the edge of Lake Erie. As a rain-splattered dawn broke on Wednesday after the first night of gunfire and sirens in Glenville, an unlikely meeting was underway inside. Cleveland's seat of power had likely hosted many sit-downs where the only faces at the table were white. Not this time. More than one hundred black leaders packed a chamber, from young Black Power militants to pulpit-pounding heavies from the largest churches in town. They were all waiting to hear what Mayor Carl Stokes wanted to do next.

Dizzy from no sleep and the conflicting scraps of information coming from seven miles away, the mayor appeared ill. For the country's first black big-city mayor, his worst fears were coming true. Carl Stokes likely didn't pass a day behind the big desk at City Hall without thinking of the Hough riot—how to patch the damage, how to avoid it again, how to use it right. Hough was the wedge that put him into office. But on July 24, 1968, Stokes was staring down the kind of five-alarm crisis no American politician—white or black—had dealt with before.

Among the black Americans who crashed through racial barriers in the 1950s and 1960s, Stokes was unique. Not a legal wizard uprooting Jim Crow from the courtroom or a preacher spinning eloquent calls to action, he was a pure politician, his instincts precisely machine tooled to the needs and fears of voting blocs well beyond his base.

The ground game of Cleveland politics was fiercely sectarian. Yes, the city was Democrat and pro-labor, but under those umbrellas were neighborhoods still clinging to their European ethnicity with white knuckles; these constituencies regularly elected city leaders from their pack, creating steady political energy behind certain candidates. The political pull of these ethnic politicians—known in Cleveland as "the cosmos"—forced the mostly white Republican business elite to cede control of the city to second- and third-generation Slavs, Czechs, and Hungarians early in the century. Not that the power shift completely sidelined the WASP pashas of the economic upper rungs. Instead, it created a two-part governance structure: let the ethnics control city hall; by establishing a series of foundations (including the first-ever city foundation), the economic elite retained influence through charitable giving. The two sides found areas of overlap. "The ethnics' rise to power ushered in a period of governance that catered to the immigrants' mistrust of politics: limited government, low taxes, and few services," historian Leonard N. Moore wrote.[16] "The industrials allowed working-class immigrants to run local government so long as they kept taxes low to attract investment, maintained services for businesses, and deferred to the wisdom of the business elite in reaching economic decisions." This tag team of interests steered city hall and dominated the thirty-three-person city council for the two decades following the Second World War. And although blacks elected a number of representatives to the city's legislative body during that stretch, the power structure largely ignored Cleveland's African Americans while pursuing a small-government, low-taxes mantra.

Stokes's particular genius was to read his position in this fractured scheme. The son of Georgia migrants who came north for work, Stokes grew up poor on the East Side, selling scrap metal and running errands for working girls to help pay family bills. A stint in the army and time as a state liquor inspector were followed by law school and a job working as a county prosecutor. He was touched by hot ambition early on, that desire twinned with the bravado to push open doors he wasn't supposed to walk through. Stokes eyed public office—first a state senate seat, then Cleveland's city hall.

His insight was to look at Cleveland's African Americans not as an ignored minority, but as an untapped voting bloc. The city's black population wasn't sizable enough to float him to higher office alone, but Stokes realized he could piece together enough ballots from different areas to carry a Democratic primary in a one-party town. Any success there, however, hinged on convincing white and ethnic voters to see Stokes as a viable candidate. He would show up uninvited to Democratic Party ward meetings in ethnic districts, neighborhoods unfriendly to the black cause. Stokes would walk in and ask to address the crowd. It was almost a taunt—if you're a racist, show me. "Those people disliked Negros," he wrote in his autobiography in a chapter tellingly titled, "How to Get Elected by White People."[17] "But they didn't dislike Carl Stokes—didn't, that is, after he had talked long enough to show them he was a real human being."

Stokes's road show was part of a strategy. The candidate spent his off-hours poring over old voting records at the county board of elections, studying how black candidates fared in specific districts, how newspaper, labor, or party endorsements tweaked the numbers in certain parts of the city. Some white voters would never check a box by his name, Stokes figured. "So even if you lose votes because you're black, you can still dip into the band of liberal whites if you can convince them you are progressive, socially committed, intelligent, and, well, one extraordinary black man," Stokes wrote later. "I had everything to gain and nothing to lose by running visible in white suburbia."

The calculus worked. Stokes served in the state assembly from 1962 to 1967. Bolstered by what he saw in the voting patterns, he ran for Cleveland mayor in 1965. In a contentious, three-candidate showdown, Stokes lost by less than 1 percent of the vote. Two years later, when it was time for the city to elect a mayor again, Stokes was confident about his chances.

The game changer proved to be Hough. Following the 1966 riots, local business leaders who had long ago ditched politics for the sotto voce influence of foundation giving were mortified. Riot damage was lost dollars. A black mayor, many in this clique believed, could be a safeguard against more racial strife. "Curiously enough, that made me the most desirable candidate," Stokes wrote later. On November 7, 1967, a major American city elected its first black mayor, with 129,396 votes to his opponent's 127,717. Overnight Stokes entered the front ranks of national African American figures. Within the week he was on the cover of *Time* magazine. Yet it's telling how far Stokes—and his establishment backers—went to frame the election not as a civil rights victory but a political score. When the Reverend Martin Luther King Jr. arrived in Cleveland on Election Night, Stokes asked him not to speak at the public festivities.

The new mayor walked into city hall with a liberal agenda that included public housing and equal opportunity employment. But police reform topped the list. In his days as a lawyer and a prosecutor in the 1950s, Stokes witnessed how the courts operated. "Few judges worked past noon, and many headed for the racetrack at midafternoon," Stokes wrote.[18] "Homicide detectives were usually willing to lower a charge from first-degree murder to second degree, or even manslaughter, if two conditions were met. The first was that the man charged with the crime had to come up with some money, at times as little as a hundred dollars. The second, but most important, was that he had to be a Negro accused of killing another Negro."

The black community's relationship with the city's police department was at an all-time low by his inauguration. Most black men and women in the city knew that if a police officer saw a suspect running from a crime scene, he would not hesitate to unload his service weapon at the fleeing target. "And all the police knew that few policemen faced charges or an appearance before the grand jury for shooting a black man while on duty," Stokes would later say. Cleveland's police chief, Richard R. Wagner, was also no friend to the black community. Before a panel of state legislators, the department's top man had testified that the death penalty was a useful deterrent for racial disharmony. "We need capital punishment in order to keep the Negro in line," he said.[19] During the Hough riots, Wagner roamed the churning streets armed with a deer rifle.

In reality, it didn't matter who sat at the top of the division. A clique of senior officers reigned. In 1966, Cleveland ordered an outside review of all city departments. The hard look concluded that the real machinery driving the police department was invisible. "Perhaps the division can best be described as a loose federation," the report concluded, built around "small empires." "It is further confused by informal arrangements, power centers, and unusual lines of communication which make the apparent structure of organization virtually meaningless." But the status quo was fortified enough to scare off any potential change in the police structure. When the city's departmental review was released to the public, the chapter on the police division was not included.[20]

The new mayor had the opportunity to make good on the symbolic promise of his election four months into his term. On April 4, 1968, the Reverend Martin Luther King Jr. was killed on a hotel balcony in Memphis. Reaction to King's murder exploded across the country: 110 cities saw rioting; thirty-nine people would eventually be killed. But in Cleveland, Stokes gambled. He ordered Cleveland police officers out of the East Side. Instead, he deputized black leaders and citizens—a peace patrol—to walk the broiling neighborhoods, urging the folks to "keep it cool." The plan worked. Unlike nearly every other American city, Cleveland saw no violence in the aftermath of King's murder.

And now, three months later, in July 1968, Cleveland was waiting to hear how Carl Stokes would calm the rage set loose by the events in Glenville. Inside his all-black city hall meeting, the assembled leaders were split on whether Stokes should again pull the police from the neighborhood. Trusted members of the department were warning the mayor to keep police out. With three of their own dead on the streets, the Cleveland police were amped up—dangerous, even. A small-scale race war was chewing through the city. The racial mood was bitter. Stokes was still confident "black people were not going to kill black people." So he issued the order: all cops out; the National Guard would man the perimeter; only black police and community leaders wearing red armbands—known as the Mayor's Committee—were allowed in.

On Wednesday night, thunderstorms knocked in early, clearing the streets. By nightfall, a thick heat stuck to the city. More than five hundred members of Stokes's peace patrol scuffled along the sidewalks and alleys of the East Side, unwinding the tension they found among groups of young blacks. No violence was reported. But the patrols were helpless to stop looters picking their way through the abandoned businesses along Superior Avenue.

At the Fifth District headquarters on the East Side, officers stewed. The city's finest had been attacked and bested—embarrassed, even— by a group of wild-eyed militants. The orders from city hall to stay away from the conflict fueled emotions. When the mayor's office swatted down a request from officers to carry high-powered rifles on patrol for protection, anger spiked. All night, patrol car radios smoked with heated words. "Tell Stokes to go piss on it," officers repeated to one another, comments reported a year later in a report by federal officials. "Fuck that nigger mayor."[21]

Thursday morning broke peacefully. The mayor's plan had prevented more violence. But the overnight damage and looting continued, angering the white business community. Under pressure, Stokes rescinded his order barring white police from the area—a retreat that effectively sank the career of the most famous black politician in America.

Glenville was in ruins. Days after the violence died off, the area was still locked down under curfew and patrolled by armed National

Guardsmen. Firefighters continued to aim lazy ropes of water at smoking buildings. The black businesses along Superior Avenue—once busy mom-and-pop shops—were now skeletal wastes. And there picking through the wrecked guts of the neighborhood were two unchaperoned boys, Wiley and Ronnie.

The Bridgeman boys played rough and tumble. No sitting inside sucking thumbs. With three years on his younger brother, Wiley was the leader, brainstorming the games. They'd string thick ropes over tree branches, then swing around like Zorro swashbuckling on TV. They did so many swan dives off garages onto beat mattresses that when they actually got near water, the Bridgemans had the high jump already down. Hard play, that's how they were wired. So while the rest of the city stayed home scared, Wiley was leading his little brother out on an adventure to the heart of the calamity.

But as the two kids jumped around the wreckage, they caught the attention of a group of passing National Guardsmen. "Get the fuck away from up here," one of the glowering young men in fatigues shouted. They were kids themselves, really, with faces that didn't seem like they could hold a beard, and skinny arms and legs sticking out from their fatigues like tentpoles. Ten-year-old Ronnie wasn't impressed. "Man, fuck you," he belted.

The guardsman who spoke walked over to the little boy, sticking the end of his bayonet right into Ronnie's breastbone. He felt the metal bite through his shirt to his skin. "You know I have the right to send you to hell right now?" the soldier growled.

Ronnie, Wiley, the guardsman, and his fellow platoon members all froze, locked into an inevitably bad situation. Another voice suddenly broke the spell. "What did you just say to that kid?" An older National Guardsman, an officer, bolted over, knocking the rifle from Ronnie's chest. "Get out of here," he told Ronnie and Wiley.

The little boys hoofed it home. But that sting on Ronnie's chest—the first hard touch of authority—he wouldn't forget.

———

Glenville did more than mow down Carl Stokes's political prospects. It also raised a curtain on a new phase in the civil rights movement.

The move to pull police out of the conflict area exposed a rift between the department and Stokes that had been percolating ever since the reformer took office. The mayor openly criticized the actions of police during the Glenville riots, later writing that their attitude had been "self-protective, corrupt and destructive."

Stokes also felt the pushback to his leadership was not about his effectiveness but the obvious—"a black mayor had pulled out the white police," he wrote in a scalding section of his book. "This had clearly been a fear all along, that a black mayor would interfere with the police function of protecting the white community against the black peril." Stokes's own position, however, was undercut when it was unearthed that Fred Ahmed Evans had actually received funding from a community program sponsored by the administration—money that may have paid for the guns and ammunition that murdered those three police officers.

The bad blood between the two sides ended any chance to reform the department. A systemic reorganization of the ranks was fought. The mayor's effort to recruit more black police candidates sparked a testing scandal involving stolen answers and resulting in the indictment of two members of the Civil Service Commission. Stokes became convinced the police had bugged the phones in his office. When the mayor ran for reelection in 1969, several hundred armed off-duty police officers sat at East Side polling sites, harassing voters about pulling the lever for Stokes—banana republic scare tactics in an American mayoral election.

With Stokes's face-off with police so public, the mayor's political enemies used it to their advantage. Soon, many local politicians eyeing city hall fell in behind the department, lashing out at Stokes as lax on crime and pro–black militant. Ralph Perk, a West Side pol who talked up his credentials as an "average neighbor and average citizen," mounted those anxieties in his own play for city hall in '69. "Here in the city of Cleveland our streets are so unsafe that residents on the East

Side, the South Side, and the West Side are afraid to come out at night," Perk said on the stump. "When I am elected we will get rid of all these unofficial armies that now are parading the city."

Crime had become political, and any criticism of the department—accurate or not—was swallowed up by the larger campaign dynamics. You were either anticop or anticrime. Stokes himself understood the untenable position he'd landed in. Although he beat Perk by almost four thousand votes to earn a second term, America's first black mayor was paralyzed after 1968. Stokes opted not to run for reelection in 1971. He would later say police reform in Cleveland had been "my greatest frustration, my greatest failure."[22]

Glenville's fallout spread well beyond the Cuyahoga River. For those viewing the march toward racial equality as a nefarious siege on the status quo, the Cleveland incident was proof that the peaceful sit-ins and demonstrations of the early 1960s were now curdling into an open race war. This was Malcolm X's bullet. As a federal report published by the National Commission on the Causes and Prevention of Violence a year after the shooting noted, up until Glenville, the spasms of racial violence in the U.S. had mostly been directed at the destruction of property. "The Glenville incident was different," the report read. "It began as person-oriented violence, blacks and whites shooting at each other, snipers against cops. And apparently alone among major outbreaks of racial violence in American history, it ended in more white casualties than black."[23]

In Cleveland, if the Hough riots had pulled to the surface the anger and distrust between the black community and the white establishment, Glenville filed the edges of those feelings down to razor blades. Jacked up by the rhetorical punches megaphoning out of politicians, the average Cleveland police officer felt besieged, targeted, hated. As one anonymous Cleveland beat cop told the *Plain Dealer* only a few months after Glenville, "We're like a British outpost in Africa."[24]

# 2

## THAT PARTICULAR DAY

Cleveland, May 19, 1975

*ON THE THIRD MONDAY IN MAY DAWN CAUGHT THE CITY RAW AND EDGY,* and already two up on the new week's body count. A thirty-year-old housewife had been found strangled on her dining room floor on East 138th, and a barkeep was gunned down on East Ninety-third—fresh whodunits in a year that was already outpacing the last in violent death. A record-setting year for murders—just what the town needed in spring 1975. More damn reasons to worry.

Troubled thoughts hounded sleep across the city. It was shaping up to be an ugly season. Buried currents were bursting open like bad pipes. That morning at the federal courthouse the families of the Kent State University students killed by National Guardsmen in 1970 were scheduled to begin a civil trial against the federal government. Down the hall in the same building, political storm clouds massed in the pre-trial stages of an NAACP lawsuit against the school district over segregation on the East Side in the 1960s. Behind the walls of the Georgian and Van Sweringen Tudor houses in the heights, business captains were restless about the start of Cleveland's first International Business Week, a bit of overseas goodwill that might, fingers crossed, pump life into a local economy that was wobbling. There were plenty of other civic worries large and small to stack on the pile: an upcoming mayoral election in November; a long-shot push to bring the 1976 Republican National Convention to town; power struggles among black politicians; gangland bombings. To top it off, the Indians were already six games back in the American League East.

But on the far edge of the East Side, as the sunrise washed the residential streets in rose-gray light, Ronnie Bridgeman was already rolling awake in bed, his thoughts disconnected from whatever larger anxieties wound through the city. Early rising was a leftover habit from his old summer gig at the Northern Ohio Food Terminal—he had to be there around 4:00 A.M. to unload the trucks. Now the teenager's eyes snapped open on bedroom walls that were a psychedelic smear of posters and black-light paint, Jimi Hendrix trashing his guitar, Wile E. Coyote with his hands around the Road Runner's neck, *Meep meep your ass!* All night, while he slept, the radio had been leaking rock station WMMS—*Where Music Means Something.* He picked up a guitar, working his fingers along the frets with the FM music, waiting out the hours until everyone else woke.[1]

Ronnie was out on Arthur Avenue around 8:00 A.M., seventeen but still baby-faced, a little swagger just starting to pop his steps. In a T-shirt and slacks, he walked from the modest two-story house he shared with his mother and Wiley, over three houses to where his older sister Beatrice lived with her own family. As usual, he loaded his sister's four little kids into her station wagon and drove them over to Bolton Elementary, just a few blocks west. He did it every weekday. His sister's kids, so he took her car.

Kids and cars—Ronnie had a funny story about that. He had a whole bulging bag of stories, jokes, riffs; he was barely old enough to drive but already a precocious street corner raconteur. Words didn't spook him—thank you, Mom—even though he was technically a high school dropout. Ronnie also didn't freeze around strangers. Words plus wit—just like his hero Muhammad Ali, Ronnie was an easy charmer who could win over an audience with gab.

This particular story was great. At the time he hadn't been much older than the nieces and nephews he was hauling to school now—four years old, probably. The Bridgemans were living then in an apartment house off St. Clair. Ronnie was always hanging around with a little bucktoothed neighborhood girl his age named Candy. Their favorite game was playing "grown-up," which was how they ended up in the front seat of Mr. Wittick's brand-new Buick.

The car was a beauty, powder blue with a checkerboard terry-cloth interior. Ronnie was in the driver's seat, pretending to drive like he'd seen adults do, his little hands twisting the wheel he could barely see over. In the passenger seat, Candy played along, too, acting as she'd seen her mother act when driving with her father. "Ahh, motherfucker!" the little girl screamed, surprising Ronnie. "Goddamn bullshit!" Candy grabbed a cigarette butt out of the ashtray and fired up the car's automatic lighter. She took one puff, hacked, then passed it to Ronnie. The smoke singed his lungs, and Ronnie tossed the butt into the backseat.

The neighbors all collected outside to watch the firefighters try to save Mr. Wittick's Buick. Ronnie stood innocently by his mother, while an old woman who'd seen Ronnie and Candy flee the burning car sidled up to Mrs. Bridgeman. "That sure is a shame," Mrs. Bridgeman said. "Yeah, it's a shame," the old woman croaked. "Now you're going to have to pay for that man's car." Ronnie fessed up right then. It seemed like the whuppin' he got lasted three whole days. He never learned how his family settled up with Mr. Wittick. But it was a hard—and memorable— lesson in accountability. Still, the story always sent Ronnie laughing, a slow-starting giggle that then broke quick like a rocket.

Just another Monday. After dropping his nieces and nephews off, the teenager was back inside his own home on Arthur. His mother was awake, but she was still in her room. Ronnie took a quick bath, then headed for the closet to pick out the day's outfit. Every self-respecting dude on the block had his best duds, and today Ronnie reached for his: jacket and pants, both matching blue denim. Sharp, slick, cool. All the guys in the street at the time were getting cartoon characters inked into their clothes—superheroes or characters from the Archie comics. Ronnie's brainstorm: get Spooky from the "Casper the Friendly Ghost" cartoons printed on this jacket. But the dude who did the drawings up behind the barbershop on Cedar was charging eleven dollars. Ronnie didn't have the money yet, but soon enough. Nice clothes meant girls. Throw in music, and you had the three legs propping up his young existence right there. No doubt, Ronnie looked good in his denims now. But once he had that cartoon, he'd be set.

Arthur Avenue was an oddball slab of the East Side. On the map, technically it was part of the Cedar neighborhood. But the street and the surrounding blacktop were tucked on the city's edge; rail tracks ran south, and Fairhill Boulevard, a four-lane runway for heavy traffic lifting off for the nearby suburbs, cut Arthur off like a river branch isolating a spit of land. As such, it was a neighborhood apart and intimate, everyone looped in with everyone else, a place booming with its own personalities.

If the neighborhood had a soundtrack in the early 1970s, it was "Bound" by the Ponderosa Twins Plus One. These were local boys made good, five guys from the block who scored a record deal with their Jackson 5–like sound. "Bound," a catchy high-whine slow burn that peaked at number 47 on the soul charts in 1971, shot them around the country on tours. Back home, it meant every smooth neighborhood kid—or wannabe smooth neighborhood kid—was in a singing group, hoping to repeat the same chart-topping dream. Ronnie Bridgeman threaded his tenor along with his brother and three other guys in a group they called the Golden Teardrops.

The homes were set close, one family's life spilling over into the next. Bloodlines weaved in and out of the block. That meant everyone's business was broadcast loud and clear. Cooking smells from open kitchen windows flowed into one another. Even the littlest twerp on the sidewalk could explain the details of the Cotton family's scheme for stripping stolen cars—ride the stolen one up front, have a truck behind it, a third car on lookout, strip the lead car of hubcaps, fenders, and other valuables by the time you turn the corner. When Billy killed Tommy, two best friends who had gone off to Vietnam together, it wasn't a mystery to anyone: the whole neighborhood knew they were being played against each other by the same woman. The block was as intimate as a bear hug. It made for a good place to negotiate the lane shift from childhood to adulthood.[2]

All the surrounding areas were just as tightly knit. That meant you had to be careful where your feet took you—go to the wrong area, you might get chased out. The way to the skating rink—everyone's favorite pastime—was dicey. Ronnie and his friends had a rink around the corner for a while, the Playmore on Cedar. But after that closed, they had to trek all the way to East Ninety-third and Sandusky to the Eureka. The truce between the Cedar guys and locals: you can skate here, but if you start talking to girls, you better beat the bus back home. Even when it came to showdowns, the knuckle-ups were pretty innocent—a few flying fists. Once Ronnie followed a group of older boys up to Harry E. Davis High School, where they were set to face off; as the brawling started, one kid pulled a little .22 pistol. It seemed like a second later he was the only one still standing there.

But Ronnie's world was still brushed by the darker currents running through city life. Just around the corner on East 108th there was a coffee shop known as a front for the local bookie. Up on Superior Avenue to the north, pimps would shark around in big gangster Caddies while working girls flagged down constant business. Stickup men—*pistoleros* was the flashy name people called them on the street—regularly robbed local stores. Some of these triggermen's street reps ballooned into legend, like Skip and Railroad King, gun-strapped brothers known for double-crossing the guys they worked jobs with.

And the police brought their own menace. An unspoken rule in the neighborhood put a wall up between the people and the law. You didn't mess with the cops, either getting friendly or telling them someone else's business. Why? Ronnie wasn't exactly sure—that's just the way it was. But there was no missing the strong mix of fear and hostility standing up in folks' voices when they spoke about law enforcement. Ronnie heard adults talk about Zippo lighter cases—when black men were shot down by officers claiming they had seen the man pulling a gun, afterward finding only a metal lighter on the body.

Ronnie had his own close call. One afternoon, when he was fifteen and walking alone on Arthur to play some badminton, he was stopped by an unmarked police car. Plainclothes detectives jumped out. They told Ronnie they wanted him to come along with them downtown. But before they could put their hands on the kid, it seemed like every woman in the neighborhood—all the moms and aunties and grannies—were on their porches yelling. "What that boy do?" the chorus shouted. "Leave him be!"

The detectives swapped a look, shrugged, got back in their car, and drove off.

Rickey stopped at the Bridgeman house midmorning. Time to fuck him up on the chessboard, Ronnie thought.

The two sat down in Ronnie's bedroom around the tree stump he used as a table. He regarded his best friend from across the arrayed pieces, wondering if Rickey was going to go with that pawn-to-king-four bullshit he always trucked out. Really, it wasn't even fair—Ronnie had been moving chess pieces around for as long as he could remember, losing early and often to his mother until he was sharp enough to play with the big boys. But hey, Rickey tried. Ronnie made his own first move—the queen's pawn up two.

Rickey was as at ease at the Bridgemans' house as he was at his own, and vice versa. They'd only been friends for a few years, but Rickey was glued to the family as if by blood. Rickey first clicked up with Ronnie when he was playing around on the street with a go-kart, crashing the rickety thing into bushes. Rickey, quiet and small yet tightly coiled, was the straight man to Ronnie's blaring persona. In spite of different hardwiring, they were now rarely apart, always willing to act as partners in whatever scheme or plan the other had cooked up—like the time Ronnie fitted out a room in the basement for smoking weed, only later to learn from Mrs. Bridgeman that they'd forgotten about the vent in the ceiling leading right into her room. "I heard *everything* you were doing down there," she told her son and his friend.

Some days were far too pretty for chess. On this morning, Cleveland was unrolling a spring day, the kind where the city is caught in a warm crossfire of sunlight and glare bouncing between the sky and lake. After knocking out a few rounds of chess, Ronnie and Rickey stepped outside. In the driveway, there was Wiley, where he always was, polishing his car. He loved that thing, a white '71 Sebring. The moment Ronnie spotted his older brother, he felt a pulse of pride. He always did. Wiley was the best—the coolest, smoothest, smartest. He dressed sharp. He could play any musical instrument he picked up. He was a tractor beam for girls. Yet Wiley wasn't the kind of older brother who clowned his siblings or bullied; Ronnie's brother always invited him along, always included him. Ronnie could say it without embarrassment: outside of Muhammad Ali, Wiley was his hero.

Nothing was going to get Wiley to budge from washing his car. Ronnie and Rickey instead began walking toward a nearby elementary school. There were always some guys scrapping on the basketball court. They figured they'd go get in on a game.

Cleveland was a tinderbox in 1975, eighty-two square miles constantly bursting into smoke and flame.

The bombings got most of the attention. In March, an underworld power struggle sparked. The city's leading numbers figure, Alex "Shondor" Birns, was killed when his Lincoln Mark IV exploded outside a bar. Six weeks later, Danny Greene, a former Birns associate turned rival, survived a retaliation bombing at his apartment. Over the next two years, thirty-seven car bombings would blow in the area—the most in the country. Federal investigators nicknamed Cleveland "Bomb City U.S.A." Dynamite packed with nuts and bolts for maximum damage was the preferred device. The explosions shattered windows for blocks. Cleveland bosses paid bomb makers extra if the detonations were big enough to make the nightly news.[3]

But another wave of calamity—less Hollywood but larger, uglier—also disfigured the city at the same time. The riots in Hough and Glenville had done their damage to the real estate value of the East Side. Landlords, most living in the Cleveland suburbs, were suddenly holding duplexes, houses, and buildings no one wanted to live in. Many were just abandoned. The city offered to help with demolition, knocking down 1,412 buildings between 1972 and 1974. But city hall couldn't keep pace with the market plunge and the decaying property.

So the buildings started to burn.

In 1962, Cleveland reported fifty cases of arson. A decade later, arsons were regularly swallowing more than a thousand properties a year. The year 1974 saw 1,593 arsons; 1975 would eventually tally 1,976. National insurance companies paid out millions a year to landlords, dubbing Cleveland the "arson capital of Ohio." At the height of the epidemic, only three full-time arson investigators were tasked with solving the crimes. At first officials blamed thrill-seeking delinquents, but the frequency and targeted areas clearly pointed to a larger pattern of "insure and burn," as one local newspaper put it. Yet as fires continued to saw through the East Side, city hall yanked away fire service in the poorer pockets of the city. Citing budget concerns, Cleveland closed five station houses and fired hundreds of firefighters.[4]

Hough and Glenville had shocked the country. But as 1975 pressed on, fires and bombings, destruction and damage, became the regular background noise in Ronnie Bridgeman's city.


Harry J. Franks's hazel eyes bounced up and down the blue receipt one last time—all there? One hundred fourteen money orders sold, $4,161.15 gross, plus $51.55 in charges, minus $30.93 in commission—before handing the copy over to the store owner. Earl Rogers looked like he was ready to get back to his checkers game. Couldn't blame him—as if pulling a living out of a drugstore wasn't enough hard enough, here was Rogers, a guy with three wild young daughters to lose sleep over, too. "Well," Franks said cheerfully to the store proprietor as he closed up his leather briefcase, perhaps cinching the straps a little tighter this time. "I've got to go to my last stop at Fairmount so I can go home."

Franks ambled out of the back room of Maxwell's Drug on Monday afternoon. A large white man in a brown suit, he moved past the short aisles of bread and beer, Drano and Spic and Span, nodding goodbye to the two young black women at the register. Outside in the hot flare of the late afternoon, the sun barreled down right onto his thinning crown of gray hair. The Benrus ticking on his wrist showed it was about twenty minutes to three. Franks climbed into his bronze 1970 Dodge and started east on Cedar Avenue. The Fairmount Cut-Rate was less than ten minutes away, a straight shot.

The fifty-eight-year-old's thoughts likely drifted over to his leather bag. The money order salesman had been in the business for more than fifteen years, six with U.S.N. Inc. He knew the company's rules on cash. The bag carried 460 money orders, blue-green check-sized papers that came in twenty-page booklets. On his weekly runs, Franks was supposed to collect payment from the store owners, minus commission, on whatever they'd sold. The company liked to see slips showing store owners had directly deposited money into U.S.N.'s bank account, or endorsed checks. But actual dollar bills? That was a liability, especially when you were dealing with these mom-and-pop stores. The Cut-Rate he was heading to now had been hit before. Hell, the brother of the man Franks had just been with, Earl Rogers, had been killed in a corner store robbery last year. But today Rogers had explained he didn't have time to go to the bank to deposit what he owed. Franks had accepted his cash payment. Unfortunately, it was now after 2:00 P.M., so the salesman couldn't get the money to a bank. He was stuck with it until morning, $429.55 there in his leather case.

Franks slid the Dodge onto Petrarca in front of the Cut-Rate, his front bumper kissing the curb near a garbage bin. The Benrus said it was just after the hour. He got out, sun blinking off the gold clip holding his striped tie down against his gut, and strolled to the front door of the white brick building. The air conditioner inside was chugging full blast as Franks entered. The first sight that jumped out at you in the small delicatessen was a wood carving nailed to the wall, two hands shaking in friendly, businesslike embrace. "WELCOME," the carving read. "WE MAKE FRIENDS HERE QUICKLY."

Karen Smith felt their eyes and anticipated the unwelcome sting of whatever rude catcalls or come-ons they were preparing to lob at her.[5]

The two young guys were leaning on the brick wall of Bob and Anna Robinson's store, strangers, not from the neighborhood—a red flag for the shy honor student who was embarrassed by any attention. Karen walked up Petrarca, clutching two empty soda bottles. After getting home from John Hay High School that day, her mother had asked her to return the bottles to the Robinsons' store. Now here she was, eyes fixed ahead, trying not to be noticed.

Luckily, the boys didn't say anything as Karen strolled by. She fixed her eyes on the door, just noticing one nod in her direction as she passed.

When the teenager walked into Mr. and Mrs. Robinson's store, a tall white man in a suit was just gathering his papers into a suitcase and heading out. Karen placed the empty bottles on the counter above the glass showcase holding cigars and cakes. She asked Mrs. Robinson for a bag of Dan Dee potato chips. The snack was up on a high shelf, so the store owner told the clerk, an old man named Clarence, to get them. As Clarence was placing the chips on the counter, a groan sounded from outside, followed by a muffled noise—the rushed foot scrapes of a scuffle. Mrs. Robinson came around the counter to the front window.

Outside, two young men twisted with Franks—one dressed in dark colors, the other wearing a flowered shirt. A metal pipe smacked into the older man's side, followed by a splash of liquid that hit his face and doused the store window. As Franks landed on the pavement, two piercing sounds snapped in the air.

"Oh my God, they're shooting," Mrs. Robinson said, turning the door lock. A third shot banged. Mrs. Robinson turned around, took a few steps, then felt her feet disappear beneath her. She was on the ground. "Get Bob," she tried to say, but the words slipped around the blood flooding into her mouth. "Get Bob."

"Don't move," Clarence told her. "The customer's on the phone trying to call the police. I'll go get your husband. Please don't move," the older man pleaded, "just be cool."

Someone screamed. Blood jetted out from Mrs. Robinson's neck and mouth.

After gassing themselves out on the basketball court for a few hours in the thick May heat, Ronnie and Rickey were ready to get back to the neighborhood. When they strolled onto Arthur, the two friends stopped by Lynn Garrett's house. He was sitting outside with his girlfriend, Sherry.

Lynn Garrett. Before Ronnie had hooked up with Rickey, he'd pretty much been inseparable from Lynn. The two were the same age, and really what eventually split them apart was nothing so much as Lynn's pure athleticism. Whatever sport he picked up, he excelled at—basketball, football, he was a natural at it all. And he rode that talent out of the neighborhood, securing a football scholarship to Baldwin Wallace University. In Ronnie's eyes, that kind of dedication—not screwing around with the usual teenage street shenanigans—was a reason to respect Lynn.

The four stood together, trading street gossip. Someone mentioned they should head up to Grant's store, a mom-and-pop up on 108th. Walking down the street, the foursome stopped at the Vernon house. Two of the family's girls, Darlene and Susan, were sitting on their porch. Lynn, Sherry, Rickey, and Ronnie stopped to talk. Whatever they were blabbing about, Ronnie didn't know. He'd tuned them out.

Instead, sex-fiending teen that he was, Ronnie was trying to catch a peek up the Vernon girls' dresses up there on the porch. His eyes cat-and-mousing for a look, Ronnie didn't notice the car pulling up in front of the house until he heard the voice shouting from the backseat. "Someone just got shot up at Robinson's store!" the passenger called out. "Y'all should go check it out."

Curious, the six neighbors—the two Vernon sisters, Lynn, Sherry, Rickey, and Ronnie—walked up 108th, then hooked a right, heading for the Robinsons' Cut-Rate.

Eyes lidded down to slits, head bent as if puzzled, Harry J. Franks lay in the store's doorway, his body a limp zigzag.

Radios in fifth-district cars crackled out the dispatch at 3:37 P.M: holdup in progress, male shot. Sirens razored apart the afternoon as police fought through the rush-hour traffic. The first Cleveland officers on the scene huddled with Mrs. Robinson while an ambulance screamed to the store. She tried again and again, but the blood coming out of her mouth kept her from telling them what had happened. Outside, Reverend Charles McCann, a retired Catholic priest just passing by, stopped to whisper the last rites over Franks's body. Called in by the bulletin, a newspaper cameraman snapped his shutter as the priest ushered Franks on. The photograph would be splashed on the front page of the next morning's *Plain Dealer*.

Police photographers also arrived, their flashbulbs blinking rhythmically over the street corner and store. *Flash:* the glass portion of the store's door spiderwebbed with a bullet hole and still dripping with an unknown liquid. *Flash:* the wide Rorschach patterns of Mrs. Robinson's blood inside still marking the store's linoleum. *Flash:* a CLOSED sign in the store window, Franks's body on the ground. *Flash:* the street corner jammed with rubberneckers, faces from the neighborhood, regulars at the store, police holding them back, everyone straining to see.

By 4:15 P.M., two detectives arrived from the downtown station: Eugene Terpay, a twenty-seven-year department veteran with a face as lined and sagging as an old speed bag, and James T. Farmer, a native West Virginian and Korean War vet with a file thick with decorations and advanced course certificates. Together the investigators started filling their notebooks with details. Karen Smith provided specifics on the two young men she spotted on her walk into the building. A cup, presumably the one holding the acid splashed in the victim's face, was recovered at the scene. An Ohio Bell employee named Tim Brzuski had been idling in his van at a stoplight on Cedar Avenue when he noticed two young "colored men" tussling with Franks. After hearing gunshots, Brzuski pulled off at a gas station to call police. A neighbor, Charles Loper, informed detectives he'd been on his porch next to the Cut-Rate when he witnessed "two col. Males accost the victim as he came from the store," the officer's notes later reported. "They appeared to beat him with an object, a piece of pipe. One of the suspects was armed with what appeared to be a 38 cal. Revolver. This suspect fired three shots at the victim and then both took a tan colored brief case from him and ran."

The detectives concluded after their initial interviews that they were looking for two young black men, between seventeen and nineteen. "Suspects last seen running SOUTH on Petrarca Ave., then WEST on FRANK Ave.," the day's report concluded. "Suspects seen entering a DK [dark] green over lite green Olds."

The crowd ringing the store continued to press in for a better view. Ronnie Bridgeman elbowed his way to the front; his attention stopped on an older guy from the neighborhood up there watching, too. He had on a plaid apple hat that matched a pair of bell-bottoms, the outfit rounded out by a black shirt and suede jacket. Man, Ronnie thought, a nice hookup. Then he saw the victim. The white man was still lying lifeless on the sidewalk, no sheet yet hiding his body. Ronnie felt ill. The dead should be respected, he believed, not left in the street. Here was a man, a stranger, sure, but another human being, the intimacy of his passing open for everyone to see.

"Come on, man," he told Rickey. "Let's go." The two black teens walked away from the store. Crime scene techs finished their duties.

Evidence went into bags. The detectives remained inside, pulling info out of the store owner, whose wife right then was under the knife for an emergency tracheotomy at Lakeside Hospital. A white sheet was eventually placed over Franks. It was too short for his tall body, and his brown dress shoes poked up at the sky.

Uniformed officers were left with the grunt work, quizzing onlookers about possible witnesses. Patrolman Robert Hassel, pen and notebook in hand, circled around to one of the small knots of neighborhood children. He asked if anyone had seen anything. Hoots and giggles came back from the group. But under the tangled voices, someone piped up.

"Yes."

# 3

## BLACK AND BLUE

Cleveland, May 25, 1975

*STABS OF LIGHT WHEELED ACROSS THE FRONT WINDOW. RICKEY ALWAYS* woke easily, and the play of beams in the dark outside fished him up from a thin sleep on the sofa. A burglar? he thought from the couch in the Bridgemans' front room. Before his mind flipped to any other possibilities, gun barrels were coming through the door.

The first officers inside rushed Rickey; the teen was shoved down into the cushions, arms twisted behind his back. From where he was pinned, Rickey could see directly into Mrs. Bridgeman's bedroom. One cop had the fifty-seven-year-old woman by her leg, the other by her arm. They handled her like baggage, dragging her out of bed while her pained moans filled the hallway. Mrs. Bridgeman's heart was bad, Rickey knew. She fell to her knees between the two cops. They yanked her up and marched her out of the room with her hands behind her back, a perp walk in her own home. Ideas crashed in on Rickey all at once. What the hell is going on? They've got the wrong house.

It wasn't unusual to find the Bridgeman brothers' best friend at their address late at night. Rickey's stepdad flipped the locks at home at midnight, so if you weren't in by then, you weren't getting in; on nights like tonight, when the three friends killed hours driving the East Side in Wiley's Sebring, Rickey would just stay over. The three had been out till nearly 4:00 A.M. before heading inside and smoking weed, the joint wrapping their heads in woolly static—and clapping more confusion over the chaos now spilling out in the home.

Wiley had actually been the first to the door when the banging started. As the cops pushed inside, the eldest Bridgeman son darted into his mother's room, hiding behind the door. Like some silent movie slapstick, officers stepped into the room, in and out, in and out, looking for anyone else, but failing to see him. Finally a plainclothes detective eyed Wiley in the door crack. He yanked Wiley roughly from his hiding spot.

Down the hall Ronnie was asleep in his room when he felt his toe twitch. Popping his eyes open, he found half a dozen cops standing over his bed. The pistols and shotguns worried him less than the sound of his mother's shouts from the hallway, and the teen shoved past the officers. Despite his repeated questions, the only information he could squeeze from the cops as they began ripping up the house was that they were looking for Rickey Jackson and Wiley Bridgeman.

"What do you want us to do with this guy?" one of the cops asked a sergeant, pointing to Ronnie.

The white-shirted cop looked over at Ronnie. "Take him downtown."

"For what?"

"Getting in the damn way."

With the handcuff metal biting their wrists, the three boys were pushed outside. A dozen police cars flung ribbons of red and blue light around Arthur Avenue. Past the blocky shadows and streetlamps, Rickey could see more patrol cars at his own house. His mother, stepdad, and brothers and sisters were all laid out facedown on the pavement.[1]

The violence in Glenville didn't truly stop when the last National Guard jeeps left and the glass was swept up. The rancor born out of the 1968 incident stamped the city. As the 1960s gave way to the

1970s, the event's weight continued to exert phantom pressure on the interactions between black Clevelanders and police. Some small part of Glenville still lingered in every car stop, house raid, and police shooting.

Cleveland wasn't alone. Harlem, Watts, Detroit, Newark. The urban unrest in the mid- to late 1960s, riding into American living rooms with the nightly newscast, jolted the establishment. Something had switched. The blue notes and gospel rhetoric of the civil rights movement were gone. A more aggressive tone muscled into the dialogue on equality. The images from the front lines were now chaotic. City blocks burning. Soldiers in the street. Black men in sunglasses and berets. "Now that they've taken Dr. King off," Black Power evangelist Stokely Carmichael declared when he learned of the assassination, "it's time to end this nonviolence bullshit."[2]

This rage shook even the top level of American power, where it would derail the best intentions of the era.

When he took office after the Kennedy assassination, Lyndon Johnson—the longtime Senate operator, a Texan gripped by massive ego and ambition—pushed ahead a progressive agenda that aimed to remake the entire country, a societal overhaul equal in impact to Roosevelt's New Deal. The Great Society forged together civil rights legislation with what Johnson termed the "War on Poverty," a series of federal programs and interventions mainlining job programs and welfare initiatives into the inner city in order to wipe out the root causes of crime and unrest. "For decades, the conditions that nourish crime have been gathering force," Johnson said.[3] "As a result, every major city harbors an army of the alienated—people who acknowledge no stake in the public order and no responsibility to others." Food stamps, Job Corps, Head Start child care, and Medicare—all were the product of Johnson's optimistic hope that the brawn of the federal government could be leveraged for the benefit of the country's vulnerable.

As much as the right morals were steering the policy, the details themselves were still stunted by racial stereotypes. As the historian Elizabeth Hinton has pointed out, the Great Society's programs were largely aimed at the individual—school, job training, housing. The cies ignored the longtime structural barriers that ran along rac_ lines—what good can job training do if the local union won't hire you because you're black? Instead, the programs "presented inequality as a problem of individual behavior," Hinton wrote.[4] Success or failure was measured by the "right" behavior; the "right" behavior was the behavior of the mainstream white establishment. They "aimed to change the psychological impact of racism within individuals rather than the impact of the long history of racism within American institutions," Hinton wrote.[5] Conceived as a release from poverty, the programs actually were a form of social control.

In the historian's telling, this faulty wiring doomed Johnson's War on Poverty. It failed to hoist young black men out of the ghetto in larger numbers, a failure that was writ large in each of the American cities burning like bonfires in the 1960s.

Johnson personally was aghast at the violence. The president refused to see the riots as collective outcry over larger structural inequalities. No, it had to be the work of instigators—communists or radical Black Power groups, Johnson felt. "There is no American right to loot stores, or to burn buildings, or to fire rifles from the rooftops," the president told the nation in a televised speech. He tasked a group of mayors and government officials—the Kerner Commission—to perform an exhaustive autopsy on the riots. The group returned with a searing 426-page report laying out the systemic causes boiling black neighborhoods to anger. The conclusion warned that the current status quo "could quite conceivably lead to a kind of urban apartheid within semi martial law in many major cities, enforced residence of Negroes in segregated areas, and a drastic reduction in personal freedom for all Americans, particularly Negroes."

But Johnson rejected the findings of his own group's report. Rather, he turned to police, dramatically shifting the administration's attention away from poverty to law enforcement. When Johnson declared a "War on Crime" in 1965, the program was just another piece of the Great Society agenda, an effort to modernize local police and

al crime data into their departments with federal
s a battle cry.

the Omnibus Crime Control and Safe Streets Act
reconfigured the national response to crime. Lift-
ing the philosophy of the War on Poverty—federal intervention in urban spaces and a focus on measured, data-driven social control—the
program offered hundreds of thousands of dollars of federal grants to
local departments through money administered by the newly created
Law Enforcement Assistance Administration (LEAA). Between 1969
and 1974, the office's annual budget would explode, from $63 million
to $871 million, money going directly to local cops on the front lines.
This new federal emphasis on crime drastically altered the tenor of
American law enforcement—permanently. The government money
went to crime deterrence rather than criminal prosecution. It was a
switch from enforcing law to maintaining order. And for Cleveland, it
would mean a flood of money and pressure on the police.

Heavy lights bleached half the room, a twenty-by-ten sweatbox on the
fourth floor of the central police station downtown. The desk sergeant
on duty stood by the door, looking like he couldn't care less, like this
was someone else's headache. He barked at the seven young black guys
inside to take off their hats, put out their cigarettes, and line up wherever they wanted on the seven slots marked out on the wall. Rickey
walked to the very end—number seven. Wiley was six spaces down—
number one. Rickey had shaken off the initial shock from the raid
hours earlier, but he was still clueless about why they were there.

The seven men faced a mesh screen dividing the room. The other
side was dark, and with the bright lights daggering into his eyes, Rickey
could only spot vague shapes on the far end. The desk sergeant ordered
the group to step forward. Turn to the left. Turn to the right. Turn
around. Face the front again. Step back. The lockstep routine over, only
silence came from behind the screen. The desk sergeant told the seven

men to follow him out of the room. It was over, but Rickey still wasn't any closer to piecing together what was happening.

Rickey was quiet, but far from oblivious. Ronnie and Wiley, with their liquid charm, could make a quick, easy peace with whatever situation they were in. Rickey tended to hang back. But inside that reserve he was alert, constantly observing and assessing. He liked to have the facts before acting or committing to something.

The reticence was a natural by-product of his upbringing. His family had moved often, hopscotching the East Side ten or more times; he got tired of the social dance routine involved in making new friends. He kept to himself, and he killed hours by aimlessly riding the city bus for as long as the change in his pocket lasted. If he got lost, he'd simply cross the street and hop a bus going the opposite way. These wanderings often took him to the Cleveland Museum of Art, probably the last place on earth you'd expect to find him, a poor black kid from the East Side squeaking his shoes down the halls, the high church of Cleveland culture, a marble testament to the buying power of institutional steel and manufacturing capital. Sun-shot Monets, glowering Dutch masters, puzzle-piece Picassos. Rickey's favorite part of the building was the Armor Court, an exhibition of medieval weaponry. There in the middle of a room stood a knight and horse fully decked for battle, the shiny metal catching the sunlight drifting down from the glass ceiling. The only horses Rickey ever saw in real life were carrying policemen.

Rickey's mother, Essie Mae Copeland, had been a fifteen-year-old girl in Greenwood, Mississippi, when she learned she was pregnant. This was the late 1950s, in the same haunted Big Cotton flats that birthed the stark blues of Robert Johnson and the White Citizens' Council movement. Essie Mae's mother and father sent her off to Cleveland to live with relatives. The baby's father, Ronald Carter, went, too.

The couple—two slow-talking southern kids 850 miles away from everything they knew plunked down in the fast-lane rhythms of the industrial North—settled near Central Avenue. Ronald got work at a nearby gas station; some of Rickey's first memories were of taking his father's lunch to him every day. Ham and cheese with mayo and a tomato slice.

Rickey learned early that if he wanted to understand his parents or what was happening in his house, he'd have to pick it up on his own. His parents weren't the type to talk or explain. In 1965, with a new baby brother in the house, stiff white people began making regular visits. New cheese and oatmeal would then appear in the cupboard. But for some reason, Rickey's father could never be around at the time. Even his clothes had to be hidden. Rickey could see these visits were putting a strain on his parents. His father was out of work. As a condition of welfare aid, Rickey later learned, an unmarried adult couldn't stay in the house. His father started coming back less and less. And then he was just gone.

Essie Mae didn't explain. They just kept on moving from place to place, Essie Mae from boyfriend to boyfriend. Sometimes the guys were nice. Sometimes they drank and hit her. When Essie Mae had had enough, she took her family—which eventually included two more brothers and a sister for Rickey—to another part of the East Side. There was no camouflaging the fact they were poor. But Essie Mae never let them go hungry or sleep on the street. The journey north hadn't rubbed out her sense of southern decorum. She was a drill sergeant about keeping her kids in clean clothes and combed hair. Even when they only had milk crates for furniture and two chipped plates to eat off, she kept them immaculate. If they didn't have a place to stay, she would get the whole family on a bus to some far-flung distant relative and march her children inside over protests or excuses.

As Rickey got older, he could read his mother better. To her children, Essie Mae yo-yoed between angry and sad, otherwise keeping her feelings out of sight. Whatever crashed around inside, Essie Mae couldn't box all that up in words, much less explain it to her children. All that surfaced was that unshakable loneliness. Rickey felt an unsatisfied yearning pulsing off his mother, a gap that home couldn't patch.

Sometimes she'd pull Rickey aside, palm him some cash, and tell him he had control of the house. Then she'd vanish. Three days. Seven days. Ten days. Once, when the family was living in an apartment on Hough after the riots—they took to calling the cratered neighborhood "Baby Beirut"—she was MIA when the power cut out at night. Essie Mae hadn't paid the bill. Rickey and the four kids laughed it off at first. Then they heard the rats. They began by chewing through food in the kitchen. Then they were bolting across the family room. Soon all the kids were huddled on the bed screaming, Rickey vainly tossing shoes at the scurrying shapes.

"Does anybody need to make a phone call?" The desk sergeant's question yanked Rickey's thoughts back to his current situation at the police station. Despite all the history between them, he knew he needed to let his mom know what was happening to him. Along with Wiley, he followed the desk sergeant to a phone bank down the hall from the lineup. Essie Mae's phone wasn't working, so they dialed the Bridgeman house, hoping Mrs. Bridgeman could relay the message.

As the call was going through, Rickey spotted two detectives enter the room with a young boy from the neighborhood. The paperboy, Darlene's brother, Ed Vernon. Toothpick arms and legs. Face fishbowled behind glasses that looked thick enough to stop a bullet. Rickey got it then. Word had been going around the neighborhood that Ed was telling folks he knew who did the killing at the Cut-Rate earlier in the week. Rickey looked at Ed. Ed looked at Rickey. Ed pointed at Rickey and said something to the detectives. Rickey knew then that this was all about the dead man up on Fairhill.

No Washington, D.C., hack bureaucrat or committee report could tell the Cleveland police much about a war on crime. Glenville drove the department to its battle stations, and they never really stood down. The department, in the words of one city hall staffer, began to "relate change to subversion, see progress as a threat to self-interest, and view civilian direction as outside interference."[6] As the years progressed, the interactions between Cleveland officers and the black community increasingly took on a furious and delirious edge.

The East Side was super-charged with ill will. Regularly, officers reported taking sniper fire from dark alleys on patrol. In September 1970, a routine car stop at East 105th and St. Clair ended with a black driver fatally shooting one officer and wounding his partner. Soon even plainclothes detectives started carrying military-style .30 caliber carbines for protection. "We will stop carrying them when the militants stop using them on us," a police officer said at the time.[7] This anticipation of violence was even formalized in the department; promotions were rarely based on anything more than how well a cop could shoot at the range. "We had some great shots," Chief Patrick Garrity later admitted. "But not that great in the brain department."[8]

Earlier in 1970, fifty Cleveland cops surrounded an East Side apartment building where members of the local Black Panther Party put together a community newsletter. Ostensibly there to serve a pair of warrants, the lieutenant leading the raid—Harry Leisman—opened fire with a .45 caliber Thompson submachine gun, tearing apart the building's second floor. He claimed later he'd seen a muzzle flash. One Panther and one cop were injured in the ensuing exchange of gunfire. Later a black Cleveland police sergeant—only the fourth African American man to reach that rank in the department—told the city's leading black newspaper he wondered whether his fellow officers were there to "execute a search warrant or to execute any blacks found there."[9] The Cleveland cop union's president, Frank Schaefer, didn't dispel the idea. "This country doesn't need a Black Panther Party," he told the press. "To my way of thinking, they have to be wiped out."[10] That same summer, in the span of a few days, three leaders of the black activist group Pride, Inc. were shot in the street. Two died, the third recovered. One journalist wondered openly in print if the city's police were either ignoring the violence or hunting down prominent black activists themselves.

Within the department, police officers witnessed their fellow officers beat suspects, coerce information, and pull over black drivers with no probable cause. "And God," one former police officer would remember years later in a court deposition. "Don't let him have a white woman with him." The same officer would later tell the story—under oath—of police officers preparing a suspect for a lineup with a witness. Realizing the suspect was wearing a different-colored pair of pants than the individual described by the witness, the officers forced the suspect to change clothes before the lineup for an easier ID. "You learn rather quickly that the way things are handled on the street is contrary to what it should be handled according to the book," the officer recounted. "Winning the case was what it was all about. It wasn't about what was fair, it wasn't about what was honest. It was about winning."

Within the department, good men and women may have been uncomfortable with such activity. But it was also clear the department was walled off by a code of silence. "You do something they don't like, you are not in the group, you are not in the clique, you get punished for it," an officer later recounted.[11] Another Cleveland police veteran would describe the attitude within the ranks as "it is us and everybody else," he said. "Us against them."[12]

Still, some whistle-blowers did leak accounts of the chaos inside the department. The *Call and Post*, Cleveland's black weekly newspaper, ran a series of articles written by "Arthur X," an African American patrolman. "Black officers have spoken privately for some time on matters involving questionable police tactics and unequal application of the criminal justice system in the black communities," the officer wrote.[13] "Most black officers are hesitant to complain or protest any police action for fear of reprisals." Arthur X's pieces later went on to describe daily violence from his fellow officers. "I saw seven or eight policemen without badges hitting some black kids over the head for no apparent reason . . . it was as if they were trying to see how many they could get. . . . If I, as a policeman, couldn't do anything about the police violence, then what the hell could the citizens do about it."[14]

It was only a matter of time before this runaway antagonism that had taken up shop inside the department began pushing officers into outright criminal behavior. On Christmas Eve 1971, a police officer—the same one who led the trigger-happy raid on the Black Panther apartment—was summoned to a bar near his home where a fight was allegedly taking place. Off-duty, Harry Leisman burst into the place with an M14 rifle—the same automatic weapon issued to U.S. military in Vietnam. Leisman sprayed the room. A twenty-five-year-old patron was killed. One of the M14's stray rounds punched through the wall into the family room of an apartment across the street, killing a ten-year-old boy watching television. When questioned by his fellow officers, Leisman—who'd already killed two people in his thirteen years on the department—claimed a mysterious stranger had handed him the hefty automatic weapon outside the bar.[15]

Less than six weeks later, in February, two white Cleveland police officers were indicted on charges of rape and sodomy. John Mandryk and Ronald Turner had come upon a young black couple in Woodhill Park. The patrolman told the twenty-two-year-old man at the wheel that he could go to jail for a year for not having a driver's license—or his nineteen-year-old fiancée could go with the cops. The girl was then taken to another, secluded part of the park and raped. When the officers' arrest hit the news, another teenager came forward; she also had been raped by the same men.[16]

Leisman, the Christmas Eve shooter, was charged with first-degree murder for the deaths of the twenty-five-year-old woman and ten-year-old boy. A jury acquitted the officer, who was taken off the street but later promoted to captain and put in charge of the city jail.

Mandryk and Turner both ducked felony rape and sodomy convictions, but a jury did find them guilty of abducting a woman for immoral purposes. They were both given prison sentences of five to thirty years. The *Call and Post* cheered the convictions, noting it was "one of the first times in Cleveland that policemen were brought to trial and found guilty."

But forty days into their prison stays, Mandryk and Turner were both released by the sentencing judge. Evoking a twist in the law justifying "shock parole" in exigent circumstances, the court ruled the ex-cops' prison terms were "cruel and inhumane" because they were being kept in solitary confinement for protection.

"It was a shock when I first heard the announcement," one of the young rape victims told the newspaper after the release. "But then, with that, by them being white, you know it was sort of expected."[17]

The first judge to see the state's case against Rickey Jackson and Wiley Bridgeman wasn't impressed.

The two appeared before Cuyahoga County Circuit Judge John Angelotta at a preliminary hearing not long after the police lineup. The case against the two was woefully thin, even for the low bar of the Cuyahoga County Court system. There was no physical evidence, and at the time, prosecutors presented no details on any witness identification. Nothing. Angelotta was ready to dump the charges altogether. But an assistant Cuyahoga County prosecutor piped up, telling the judge that one of the victims in the crime—Anna Robinson—was still in the hospital recovering from a gunshot wound and hadn't yet had an opportunity to view the suspects. He asked Angelotta to hold Rickey and Wiley for two more weeks. The judge agreed. So the two were shuffled back to the city jail, where they were slotted into individual cells on the fourth floor reserved for murder suspects. Rickey was left alone, mulling over the irony. All this could have been avoided had he made a different choice three months earlier.

After years of knocking around the East Side, Rickey's family had settled into a stable life by the time he was in his teens. Essie Mae met Milton Copeland, a sanitation truck supervisor. Not only did he bring home a sizable city paycheck, he was a pro at gaming the system: Milton's routes stretched into the suburbs, where folks would junk perfectly good furniture and other items for no reason. When Essie Mae and her kids moved into the house with Milton on Arthur Avenue, the whole place was fitted out with quality castoffs from the county.

Milton and Rickey got along fine. Unlike some of the other men his mother went with, he didn't press a dad act on Rickey. Milton's unsaid message seemed to be: *Look, I'm the guy who's with your mom, I would appreciate if you occasionally listened to me.* Fine by Rickey. He respected that. Actually, he would always think of Milton as his stepdad.

Rickey himself was rounding into the last stretch of childhood. Already that adventurous streak was pointing him elsewhere. He liked to watch *Star Trek* with Milton, and Rickey felt the pull to boldly go where no Arthur Avenue kid had gone before, way past the county limits. The U.S. Marine Corps was recruiting heavily out of Cuyahoga County. Rickey had seen the guys who came back from Vietnam, strutting in uniforms and unrolling war stories. The military looked better and better as his home life started cracking with familiar strain.

Like so many of the men Essie Mae had been around, Milton liked to drink. The fights didn't usually get physical. But one night at the end of 1974, Milton was into Rickey's mother about hiding money again. "Don't touch my mother," Rickey preemptively warned his stepdad. Milton palmed Rickey's head like a basketball. Rickey blinked, suddenly finding himself on the floor, his mother shaking him awake. There was an imprint of his head burrowed into the wall. On his feet, Rickey immediately went to get some lighter fluid. Milton had a new car in the driveway, a Deuce and a Quarter. Rickey doused the car with the fluid, but he hesitated before flicking a match. He looked around. Assessed the scene. If he turned Milton's Deuce into a fiery blaze, the flames might torch the house as well. He walked. Milton later apologized, but Rickey was signing those enrollment papers soon after.

Marine recruits were funneled to Parris Island in South Carolina, the basic training meat grinder for the military's fiercest branch. At first Rickey could handle the brutal physical routines. But soon he began getting headaches, red storms of blinding pain that crawled all the way down to the tips of his fingers and toes. When military doctors examined him, they asked if he'd had any recent head trauma. He relayed what happened with Milton, and the doctors concluded he was likely suffering the mental aftershocks of an untreated concussion. They couldn't clear him for combat. The marines handed him an honorable discharge.

That was how Rickey found himself sitting in a South Carolina bus station in February 1975, waiting to catch an all-nighter home. A single thought stood up in his mind, waving its arms around, trying to be heard: *You don't have to go back.* He could go anywhere. This time the change in his pocket could actually get him someplace. He could *boldly go.* But home was Bitzie and Buddy. The house on Arthur furnished with great sidewalk finds. His mother planted on the couch all afternoon watching her soap operas. His own bedroom down in the basement where Milton had his prize possession, a big-ass color Curtis Mathes TV that he'd rescued from a burning building. No matter how much Pine Sol Essie Mae rubbed into the wood the console still stank of smoke. He got on the bus for Cleveland.

Now, sitting in the city jail three months later, Rickey figured this was just like Parris Island, a trip outside his orbit before heading back. It was just a matter of time before he was on Arthur Avenue again. But the days pooled into weeks. Eventually he asked one of the jail guards when his family was coming to get him. "Coming to get you?" the deputy said. "You've been identified and charged with murder."


On his second run for office, Ralph Perk was propelled into city hall in 1971 by the West Side fear of black unrest.

A Republican county pol with little campaign or party machinery at his back, he leveraged law-and-order rhetoric to a surprise win in a three-way contest. The momentum tilted to Perk largely because his campaign pressed many of the same emotional buttons Richard Nixon hit in his 1968 White House run, including sharp criticism of black radicals and war protesters.

In Washington, D.C., the Nixon administration had fully embraced the previous president's federal law enforcement funding programs, supersizing the pile of money available for local departments waging the war on crime. The Law Enforcement Assistance Administration would become the fastest-growing government agency throughout the 1970s. And as one of the few big-city Republican mayors, Perk was sure his party affiliation would open the right doors in Washington.

But when the new mayor arrived in the capital for a sit-down with Attorney General John Mitchell about enlarging Cleveland's take of federal money, the country's top lawman had concerns. Cleveland police, he told Perk, had the worst reputation in the country.[18] This wouldn't help with grants, Mitchell indicated. As if to hammer in the point, when LEAA announced the first eight cities that would receive funding in 1972, Cleveland was left off the list. Perk personally rushed back to the capital to beg the administration to reconsider. Cleveland was eventually included, receiving twenty-one million dollars for crime prevention. The funding went directly to "target areas" on the East Side, increasing the numbers of patrols. Drug arrests alone tripled by 1974 thanks to this influx of federal money.[19] But Perk realized a dirty department would risk losing any additional money from Nixon's war chest.

And Perk—and Cleveland—needed every dime. Cleveland had been bleeding businesses and residents to the suburbs for years. The city had never passed tax increases to compensate. Perk's administration would be remembered for its desperate bookkeeping. During his years in office, the city's debt grew modestly—$326 million in 1971 to $434 million in 1977. Perk, however, ran up Cleveland's short-term debt—$14.6 million in 1971 to $140 million in 1977. At the same time, Perk became overly reliant on federal money, fiscal blood transfusions that by 1975 were covering one-third of the city's operating budget.[20] But this funding was constantly threatened by bad headlines about police misconduct. Perk was left tiptoeing the fine line between corralling a wayward department and keeping law enforcement's reputation clean.

There were few practical blueprints available for cleaning up a police department. Washington, D.C., didn't help. During the Johnson years, as commissions and task forces put microscopes on the riots, there was an almost uniform official blind eye to police misconduct during the uprisings. These government brainstorm sessions—which would set the national policy—were also staffed by law enforcement, so progressive ideas like civilian oversight were never seriously floated. And finally, both the Johnson and Nixon administrations pressed local and federal law enforcement to adapt to stricter crime reporting requirements. The influx of data, it's been argued, created the first detailed picture of American streets—while also suggesting that crime rates had spiked when really crime was just being more thoroughly reported.

In October 1972, a few months after his meeting with Attorney General Mitchell, Mayor Perk sent a testy confidential memo to both the city's chief of police and safety director. "Events," the mayor wrote, "have taken place in recent months which reflect upon the operation of your Department and Division respectively." Park continued: "These events have included the actual indictment of Cleveland policemen for offenses such as armed robbery, rape, and manslaughter, the damaging of a bar by members of the Cleveland Police Department, and continuous citizen complaints of poor or no response to calls for assistance and help."

Perk's first order was that no officer on duty should henceforth be "seen or found in a bar or cocktail lounge unless he is there on a specific complaint or request for assistance." The mayor also reminded his subordinates that police officers could only carry city-issued weapons; all other firearm requests were to be reviewed. Most dramatically, he ordered the entire top layer of the command staff, from captains on up, in both districts and detective bureaus, to swap positions every few months. The juggling would hopefully eliminate comfortable cronyism.

But the chronic problems rotting out the department like a bad tooth were immune to hard words from city hall or command staff musical chairs. That was the lesson of Carl Stokes's administration. The extent of the division's discord would become painfully, embarrassingly clear to all of Cleveland within eighteen months of Perk's memo.

March 1974 was a strange season for both the country and the city. Americans coast-to-coast reached for morning newspapers splashed with headlines on President Nixon's slow-motion implosion, triggered by Watergate. Confidence in the basic American institutions was in a tailspin. Downtown at Cleveland city hall, the basic municipal decision-making was on pause; Perk, a famously hands-on mayor, was in the hospital recovering from viral pneumonia.

Into this patch of dead static, the *Plain Dealer* began dropping a series of above-the-fold blockbuster reports on police corruption. The first salvo tied a handful of police officers to an East Side burglary ring responsible for a string of jobs, including knocking over a bank branch for more than seventy-one thousand dollars, stealing twenty-three thousand dollars' worth of goods from a jeweler, and lifting twenty thousand dollars' worth of suits and topcoats from a men's store. The next day the paper ran a piece on four high-ranking officers who were allegedly receiving payoffs to keep an illegal gambling house open. When a lower-ranking patrolman attempted to close down the East Side spot, the paper reported, someone dropped a concrete block on his car as he was driving home after a shift. Follow-up reports from the *Plain Dealer* showed how officers—despite Perk's prohibition—were still spending their shifts bellied up to bars and carrying military firepower. A later piece recounted how fifty-to-one-hundred-dollar weekly payments from pimps were keeping officers from arresting working girls, and pointed out the city's busiest prostitute stroll was only two blocks from the vice unit's headquarters.[21]

As the series continued through March, anonymous cops approached the paper to unload their own horror stories of working with bad partners. One officer told the paper it was common for police to fill their own pockets at crime scenes—even murder sites. "The police at the scene ransacked the house looking for any money that had been hidden. They would even go so far as to look into the mouth of the corpse for gold teeth," the patrolman told the paper. "As funny as that may sound, I've seen it happen."[22]

"I would fear being shot at," another patrolman said when explaining why good cops didn't turn in the bad ones. "Or set up as being involved in a crime which would ruin my career."

So much ugly press just confirmed Attorney General Mitchell's assessment of the department. Hot panic flashed through the ranks of local government. Thanks to Watergate, public opinion was also particularly sensitive to public corruption. A solution to the police problem—something, anything—was imperative. Or at least the appearance of a solution. Both inside the administration and on the city council, eyes turned to New York City and Mayor John V. Lindsay. In April 1970, a *New York Times* article revealed extensive corruption within the NYPD. Police whistle-blowers—including Frank Serpico—related tales of bribery, payoffs, shakedowns, and worse. Mayor Lindsay met the problem head-on, using a mayoral executive order to create an independent commission to investigate the claims. Known as the Knapp Commission (after its chairman, former assistant New York district attorney Whitman Knapp), the commission spent two years investigating the department's practices and policies, eventually indicting fifty officers and rewiring the NYPD. The Knapp Commission was the gold standard for police reform. Even as Cleveland's politicos were wrestling with their options in spring 1974, Chicago was staffing up its own thirty-person civilian unit to address law enforcement corruption. Perk's law director and members of the council urged the mayor to similarly adopt the Knapp blueprint.

Instead, Cleveland's mayor bricked the play. Rather than hire experts to tackle the problem, Perk announced he would ask four local clergymen and a rabbi to sit on a commission tasked with investigating police corruption. Rather than open the city's bank vault to pay for the committee, Perk decided to apply for federal funding, essentially tying the abilities of what came to be known as the God Squad to the LEAA's willingness to foot the cost.

Other city leaders were unhappy. "I think the committee idea is utterly ridiculous and basically insane," George Forbes, the city council president and inheritor of Carl Stokes's black political machine, told the paper. "Perk is either losing his mind or is still under sedation . . . the clergy have the ability to save souls, but right now we're trying to save a city."[23]

Obviously the God Squad was bound to fail. The federal funding never came through. And when the committee issued its first of what was expected to be many reports in June 1974, the clergymen made it clear they weren't advocating for an NYPD-like overhaul. "The Cleveland Crime Commission," the recommendations began, "preliminarily concludes that a long-term investigation of corruption in the Cleveland Division of Police, such as conducted by the Knapp Commission over a period of a year and a half, will only delay the inevitable departmental reforms which can have the greatest impact in eliminating corruption and misconduct." The God Squad also punted the responsibility for a serious investigation back to the existing power structure. "We believe that such a criminal investigation of these practices primarily rests in," the same early report noted, "and should continue to be a function of the Cuyahoga County Prosecutor's Office and the Cuyahoga County Grand Jury."

Cuyahoga County Prosecutor John T. Corrigan hustled together a grand jury in April. Four officers were indicted on charges related to the burglary ring. But a second grand jury tasked with sorting through evidence of widespread payoffs and bribes tied to gambling and prostitution proved as ineffective as the God Squad. In late May the panel announced there was insufficient evidence for charges against any officers. Instead, the grand jury released its own report blasting the department's "atmosphere of toleration, condoning, and indifference, if not an atmosphere of favoritism" toward some illegal gambling operations. "It did not surprise us that such qualities as discipline, respect, competency were replaced by disrespect, incompetency, indifference and something less than quality police work," the report fumed.[24] But again, instead of criminal indictments, the grand jury served up organizational and policy recommendations.

With outside committees deferring to grand juries, and grand juries opting for recommendations rather than criminal indictments, concrete solutions to the 1974 police scandal seemed a long shot. Exacerbating the situation throughout the spring and summer was a crime wave that political leaders couldn't ignore—and begged the question, corruption or not, of whether the department was actually doing its damn job.

Cleveland notched its record number of reported crimes in 1969. A year later the city watched those numbers slip. But as 1974 pushed on, and while the police were being roasted in the newspaper, reported crime citywide jumped 22 percent.[25] The most eye-popping aspect of the new figures was that they had skipped across the Cuyahoga River. Between 1970 and 1974 on the West Side—the fortressed hub of the white ethnic constituency—there was a 17 percent increase in overall crime, including a 117 percent climb in break-ins, 138 percent in rapes, and 80 percent in robberies. "Things are changing," a white West Side reverend told the *Plain Dealer*. "A fair number of older women here have simply refused to go out at night. They will not even come to a meeting here [in the church] at night, and they only live down the street."[26]

Citywide patience was running low. Forbes publicly took aim at the department, going after their paycheck and civil service protection. Throughout the year, the outspoken council president threatened that if crime rates didn't drop, he'd hack a sweetheart provision out of the city charter forcing Cleveland to pay its police officers the highest salaries in the state. In news reports, a peevish frustration flashed in the tone of commentators and reporters when writing about the department—culminating in a *Plain Dealer* series a year later titled "Do Police Give Money's Worth?"

The political finger pointing in newsprint and council chambers did little to fix the situation on the streets.

Crowding into the news cycle on the same May afternoon as reports of the grand jury's failure to bring indictments was news of another gun battle on the East Side.

Three black men who identified as devout Sunni Muslims—Craig Fowler, Larry Johnson, and Charles Jordan—abducted Schoolboy Jackson, a local drug pusher who sold to teens out of an East Side shoe store. The message: stop selling, or else. But Jackson slipped away from his kidnappers. Alerted to the possibility of armed black militants in the area, police were already piling into the neighborhood, more than seventy-five officers. Adrenaline spiked. Here was Glenville, round two. The cops arrived with guns blazing. "Cleveland police ran up the street shouting, 'We'll get those bastards,'" a witness told reporters. "It appeared that nobody was in charge. The cops ran up the hill shooting—pumping shotgun shells like mad."

The three would-be kidnappers barged into a house on Union Avenue for cover. Inside were a mother and her eight grown children. With gunfire already raging in the street, the three barricaded themselves inside, using the family as hostages.

Police and the hostage takers traded gunfire for eighty minutes before negotiating the family's release. The two oldest hostages walked out the front door with their hands up—and into a wall of bullets fired by confused Cleveland patrolmen. Reporters later confronted Police Chief Gerald Radenmaker about his officers' trigger fingers while the two hostages struggled on feeding tubes in the hospital. "We got the people out, didn't we?" he snapped.[27]

Fowler, Johnson, and Jordan's trouble was just starting.

After they were roughly piled into separate patrol cars and taken to the East Cleveland police station, after they were arraigned on thirty-three felony counts and put through an exhausting trial and found guilty on six counts and each sentenced to fifteen to one hundred years in prison, after nine years inside and appeals and hearings and rejections and a last legal shot, Fowler, Johnson, and Jordan were finally allowed to tell their stories in a federal court in September 1983.

All three men described beatings and torture by Cleveland and East Cleveland police on the night of the shooting. The men were dragged down hallways lined with officers swinging flashlights, clubs, and fists. Charles Jordan recalled being clubbed so badly with a shotgun that the stock broke. Fowler detailed his interrogation. He wasn't Mirandized. He was told he had to make a statement. He was told his friends were already cooperating.

"I told them that I knew my rights and I would like to have a lawyer," Fowler testified in 1983. "They said, 'Nigger, you have no rights. Give us a statement.'"

The man across the table from Fowler, he told the court in 1983, was a Cleveland Police detective named James Farmer.

"Detective Farmer was beating me with a blackjack on the head down the hallway. They told me that if I would not make a statement, 'Nigger, we are going to finish what we started downstairs,'" Fowler told the court. "'You're going to make a damn statement or we are going to beat you half to death.'"

A year later, Rickey was sitting at a small table in a murky room, in nearly the same situation. He wasn't Mirandized. He was told he had to make a statement. He was told his friends were already cooperating.

"The brothers have already told us everything," the detective named Terpay told Rickey. Detective James Farmer nodded.

The teen had sat through enough hours of television to know the good-cop-bad-cop routine. He didn't even bother reading the piece of paper the detectives were waving at him to sign in the windowless interrogation room. Terpay was sliding him lines about how this was all to help him.

"What could they possibly tell you?" Rickey snapped.

"They said you were the triggerman. You planned it. You had the gun." The detective pushed the paper across the desk. "Just sign right here."

"If I know anything about these two, I know that they aren't going to do something that stupid," Rickey answered.

"The guy's trying to do you a solid," Farmer chimed in. "You can still have a life after prison."

Bullshit, Rickey thought. Bullshit. Terpay then switched into bad-cop mode. The table jumped under his slammed fist. "Goddamn, you are wasting my fucking time!"

They had been swatting around this volley for hours. Rickey knew Wiley and Ronnie weren't anywhere in the police station talking because there was nothing to talk about. Fairhill was just a street to them, Mrs. Robinson a friendly face behind a counter, Harry J. Franks a shape under a sheet. Nothing beyond that. But the detectives only seemed interested in getting his signature on the paper. Exhausted with the banter, Terpay finally called for an officer to take Rickey back to his cell. But before he could leave, Terpay ordered the uniform out again.

"Stand up," the detective said.

Terpay cuffed Rickey's hands behind his back.

"A good man was killed, you fucking nigger," the detective said tersely, now picking up a hefty phone book from a nearby shelf. Nigger, Rickey thought, feeling like the word had kicked down an unseen door, letting something new and serious into the room. Terpay opened the thick, flimsy book, settling it carefully over Rickey's shaking chest like a carpenter lining up a board. Farmer held the pages in place while Terpay slammed his knuckles against Rickey, shocking the air out of his lungs and freeing a rush of tears from his eyes. He kept his lids shut, cinched tight, glued, while fists continued rolling into him like beats of a drum.

"You ain't shit without a gun."

# 4

## X-RAY EYES

THE BOY'S WORDS WERE SO QUIET THEY DIDN'T CARRY ACROSS THE courtroom, dropping out midflight like flimsy paper airplanes. Tall windows threw down rectangles of August light that stretched and yawned onto the wood floor while Ed Vernon tried to speak. Small already, he seemed now to be collapsing in on himself, hunched over, head angled away from the rest of the room. Despite prompts from Judge John C. Bacon to raise his volume, Ed's voice continued to falter. The courtroom leaned in to hear—the law students scribbling notes in the gallery, the jurors in the box, the lawyers at the two conference tables, and the defendant, Wiley Bridgeman, on trial for murder.[1]

"What did you see them doing?" Cuyahoga County Prosecutor Charles Mathay prompted.

"I seen them throw a pop in the man's face after he came out of the store and then they hit him with a stick," the boy said. "Then one of them—both of them rather, pulled a gun and tried to pull a briefcase away from him and then he wouldn't let go of it so he shot him twice."

"Who shot the man?"

"Rickey." Ed then explained that he saw Ronnie Bridgeman throw liquid in the man's face before hitting him with a pipe.

"When you saw this happening, what did you do?"

"I went back to the bus stop and peeked out," the boy said. "I seen them take the briefcase and run down the street." The words were marching out of him like he'd been programmed, Wiley thought.

"Where did they run?"

"To the car," he mumbled. "I seen Buddy standing out and then when they shot—"

"I can't hear," Bacon moaned.

"When they started running down here, he got in the car and started the car."

"Who did this?"

"Buddy."

"This man here?"

"Yes."

Wiley looked at this boy. The kid from a block over. The paperboy. One of the neighborhood boys who jokingly called Wiley "Bruce Lee" while they watched him practice martial arts in the yard. Wiley's frustration had already made the short leap into hatred for everything that was happening to him, all the more so because he could feel the oppressive big-picture machinery clanging underneath it all. But still, Wiley looked at this boy and felt a tiny pang of sympathy. Damn, he thought, they made this little kid so scared.

At seventeen or eighteen, you're still a work in progress. Mostly what-ifs and we'll-sees. A bag of foggy inclinations, unfinished emotional infrastructure. The coming attractions, not the main event. But by twenty-one, you're *you*. Ronnie and Rickey were still kids. Wiley was a man.

To the neighborhood Wiley was something of a star, the closest anyone on Arthur could reasonably label "genius." Wiley was a looker: just under six feet, he was stout but fit from—of all things—martial arts and yoga. When he was suited up in his National Guard dress blues or one of his funky white velour suits, he turned heads. Add his car into the mix, the '71 white Sebring he was always polishing in the driveway, and it was no surprise that Wiley was a favorite with the ladies.

But the style packaged a sharp mind. Wiley seemed to know about everything. He could tell you how to fix your car's engine. He could pick up a bass guitar and effortlessly riff a Top 20 groove. He was unbeatable on the chessboard. He was a voracious reader; Ayn Rand and Kahlil Gibran were two of his favorites. The summer he spent working at the Cleveland State University library, he snuck off whenever he could to play the classical collection in a listening booth, Beethoven and Tchaikovsky crashing through the headphones. Wiley's interests and his intensity really kept him somewhat apart from friends and family. It was like he was plugged into some higher plane of thought.

Bessie Bridgeman picked up early on her second oldest son's precocious mind, a little boy who never seemed to give up once he was set on something. "It's a hard road to go, if you really are going to walk it, but you don't turn around," she advised him.

The road was usually Wiley's own, in spite of course corrections from others. His elementary teachers saw he was smart, so he was enrolled in advanced placement classes at a local Catholic school, St. Aloysius. But Wiley didn't take to the environment—he felt like education came with a heavy helping of religion. Daily Mass wasn't for him, period. You might get a good education, but you were also force-fed their agenda. The deal wasn't worth it to Wiley.

This mix of personal resistance and independence found a home in the changing energy of the era. Cleveland's early disappointing experiences in the 1960s with school desegregation and police violence had shown the limits of nonviolent protests. By the decade's end, a younger generation was remaking the idea of black identity, retrofitting it from the pavement up. The flip side to the anger of Black Power was self-reliance. Integration was out. Independence was in. This bent into all kinds of shapes, from Afro-cultural organizations to community betterment programs. Wiley hooked up with one group, Cleveland Pride, which was run by a man named Baxter Hill. One of Stokes's personal connections on the East Side, Hill drilled youngsters in marches and schooled them on community improvement. They would pick up trash out of empty lots. Across the East Side, you'd see telephone poles painted white five feet up from the sidewalk—the better for drunk drivers to avoid, and as high as most of the Cleveland Pride kids could reach. It was all, Wiley thought, about corralling the wayward possibilities of the youth, presenting *structure* and discipline that could lead to a healthier community.

As he got older, Wiley started spending hours at the East Seventy-ninth and Central Avenue office of the local Black Panther outfit. He was less interested in the group's in-your-face militancy than the social agenda. Wiley volunteered to cook breakfast with the Panthers for elementary students at a school off Quincy Avenue. He also drove a bus for families visiting inmates at the state prison in Marysville. But Wiley never officially joined the group—to his mind, the message was scrambled in the delivery. How do you expect people to listen to you when you roll up on them with all that heavy militancy shit?

Through his own reading of W. E. B. Du Bois and Richard Wright he was drawn to dialectical materialism, the grand Marxist theory of class struggle and exploitation. Wiley had a knack for boiling intellectual heavy lifting down to terms regular folks could understand. For the Panthers, he led community meetings on the topic. At first, when he started in with the petite bourgeoisie and lumpenproletariat, people would roll their eyes at all that foreign talk. "It's the history of the world," Wiley would tell them. "You got the people who snub you, the people who play like they don't snub you, then you got the people that you think are cool with you."

Structure, codes, philosophies—these were the registers his mind worked in, slots you could organize experience around, categories where he could neatly park all the oppression he'd already run across in his life. By the time he was twenty-one years old, Wiley had felt out the larger political edges of being a black man in America. And when he found himself stuck in a courtroom fighting for his life, the situation wasn't terrifying and painful because he was confused. It was terrifying and painful because Wiley understood exactly what he was up against.

The Cuyahoga County Courthouse on Lakeside Avenue was a grand showpiece of civic muscle, ornately self-conscious in its display of power symbols, knowingly synced with national backstory.

Thomas Jefferson and Alexander Hamilton both shot stony gazes from colossal plinths on either side of the building's stone steps. Inside, marble hallways ran around a two-story atrium propped on Corinthian columns. The building went up in 1913, the era when the national imagination idealized the Midwest as the stage for the democratic experiment, and the courthouse wore those aspirations. A second-story mural depicted King John signing the Magna Carta at Runnymede in 1215. Opposite the atrium, another mural showed the Founding Fathers inking the Constitution in 1787. Quotes from Aristotle were chiseled into the walls. A two-story stained-glass window featuring the figure of Justice—a pale woman topped in a gold crown—colored the landing of a majestic staircase. The architecture signaled history and ideals; it also was a clear reminder to the accused felons walking into the building of the government power massed against them.

The two attorneys assigned to represent Wiley couldn't have been more different. Jerry Milano was a hard-nosed street lawyer, all jagged edges and bulldog instincts inside a courtroom. It was a style that matched his rise. He had worked his way through law school tending bar and working at a chemical factory. His aggressive tactics earned him a client list that included local Mafia heavies and NFL legend Jim Brown, who turned to Milano when he was charged with assaulting a girlfriend. Milano won the sports hero's case.[2] Daniel McCarthy had also hoisted himself up from his own meager background in Cleveland; now in his fifties, he was a Shaker Heights patrician and father of eight, a former IRS man who mostly handled corporate tax law. Two years before Wiley's arrest, McCarthy had become a minority owner of the New York Yankees.[3]

The first consequential witness to testify in Wiley's trial was Charles Loper, a retiree and rumored alcoholic who lived in a home attached to the western side of the Robinsons' store. As Loper explained to the courtroom, on the afternoon of the robbery, he'd been sitting on the steps watching his grandson play in the yard facing Fairhill. "I heard some shots," Loper told the jury. "I heard shots and the man fell and I grabbed my grandson out of the driveway and started running up to the porch, and tried to get in the house."

Loper, however, claimed he couldn't identify the attackers. "Only thing I saw was a hand grab his briefcase and run down Petrarca. They had to go down Petrarca 'cause they didn't go up Fairhill."

"Did you ever see this boy in the neighborhood?" Milano asked, pointing to the defendant. "Look at him carefully."

"No, I haven't."

"Did you see him on that day?"

"No, I haven't."

Still, Loper's testimony moved the state's case forward in a significant way: the old man testified he'd seen Ed Vernon get off at the bus stop a few feet from his lawn and walk toward the store—placing Ed at the scene.

The other main player in the prosecution's early case was Anna Robinson. Still frail from the bullet that had ripped through her throat, the store owner described for the jury the harrowing details of how she'd heard a scuffle outside and peered through the glass door to witness the attack. "I walked to the door and I saw this tall party standing there. I saw a flowered shirt. I didn't notice the face," she said in court. "I looked down the left-hand corner of the glass and I saw Mr. Franks's body on the ground and someone bending over him, stooping over him real low that had a black coat on and a black cap."

Robinson explained that she tapped on the door to get the attention of the attackers. That's when a bullet punched through the glass. "The blood ran all down my arm and everything," she said. "The blood ran towards the bread rack which was in front of the dairy case. It's a long dairy case."

This witness, however, could not place Wiley, the alleged getaway driver, at the scene.

Down the hallway in the courthouse, Rickey Jackson's trial was going through similar motions. Seated between his two lawyers, Robert Loeb and Joel Garver, Rickey watched as Mrs. Robinson unraveled the same horror story for the jurors—with one key difference. Rickey, the state maintained, was the alleged triggerman who not only killed Franks but maimed Mrs. Robinson. The store owner told the jury she'd known Rickey for almost eighteen years. But she could not identify either of the men scuffling with Franks.[4]

"I believe you testified that you cannot identify Rickey Jackson?" Garver, the defendant's attorney, asked Robinson, the lawyer's hand resting on his client's shoulder. "You cannot identify Rickey Jackson as either of those two, is that correct?"

"I didn't see the faces, no."

Karen Smith, however, testified that she could. The Arthur Avenue neighborhood girl was called to the stand to recount her own experience that day by Rickey's defense. Smith, who knew both Bridgeman brothers and Rickey Jackson—she had even shared a class with Ronnie in elementary school—was adamant that the two men she saw outside the Cut-Rate weren't the defendants.

"It was not Ronnie Bridgeman?"

"No."

"And it was not Rickey Jackson?"

"No."

"How close did you get to those two people?"

"I had to pass around them," she answered. "It was close."

"Are you absolutely positive when you state that the two men who were outside that store as you went in were not Rickey Jackson or Ronnie Bridgeman or Wiley Bridgeman?"

"Yes."

Smith—the shy girl easily embarrassed by just a look from a stranger—

held her ground when the prosecutors tried to insinuate she was just trying to help her friends. They also went after her character. "If you had an opportunity to do Rickey Jackson a favor, do you think you might do it?" the prosecutor, Dominic Del Balso, asked the teen.

"What kind of favor?"

"Any kind," he said. "You are doing him a favor today, aren't you?"

"No," the girl answered, grabbing hold of where Del Balso was going. "Not a favor for him. I am not—I wouldn't come up here and lie for him."

"Do you date a lot of guys? Go out with guys a lot?"

"No."

Ed Vernon was the prime witness for the state's cases against each of the three young men—really, the whole case. In each trial, the recently turned thirteen-year-old told a story that laid a straightforward line of facts stringing points A to B to C.

Instead of riding the school bus home on the day of the murder, Ed claimed he'd left his elementary school early, catching a city bus home alone. At the stoplight at Cedar and Fairhill, the boy had recognized Wiley Bridgeman behind the wheel of a green car. The two even waved. Then, Ed claimed, he'd stepped off at the bus shelter on Fairhill, a short walk from the Cut-Rate. From there, he'd seen Rickey and Ronnie attack Franks as he was leaving the store. Ed claimed he'd seen the two run away, reappearing later in the same green coupe he'd just seen Wiley driving, as Harry Franks bled out on the pavement. Ed also explained that when he had been shown Rickey and Wiley in the lineup, he had not picked the suspects out initially because he was afraid. It was only later, after seeing Rickey and Wiley making their phone calls in the police station, that Ed identified the men to police.

But there were issues with the boy's testimony that first surfaced a week into Wiley's trial. Milano discovered a piece of evidence that seemed to derail Ed's testimony: a statement Ed gave police and signed on May 25, the day of the lineup. Milano believed the statement was so explosive that he was worried the state would try to manipulate the witness. "I request of you to advise the prosecutor, Judge, not to talk to this young boy during the lunch hour, please," Milano dramatically asked before testimony resumed. "Or any detectives, please, sir."

When court resumed, Milano passed a single-page statement to Ed. "Would you read that first paragraph to the jury, please."

In a voice wavering like bad FM reception, the boy read from uneven clumps of hastily typed text. "On Monday, May 19, 1975, at about 3:50 P.M., I was getting off the bus at Fairhill and Petrarca. I seen two guys, Rickey and Vincent, they were at the side of the store. They were waiting. A white guy got out of his car and was walking towards the store. When he got up to the guys Vincent threw pop in his face. Then Vincent hit him with a stick. Then Vincent tried to take a briefcase from him. Then Rickey shot him twice."

Milano waited a beat before diving in. "Now," the attorney said. "You told us and you told the prosecutor, you told me that you saw Mr. Franks coming out of the store here in court, didn't you?"

"That's where they made a mistake at," Ed replied.

"You are telling us the police made a mistake while they were typing it?"

"Yes," he said. "I told the detectives, too."

"You are saying that first paragraph was just a figment of their imagination?"

"No, not all of the first paragraph, just those few words."

"Those few words are that you saw poor Mr. Franks get out of his car, walk up to these two boys and have acid thrown in his face and shot, is that correct, Edward?"

"No, he was coming out of the store," the boy replied. "They said just go ahead and sign it."

"You are telling us, then," Wiley's attorney drilled in with evident sarcasm, "you told the detectives before you signed your statement, 'Gentlemen, this isn't the truth, this isn't what I said.' And they said, 'Oh, go ahead and sign it anyhow.' Is that what you are telling us?"

"They wouldn't type it over."

"They wouldn't type it over?"

"No," the boy said. "I told him to type it over and he said he didn't have time."

After Ed left the witness stand, Detective John Staimpel was quickly called. No, the detective testified, Ed did not indicate there were any issues with his written statement.

Following the close of the state's case, Milano moved for the judge to issue an immediate acquittal on the grounds that the prosecution had not proved the charges. "The issue here is have they proven beyond a reasonable doubt that either Wiley Bridgeman did it or aided and abetted in the commission of the crimes," Milano argued after the jury had been dismissed from the courtroom. "The only evidence on that is what Vernon has told you. Now, can you believe Vernon? The Court may think, 'Well, let it go to the jury.' Judge, you know what happens with juries. How many times have lawyers said, 'Jesus Christ, how in the world did they arrive at this verdict.'" The attorney pressed on about the witness's credibility. "You have the boy's testimony, and either he or that policeman is a liar. I won't change the language, I don't think it's too strong."

"Mr. Milano, the matter of credibility of the witness actually is for the jury in a jury trial," Judge Bacon replied. "There has been some impairment, I think we'll admit. There have been some inconsistencies, but then there's also the question of the boy's positive testimony. Whether he's going to be believed or not, why, that is not my function." Judge Bacon ruled against the defense request. "I believe the jury is going to have to decide this one, Mr. Milano."

Both Rickey's and Wiley's defense teams aimed to upend Ed's credibility. A parade of the boy's classmates cycled through both courtrooms, each relaying a variation on the same story. These middle school kids from the neighborhood told the court that Ed had not gone home early on a city bus. He stayed until the end of classes as usual and rode the school bus home with the rest of the kids. The day stood out for the witnesses—they saw the murder. According to at least three children, as the school bus crossed Fairhill down Cedar, the kids glued their eyes to the driver's-side windows as two black men attacked a white man outside the Cut-Rate. Distance, angle, traffic—none of the children could identify the men, they all claimed. But as the bus passed, the children said they heard pops—gunshots.

Ed was there rubbernecking at the bus window with the rest. "Was Eddie on the bus with you on the way home?" Wiley's attorney Daniel McCarthy asked a girl named Kim Dickson.

"Yes," the girl replied. Dickson explained that she, Ed, and another neighborhood kid named Tommy Hall then got off at their usual stop—East 108th and Cedar—and ran up to the Cut-Rate to join the growing crowd.

"Me and Edward went to my house to put my books down and we came back down and went up Frank to the Robinsons'," Tommy Hall later testified in Rickey's trial. "We seen the man dead and a detective took his coat off and put it over his face." Tommy relayed in both Rickey and Wiley's trials that Ed began to claim to know who the killers were. "We was coming up the street and we said, 'How did you see it if we didn't?'"

"And what did he say?" a defense attorney asked.

"He stopped playing," Tommy answered, "and said, 'I have got X-ray eyes.'"

Wiley's feelings were sharp to the times—all that thinking and reading had arranged the world in a way so he could see the racism, the victimization, the atrocities. But now he was experiencing it himself. Rickey and Ronnie might have felt their plight as a stand-alone nightmare. Wiley saw his situation connected to something larger. Worse, he felt the conclusion was preordained. It's dialectical materialism all over again, like he explained to the bewildered audience at the

Panther meetings. I know exactly what is happening, he'd tell himself. I just can't do anything about it; I can't explain it. It was all piling up at the front of his brain—lineups and Ed Vernon, petite bourgeoisie and lumpenproletariat, the racism, the victimization. And Wiley knew the stakes here were life and death.

At the time, Ohio's death penalty law was less a responsible piece of legislation guiding the state's ultimate act than a slingshot indiscriminately hurling felons at the electric chair.

Ohio had been wielding the death penalty since before it was an actual state. But in 1972, the law was scrubbed from the books thanks to a U.S. Supreme Court decision that invalidated statutes across the country on the grounds of arbitrary sentencing. Undaunted, the Ohio Legislature simply rewrote the law in 1974, retrofitting it with new language patching over the weak spots; this new statute had three mitigating circumstances that judges could refer to when declining to impose a death sentence for an aggravated murder case: if the victim caused the murder; if the offender was under duress; or if the murder was the result of the offender's psychosis or mental deficiency. But those three outs were not there for leniency. By narrowly defining the exemptions to capital punishment, the state ensured nearly all defendants in murder cases were headed for death row—including Rickey, Wiley, and Ronnie.

On August 12 Wiley stood in the courtroom for the jury's ruling: guilty. As he was led from the chamber, the older Bridgeman brother stumbled, calling for his attorney. "I'm on your side," Milano told him. "I don't think you did it. I don't think anybody in the courtroom thought you did it, except the jury."[5]

Within the week, Rickey's jury delivered the same verdict.


Six weeks after juries delivered guilty verdicts against Rickey and Wiley, Ronnie's own trial started in the same courthouse.

On paper, the delay could have given Ronnie an edge. In the two earlier trials, defense attorneys could only zero in on the inconsistencies between Ed's testimony and the typed statement to police introduced by Milano; Ronnie's legal team had more material to work with: they could fish for errors and mistakes in both of Ed's trial testimonies as well, giving the attorneys more possible ammunition to impeach the witness.

That job fell to one of the loudest personalities in the courthouse. Through the random assignment system, Thomas Shaughnessy was placed on Ronnie's case. A hulking Irishman capped with a swirl of light hair, Shaughnessy was a workhorse who took more cases to trial every year than whole divisions within the prosecutor's office. Based out of a cluttered office on a dicey stretch of Buckeye Avenue in Cleveland's black East Side, a .38 in the drawer and a shotgun under the desk for protection, the attorney liked to boast that he was the Woolworth's of Cleveland's legal world: "Nobody can touch our low fees and high volume."[6]

He was less renowned for trial prep or legal smarts than courtroom showmanship; his cross-examinations were pure working-class vaudeville pitched to Cleveland juries, equal parts blood sport and stand-up—but always entertaining. These performances were well lubricated by the lunch hours Shaughnessy openly spent hefting beers in the bar. "He'll say, if I don't blow a .14 or .15 after lunch, I'm useless for the afternoon," a friend recounted Shaughnessy once boasting to a jury.

As Ronnie's trial started, Shaughnessy made it clear out of the gate that he was preparing to swing a wrecking ball at Ed. He opened his cross-examination with a series of seemingly innocuous questions. The attorney pointed out that the boy had told the court his school was located on East 116th Street. "Actually it is on East Boulevard, isn't it?" Shaughnessy asked.[7]

"Yes."

"About a half mile from 116th, isn't it?"

"Yes."

"And you told the ladies and gentlemen before that Audubon was on 116th and you just made a simple mistake, didn't you?"

"Yes."

"And you weren't intending to deceive them or you weren't lying, you made a simple, honest mistake?"

"Yes."

"About a half a mile mistake, didn't you?" Shaughnessy managed to get in before the prosecutor, Charles Mathay, cut in with an objection.

Not long after, the attorney reminded Ed that he had testified he received straight As in all his classes. "And your mathematics class, Edward, did you ever have any discussion or training relative to inches, feet, yards, rods, miles, and centimeters?"

"Yes."

"Well, how many inches are there in a foot?"

"In a foot?"

"Yes."

"Six."

"Six inches in a foot and you got an A in mathematics?" Shaughnessy said.

"Yes."

Later, as the attorney was pointing to a map of the crime scene, Shaughnessy again used it as an opportunity to embarrass the thirteen-year-old.

"Incidentally," he asked Ed. "How do you spell 'Cedar'?"

"S . . . e . . . a . . . r . . . d."

"How do you spell Fairhill?

"F . . . r . . . i . . . r . . . h . . . i . . . l . . . l."

"All right," Judge Angelotta cut in. "Let's cease and desist. I think it is obvious, Mr. Shaughnessy, what you are trying to show."

Shaughnessy's clinical dissection of the witness's testimony picked at the smallest of statements. First the attorney noted that Ed had testified in the current trial that he had seen Mr. Loper on the day of the murder. In the August trials, however, Ed had told the court he had not looked at Mr. Loper's house and didn't see the old man. "But Edward," the lawyer said, "that's exactly the opposite of the answer that you gave us today, isn't it?"

"Yes."

"Well now, tell the ladies and gentlemen here, if you will, Eddie, did you wave to your old pal Mr. Loper or didn't you?"

"Yes, I did."

"You did. So on the seventh day of August, Thursday, 1975, you made another mistake, didn't you?"

"Yes."

"Did you make a mistake, Eddie, or did you tell a lie?"

"Objection," the prosecutor cut in.

"I . . ." Ed said, stumbling for words. "I made a mistake."

The defense attorney continued in attack-dog mode. He challenged Ed on the previous testimony in the other trials: that after the murder, Ed had seen Rickey and Bitzie at the store in the crowd of onlookers. "Yet Eddie, once again you have told us here today that it wasn't Rickey that was there at the time," the attorney said. "It was Buddy, and you have said that ten times."

Shaughnessy also went after Ed's original police statement. In the document, the witness had said he saw Wiley driving a car with Rickey and Bitzie. But in Ronnie's trial, the boy said he couldn't see the faces of the passengers in Wiley's car. The attorney also blasted the boy for saying in his typed statement "Vincent" was the second attacker, not Ronnie. Ed continued to deny the substance of the statement. "Is your memory, young man, better today than it was six days after this incident on May the twenty-fifth?"

"Today."

"Tell us, if you will, Edward, what has happened or who have you talked to or what reports have you read that would cause your memory to be sharper today than it was five or six days after this incident happened?"

"Nothing."

By the time the defense attorney was done with the state's main witness, even the judge was shaky on Ed's credibility. "If this is an example of someone who gets straight As in the Cleveland School System, the Cleveland School System is a disgrace," Angelotta grumbled to the lawyers after the jury had been dismissed for the day. "It is quite obvious that this boy says things that are untrue," the judge continued. "There are many areas of discrepancy in this testimony for whatever reason. That doesn't make him a liar. That doesn't mean that he didn't see what he said he saw."

Angelotta continued to ruminate before the attorneys, with the stenographer snapping down his thoughts into the transcript. "I frankly don't know what to think," he said. "And I am not going to substitute my judgment for what these twelve people think."

The rest of Ronnie's defense cut a similar path as in the previous trials. Karen Smith again reiterated that the men she saw outside the Cut-Rate were not Rickey or Ronnie. A number of Ed's classmates repeated that he'd been on the school bus, not on the sidewalk, when the bullets started flying. Ronnie himself took the witness stand to deny the allegations.

But from his seat at the defense table, concerns were marching to the front of Ronnie's mind. His confidence in his legal counsel shrank as the trial progressed. He could smell the booze coming off Shaughnessy. The lawyer's face seemed to get redder as the day wore on. Ronnie would later say he watched his attorney nod off during portions of the trial. And despite Shaughnessy's assurances, Ronnie couldn't escape the fear that the verdicts in Rickey's and Wiley's trials had sealed up his own.

His attorney also seemed to second-guess his own work, especially the hard press on Ed. The cross-examination threatened to leave the impression on a jury not of a cunning lawyer torpedoing a lying witness, but a grown man mocking and steamrolling a scared little boy. In a rambling, disjointed closing statement to the jury, Shaughnessy admitted as much. "I made a few mistakes," he told the jury. "I am sure I am going to be castigated as a beater of children or something like that because I devastated that boy on the witness stand."

In the end, that was what mattered: Ed. If you believed the boy or not. If you believed the boy, the state's witness, the nebbish paperboy with thick glasses; or if you accepted the credibility of the three young men who had trouble articulating why they were innocent because they all still had trouble understanding why they were there at all. The choice before the jury was one of belief—Ed or Ronnie?

On September 27, Ronnie was found guilty.[8] Shortly after Christmas, all three young men were sentenced to death by electrocution.

# 5

## WE YET EXIST

THE SEVERED PINKIE FINGERS WERE ADDRESSED TO THE PRESIDENT OF
the United States. How far the packages made it into Jimmy Carter's
White House bureaucracy, no one was ever able to figure. But the four
mutilated digits came with a clear return address: J Block, the Southern Ohio Correctional Facility, Lucasville, Ohio.

The state's newest high-security facility was located at its very bottom, a straight two-hundred-mile drop south from the Lake Erie
shoreline. The town itself was little more than a rural pinprick with
fewer than fifteen hundred residents in Scioto County, a sparse section of Ohio that pulls its cultural DNA less from the Midwest than
from Appalachia. Hills crowded with trees and hung with scraps of
mist in the morning cupped the thirty-two-million-dollar facility on
all sides. The prison sat on sixty-nine acres boxed in by an octagon of
parallel twelve-foot-high cyclone fences curling at the top with barbed
wire. Long hallways ran the length of the complex, hospital-like run-
ways soaked in overhead fluorescence, the polished floors squeaking
underfoot. Three main residential blocks branched off the corridors—L,
K, and J Blocks. Forty units ran on each cell range, twenty above,
twenty below.

It was a modern design packaging medieval conditions. After the doors opened in 1972, the facility quickly earned a reputation as one of the fiercest lockups in the country.

Lucasville—officially known as SOCF, but everyone just called it Lucasville, or "The Luke"—was designed to replace the old Ohio State Penitentiary in Columbus, a castlelike Gothic pile of stone built in the 1830s. In 1968, the hard-core lifers and cons, Ohio's worst, rioted inside the limestone walls over conditions like overcrowding, vermin, and lack of water. Guards were taken hostage. The National Guard broke the standoff after twenty-eight hours. Five inmates were killed in the incident. These same men who had torn up the OP were the first to fill the bunks at Lucasville.

The new prison's ribbon cutting was coincidentally timed to an eye-popping jump in the state's prison population: in 1974, Ohio's facilities held 7,700 people; by 1976, the number was more than twelve thousand. These were the early boom years of Nixon's accelerated federal crime policies. Although Lucasville was designed to bed around sixteen hundred inmates in individual cells, by the middle of the decade the prison was housing two thousand, many double bunked. Within a year of opening, three guards were taken hostage; one was killed in a rescue attempt. In 1976, members of a finance subcommittee from the Ohio General Assembly investigated allegations of abuse and mismanagement at the facility.[1] Their report concluded that "serious and volatile problems exist" at Lucasville, and that there were "clear danger signals that the penal system is overburdened beyond present capabilities." The elected officials focused on the vicious tensions flowing between the prisoners, many black and from urban areas like Cleveland or Cincinnati, and the guards, drawn from the white and rural local population. "There is substantial evidence that a disturbingly high number of violent physical acts are committed within SOCF walls, by and against inmates, resulting in further tensions and fears among the inmates, guards and the community," the report concluded. Between May 1975 and June 1976, state investigators counted three murders, four suicides, thirty-six cuttings, four serious assaults, ten minor assaults, forty-two fights, and two employee stabbings.

Even though the problems at Lucasville were well known to the state, the ballooning prison population put up logistical roadblocks to any solutions. The violence continued; most seemed to be centralized in J Block, the area housing inmates in Administrative Isolation (the "hole") and death row. "It was here that most of the guard-on-prisoner brutality and murders occur," an inmate would write years later.[2] "The guards are allowed free rein to use violence on prisoners and it was a custom for them to run in a prisoner's cell and beat him, or beat a prisoner while he was handcuffed."

By the late 1970s, a group of prisoners known as the Lucasville 14 had had enough. Citing the recently inked Helsinki Accords, an international agreement between Western nations and the Soviet bloc, the Ohio inmates formally renounced their American citizenship and asked to be released behind the Iron Curtain. When the government ignored the request, three men—Richard Armstrong, August Cassano, and David Cattano—each hacked off a pinkie finger (Cattano cut off two) and mailed them to the U.S. president in protest.[3] Word about the self-mutilating defiance shot quickly through the prison; the men became heroes on the turbulent ranges of Lucasville—particularly on death row.

There, any sliver of good news or the smallest provocative fuck-you to the powers upstairs and beyond was a needed lifeboat. The inmates—including Ronnie, Rickey, and Wiley—were playing out a terrifying waiting game. Because although the state hadn't executed anyone since 1963, the chair had been moved from the Ohio Penitentiary to Lucasville. Nailed together in 1897 from wood as dark as aged whiskey, it was the last seat for 315 condemned men and women. They called it "Old Sparky."

Ohio's revamped death penalty statute worked as planned, transforming the state's felony homicide dockets into conveyor belts feeding directly into death row. By summer 1976, nearly sixty Ohio inmates had been sentenced under the 1974 law, including fifteen from Cuyahoga

County. But their cases were all essentially stalled while capital punishment itself became the subject of a court battle.

Two opposing currents collided in the federal courts in the 1970s. The first was the effort by progressive activists and attorneys to dismantle capital punishment statutes across the country. The other was the momentum coming from state legislatures. The lessons of Nixon's two overwhelming presidential campaign victories were easy to read: tough-on-crime politicians fared well with voters. In spite of the administration's War on Crime and the increased rates of incarceration, felonies continued to rise as the decade reached its midpoint. State officeholders eager to polish their credentials defended capital punishment with zeal. Whenever opponents depleted the government's punitive might with a court victory, state legislatures fast-tracked replacement laws recalibrated to cover whatever vulnerability the legal challenge had exploited. This was the cycle: court challenge, new laws, and new court challenge. The stakes—the state's moral right to take a life—were immense. Yet the debate played out quietly. This was a fight hinging on pretzel-twisted concepts of due process and chain of custody; powered by ideology, yes, but at its high-noon moment not settled in passion but with dense legal briefs or the sober debate of a court hearing. It was a bloodless, academic struggle, removed by more than miles and electrified walls from the cellblocks where the bullshitting dipped low when the news bulletins squawked over the radio, every ear searching the broadcast for anything on a U.S. Supreme Court decision that could file their lives down to a small window of time. In July 1976, Ronnie, Rickey, and Wiley were on J Block when a broadcast echoed down the range about a high-court ruling upholding another state's death statute, one mirroring Ohio's own.[4]

They all knew what it meant. By now each was an armchair appellate scholar. This decision was the cue for Lucasville's warden to warm up the chair.

———

Morning, afternoon, night—you didn't fix a name on the hours. Clock time had slipped from its routine, the minutes piling up uselessly at your feet. Hard to tell the difference when you spent nearly every hour of the day inside your cell.

Whatever time it was, at this particular moment, the death row inmates were playing chess. Not together over a board. No way. Not here. Instead, the players shouted their moves about the range. Ronnie was tuned into this particular contest. "Move my queen's bishop five to forty-seven," one of the players cried. Suddenly, screams started ripping through the cellblock.

The noise came from Mr. Collins's cell, Ronnie realized. Mr. Cleophus Collins, one of the old-timers on the row. Mr. Collins, the man who used to own a restaurant in Cincinnati before getting into a shootout with some guys he didn't know were undercover cops, to hear him tell it. Mr. Collins, who killed one of the cops but took six bullets in his own gut. Mr. Collins, who they brought back to life so they could send him to death row with his stomach so jury-rigged with tubing that when he broke wind it made the whole cellblock smell like an exploded sewer. Mr. Collins, Ronnie now realized, was the prisoner in cell 47. When the old man heard the number bounce down the range, he must have thought it meant they were coming for him, his time all up.

"Oh, Jesus, please!" Mr. Collins begged through tears. "Pleeeeeease!" The row was dead quiet except for the pleas. No one corrected the mistake, perhaps because the condemned men felt they were getting a peek around the corner at what would be coming their way soon enough. Guards eventually dragged Mr. Collins off for sedation.

Ohio's condemned men were confined to single cells arranged around an open two-story central room. Twenty cells ringed the bottom ground floor, twenty above, these opening out onto a walkway. Each prisoner's space extended ten feet from the cell door to the back wall, nine feet from the floor to ceiling. It was enough room for a bed and mattress and a wall-mounted bookcase and dimensionless private grief but little else. A sheet of light warmed the white concrete walls and floors through a single barred window for those hours of the day when the sun trucked into view. Otherwise it was dark and cold and empty. Wall-mounted televisions gurgled away between every five cells on the range. Most of the talk snapping between the condemned men was arguments about what to watch. This guy wanted the news. That guy wanted cartoons. The next guy over wanted a cowboy show.

The inmates were locked into their spaces for twenty-three hours out of every twenty-four. That meant someone was always on recreation—or rec. When your rec hour came, you had to get yourself a shower and clean your cell, but after that, the death row inmates were running up and down the range, doing favors for guys and delivering messages or passing notes between cells. It was the only face-to-face socializing anyone ever got. They waited for it like Christmas. Not long into his stay on the row, rec inmates were delivering notes to Ronnie's cell that left him scratching his head. Notes scribbled in Wiley's hand. Warnings about poison in the food.

The men talked out their own appeals. They updated one another on cases climbing the twisty ladder of the lower courts, cases that might nudge their own in one direction or another. And they banded together when they needed to—surprising, considering they couldn't even assemble in a group. When the prison slashed the visiting hours for death row inmates and prohibited their families from bringing food, the condemned men united for a hunger strike.

"We are only asking that we be given the same privileges and treated the same as the rest of the prisoners," four J Block inmates wrote to a Cleveland newspaper regarding the strike.[5] "We are not dead yet; we yet exist." Two of the names on the letter: Ronnie and Wiley Bridgeman. Within a few weeks, the hunger strike spread to the rest of the prison. The Lucasville administration eventually relented. But the successes and moments of unity were minor breaks in the total isolation of the row.

Wiley—Ohio Department of Rehabilitation and Correction's inmate #A143810—poured himself into words. When the range stirred at 5:00 A.M., he was up, exercising in his cell in the hour before breakfast.

Afterward, he sat at this desk cramming words onto legal pads, his long looping sentences charging forward, clause after clause, with a precise, stately diction. He wrote poems, short stories, and letters—dozens of letters to journalists, politicians, attorneys, even other condemned men and women. By afternoon, he'd jump to novels; the librarian was a good guy, came twice a week. Wiley was always working through a large stack of books. He liked to step into the espionage world of Robert Ludlum or Robert A. Heinlein's space fantasies. These were escape routes out from the thoughts that clamored against his head, including a crushing sense of responsibility. He was the oldest. His brother and friend were here as well, both younger guys. I've got to make sure nothing happens to them, Wiley thought. But there was nothing he could do from his cell. All the complex depth and bold strokes of his personality, the marks his mother spotted so early, the parts of Wiley that made him so unique in the eyes of the neighborhood and especially in the eyes of his brother and Rickey—all that counted for nothing here. Prison took distinction and pride from you. Wiley was just another cell number waiting for his rec days. It was so humiliating, he couldn't help wishing he were alone.

For Rickey—#A144061—the confinement itself was excruciating. He was always mobile as a kid—all those independent one-man missions to other parts of the city on the bus. Now Rickey was stuck in place, looking at the same four walls. His days passed in a flurry of exercise. The straining muscle, the heat from his body, his lungs knocking back breaths—the physical work kept his mind away from what he didn't want to think about.

Still, blinding sheets of anger would cover him when he heard the other inmates hopefully discussing appeals or Supreme Court cases. These guys were conning themselves into rosy thinking by ignoring the facts. He took a macabre sort of pleasure in making light of their situation; on his rec walks, if he caught a guy writing a letter in his cell, he'd tell him he'd better hurry up, time was running out. Or he wouldn't hesitate to tell someone they had a pretty nice radio, who was getting that after their big date with Ol' Sparky?

Despite his gallows humor, Rickey saved himself a narrow portion of hope, thinking about what would happen if they were released from the row. Prison, he resolved, might be its own strange adventure. But the same string of thoughts always led him back to the execution date and Ed Vernon. If it came down to it, would the kid really let them take that walk? Would he stay silent?

Ronnie—#A143953—dealt with anxiety that was always coding red. The zigs and zags of Ohio's capital punishment fight were enough for that. But Ronnie was really still back in the Cleveland courtroom, his mind stuck like a snagged record, trying to understand how the state could say he did something he didn't do. But how could he prove it? Especially now? They had him in checkmate. He was still back trying to make sense of the first move.

He filled his time in one-sided dialogue with God. He begged. He cussed. If you can't do nothing for me, fine, I'm fucked, Ronnie resolved. Look, God, if you are real, okay, I'm praying for Rickey, and I'm praying for my brother. Cut them loose. Get them up out of this shit. But all three stayed. Ronnie felt like he couldn't fit the correct words together to make his prayers effective. So he waited—waited to die, or waited to see if he was going to die while listening to the anguish the same waiting was igniting over in the other cells. The tears and screams. The guards rushing to one cell so this guy doesn't hang himself with a bedsheet, or running to stop another from slashing open his veins. This all rode his body hard. His shoulders sagged under the weight. Each night, the bed felt harder. And was it getting darker earlier? Night seemed to swoop in sooner than on the outside. Ronnie was having trouble seeing. Maybe if he could get a deep breath down, but the air felt heavy, like smoke off a burning trash pile. Each breath he struggled to get down sent his heart bashing around his chest. It got so bad sometimes that guards had to pull him from his cell for fresh air.

After months inside J Block, waiting to learn if he'd die or not, waiting to wait more, Ronnie figured he had been going about this prayer thing wrong. Faith couldn't be taken lightly; you couldn't scattershot your pleas like darts against a board. It was serious. Then one day, leafing through a copy of the Koran that was making its way through the cellblock, his eyes were hooked by a line. The words rang his brain like a bell. *Indeed, Allah will not change the condition of a people until they change what is in themselves.*

Good news graced J Block in April 1977: Wiley won a retrial. He was going back to Cleveland.

Along with his attorneys, the street-tough Jerry Milano and the corporate boardroom number cruncher Daniel McCarthy, the older Bridgeman brother successfully pressed the Ohio Court of Appeals to reconsider the case due to errors from the bench. Wiley argued that Judge John C. Bacon had erred when issuing instructions to the jurors tasked with deciding Wiley's guilt or innocence. The jurist, a visiting judge from rural Meigs County, had told the Cuyahoga County panel that all they had to do was identify whether Wiley was the perpetrator because the robbery and murder were undisputed. The higher court found that Bacon's bungled wording had incorrectly assumed elements of the crime had already been proven. The technicality was a possible lifesaver. The reversal was one of three cases overturned in a few weeks tied to visiting judges shipped in to assist an overloaded Cuyahoga County Courthouse in 1975.[6] Wiley set out for his new court date in autumn unsure what to expect. Hope and fear had fought to a standstill in his gut.

He was returning to a city teetering through another seismic shift. The Perk administration's overreliance on federal funding had only temporarily offset the dire financial condition sparked by hundreds of businesses fleeing to the suburbs and beyond. Tax increases failed to keep pace with the demographic changes; a close read of Cleveland's books showed that the city was speeding toward financial default. Blood was back up in the neighborhoods, too, now in the ethnic West Side wards. The federal lawsuit over school desegregation filed in 1975 had reelectrified racial lines; car bumpers around the city wore stickers proclaiming "NO!"—a simple, declarative antibusing slogan. The suit wasn't the West Side's only grievance. While the suburbs continued to soak up business and population, the Perk administration had offered substantial tax abatements to corporations to keep downtown development flowering—another blow to the tax base. Feeling ignored and sidelined in favor of deep pockets, neighborhoods organized into community action groups, less polite block clubs than grassroots shock troops given to shouting down city hall officials at meetings or picketing their homes. Dennis Kucinich, a boy-wonder Democrat city councilman representing the West Side's Tremont, tapped this aggression in his 1977 campaign for the mayor's office. "Urban populism," as he dubbed it, was about empowering the neighborhoods, not downtown business interests, to decide how they wanted to develop their blocks. It was a politics that mobilized the same white resentment fueling the desegregation debate, tossing race and issues of civil rights in the backseat in favor of economics.

Squinting out the window of the prison transport bus as it motored north into town, Wiley thought Cleveland looked the same. Terminal Tower's thin spire at attention on the skyline. The acres of factories coughing smog from the winding riverbanks, a thick taste that hit your throat as you pulled closer to downtown. Municipal Stadium, the soot-stained colossus, hulking at the lakeshore. The only noticeable change to the city was the building where he was heading. That summer, the city proudly opened the doors of a new Justice Center, planted directly across the street from its predecessor on Lakeside Avenue, one of 480 new jails constructed nationally in the first half of the decade to keep pace with the War on Crime. Whereas the county's old legal seat wore its American history like a proud coat, the new courthouse rose twenty-four bland stories into the Cleveland skyline, a featureless cube that screamed out technocratic banality of seventies chic.

As the pretrial motions began in one of the new windowless courtrooms, it was clear Milano and McCarthy had shifted their strategy for Wiley's second chance at an acquittal. Before jury selection, the attorneys notified the court they would be presenting an alibi defense. Instead of exclusively ripping away at Ed Vernon's credibility, the defense team also charged into the retrial aiming to topple other parts of the state's case. This included raising questions about the propriety of the police investigation and the lack of actual physical evidence linking the defendant to the crime.

Wiley wasn't completely sold on the strategy. Through his own constant letter writing, he'd learned from his family back home about a neighborhood girl named Angela Bennett. After the convictions, she told friends she had seen the actual getaway car both as the crime was happening and later around Arthur Avenue. Wiley was so excited by the information, he wrote his own motion for a new trial based on new evidence. The courts ignored the filing, and Milano and McCarthy were uncertain on how Bennett could factor into the retrial. One of the attorneys was also under extreme pressure. In 1976, McCarthy had been tasked by a federal judge to oversee the dramatic desegregation of Cleveland's public schools. Those "NO!" bumper stickers were aimed directly at McCarthy. The attorney was receiving death threats.

October 4 was sun-shot and stirred by lake breezes, the temperature stalled out pleasantly in the low sixties. Across the city, Clevelanders walked to polling sites for a four-candidate mayoral primary that would deliver a roundhouse loss to Ralph Perk and put Kucinich on track to election in November. The white ethnic wards, once Perk's base, turned to Kucinich. This "urban populism" springing out of the West Side would also unseat seven incumbent council members, "the biggest political bloodbath in years," one commentator called it.

Up on the twenty-second floor of the new Justice Center, Jerry Milano and Daniel McCarthy opened the proceedings by trying to pull information out of the state that could point to their client's innocence. Under legal procedure, however, the defense couldn't see the police files related to the case; the new judge, Sam Zingle, combed the pile himself to decide what was relevant. The attorneys were left groping blindly. How could they know what to ask for if they couldn't examine the file?

Topping the list of what the lawyers wanted to know was information on other suspects police had identified for the Franks killing. The lawyers had learned about a mother coming forward at the time of the shooting saying her son was involved. The lawyers also learned the FBI had told police the robbery may have been done by Skip and Railroad King, the local stick-up men. Bennett provided yet another account. All pointed to other suspects—yet the attorneys could not access the information police developed about the tips. "Now we have three people saying these guys didn't do it, that we weren't told about it until this morning," Milano argued before the judge.[7]

"In all police investigations there are all sorts of tips and leads," county prosecutor James Sweeney shot back. "I don't think each anonymous phone call is necessarily exculpatory."

"I agree, but he said he had information that three other guys did it," Milano said, referring to the FBI tip. "If that's not exculpatory, what is?"

Wiley's lawyers were also suspicious of a lack of forensic reports from the investigation. In the 1975 trials, officers testified they had both tested the paper cup found on the scene as well as hunted for fingerprints on two cars, Franks's and another vehicle suspected of being involved. None produced usable prints. But the defense wasn't provided paperwork on the results.

And now the paper cup—the only piece of physical evidence from the crime scene—was missing. As Wiley's second trial opened, the Cleveland police officers responsible for processing the evidence failed to serve up a convincing reason why. A detective named Marvin said he had given it to a police tech named Frank Muhlhan. The tech's testimony, however, provided no clarity.

"You never saw this white cup?" Milano pounded into Muhlhan on a cross-examination early in the trial.

"I never saw a white cup," the officer responded.

"Do you know Detective Marvin?"

"Yes, I do."

"And if he said he gave you a white cup to examine, you just don't know anything about that?"

"I know a white cup was processed," the witness said. "That's all I know."

Milano kept pressing. "And where is it, do you know?"

"I have no idea."

The Cleveland police had an equally limp explanation for why the tip from the FBI linking the robbery to Skip and Railroad King was ignored. As Wiley's second trial progressed in the first week of October, Detective Eugene Terpay again took the witness stand. When Milano initially asked whether he had followed up on the lead, the detective answered that this informant was not always reliable.

Yet when Judge Zingle questioned Terpay, the officer clearly contradicted himself. "Did the FBI indicate who the informant was?" the judge asked.

"No, sir, they never do."

"Not knowing the informant, did you have any way of knowing his reliability?"

"I had no way of knowing how reliable the information was," the detective admitted.

Milano jumped on the admission. "Then it may have been the most reliable information in the world, as far as you know? Isn't that correct?"

"It could have or could not have been, yes," the stone-faced cop answered.


Now for the fourth time, Ed Vernon was the key voice for the prosecution. This time, however, the boy was on his own with his story: Charles Loper, the neighbor who claimed to have seen Ed by the store during the robbery, had died. His previous testimony from Wiley's 1975 trial was read to the new jury.

The intervening two years had also revealed another problem with the state's star witness. Wiley's attorneys had learned that Robert Robinson, the store owner, paid Ed fifty dollars after the first three trials. Although Robinson claimed the money was just to reward Ed for his courage in testifying, it was hard not to look at the payout as a bribe. The elderly shop owner claimed this wasn't the case when the prosecution questioned him. But when Milano began his cross, he battered Robinson on why he hadn't mentioned it in Wiley's previous trial. Robinson also wasn't clear at all on when he had offered the boy the money. If it was before Ed identified the defendants, Wiley's attorneys suggested the fifty dollars was tempting enough for a greedy little boy to name three random neighborhood guys.

But ultimately the strategy depended on cracking Ed Vernon, and the Ed Vernon who walked into the Justice Center was much different than the Ed Vernon who had originally testified.

He was now fifteen. His arms and legs had sprouted. His voice had gravel in it. And whatever stress he'd been experiencing over the case, by now it had ground away his patience. Gone was the spooked little boy who mumbled before a courtroom of adults; here was a teenager, combative and surly, telling a new jury all about how he'd left school early on May 19, 1975, taken a city bus home alone, spotted Wiley behind the wheel of a green car at the stoplight before witnessing Rickey and Ronnie kill Harry Franks.

"You told the prosecutor, you just told me, that you got out of school and you caught the bus and went to Fairhill," Milano asked as he began his cross-examination.

"I didn't say that," Ed cut him off.

"Tell us what you did."

"I have to tell you what I did every day?" the witness shot back.

"No, sir," Milano answered. "Now, listen to me, Edward. You said you got out of the school at two forty-five and arrived at Fairhill and Petrarca at a quarter to four. What did you do for that hour?"

"You want to know?"

"No, these ladies and gentlemen want to know."

"I told you, I was playing around."

"What do you mean by 'playing around'?"

"Can't I play?"

"Yes, you can. With whom were you playing?"

"I don't recall."

The attorney and Ed continued the hostile salvos. Eventually, Ed admitted he had gone over his previous testimony with police and prosecutors before the retrial. Milano's patience seemed to give. "Now, to you this might be funny," the attorney snapped. "This man could be sent to the electric chair."

In a final blitz on the boy's story, Milano again slashed at the inconsistencies in Ed's various accounts; the differences between Ed's original statement to police and his testimony; the changes to his testimony; his reluctance to tell his friends or family about what he claimed to have witnessed; even the boy's debunked boasts about straight As.

"Tell us how many times you lied to the jury or lied to the police and lied to your friends in this case," Milano ripped. "Would twenty be a fair estimate?"

"I don't know."

"You lied, that's not true, Edward?"

"No."

"You admit that you have lied in this case to the police, to the lawyers, and to the investigator, haven't you? And to your dad, haven't you?" Milano said. "Do you deny admitting in this court that you have lied in the case on many occasions?"

"No."

"Do you admit, sir, that you were offered fifty dollars to do something in this case?"

"No."

"You don't deny that, do you?"

"No."

"Do you admit to this jury that you never mentioned anyone's name in this case to any police until after you were offered fifty dollars? Is that the truth? Isn't it?"

"No."

"It's not?"

"No."

"When did you tell the police who you say committed this crime?"

"It was Wednesday."

"Wednesday?"

"Yes."

"Didn't you tell the jury that the day of the crime you went back and talked to Mr. Robinson and he said that he'd give you fifty dollars?"

"True."

These heated exchanges were a gamble. They could confuse the jury more than spotlight the holes in Ed's story. Or, once again, the twelve panelists may have felt sympathy for a young boy being slapped around by questions coming from an aggressive lawyer. Behind the courtroom testimony, a rift was also breaking open between Milano and McCarthy. The criminal trial vet felt the state had failed to put together a strong enough case to seal a conviction. He decided there was no need to mount a strenuous defense. McCarthy, however, wanted to develop Wiley's alibi as originally intended. Wiley was jammed between the two. He knew enough of the law to see that if you announced to the court and jury that you were going to present an alibi defense, you had to—if you didn't, you looked guilty. But although the defense put on Angela Bennett to counter Ed Vernon's story, they didn't nail down the alibi. Wiley could see that his attorneys were clearly furious with each other by the trial's close. The defendant wasn't hopeful.

The jury received the case on October 12. There was little deliberation. They believed Ed. Once again, Wiley listened as the foreman announced that the defendant had been found guilty on all counts. He felt himself shrink under the weight of the sentence, saw the final end lying there under the words. A powerful twenty-three-year-old was now something tiny enough to be crushed between two fingers. He felt himself slip to nothing. Erased.

Wiley's sentencing was wired for picture and sound. In a macabre move, perhaps calibrated to show off the new Justice Center to the swath of Northeast Ohio who didn't regularly fill its hallways, the court broadcast the hearing live on television, reportedly for the first time in local history.

"Send me to the chair," Wiley told the courtroom before the judge ruled, his dark face cemented in a stern and stoic look.[8] "I don't want to be reminded each day of my innocence." Judge Zingle had little choice. Wiley didn't slot into any of the mitigating circumstances outlined in the 1974 capital punishment law. Once again, the state of Ohio condemned Wiley Bridgeman to Old Sparky. His execution date was set for July 3, 1978.

Wiley managed a final word. He went back to his legal pads. A few days after he was condemned, Wiley posted a letter to Cleveland's *Call and Post*. In his chiseled handwriting, he maintained his innocence. Yet the message also betrayed a mind struggling to fit everything he wanted to say, needed to say, into simple words. "My insinuation was clear that I believed the jurors were inflamed, rather than (the verdict) honestly decided," his prose trumpeted. "The fact stands plain to see, I will give out before giving up. It's only the getting up [that] counts anyway. Not the fall—I fell . . . I know."[9]

Back in Lucasville, hope buzzed J Block like a static charge.

On the day Wiley's case went to the jury in October 1977, the U.S. Supreme Court announced the list of cases accepted for review in the second half of the 1977–1978 term.[10] Two Ohio petitions challenging the death penalty were on the stack.

As the justices mulled a decision, the death row inmates in Ohio watched closely, discussing the points of the cases like baseball fans weighing batting averages. The first case was on behalf of an Akron woman named Sandra Lockett who had been convicted for her role in a 1975 robbery-homicide. Although Lockett was waiting in the getaway car while her two accomplices killed a store owner, she was sentenced to die under the statute.[11]

The second case pulled Ronnie Bridgeman away from his chessboard and Koran. Many of the details mirrored his own. Like Ronnie, Willie Lee Bell had only been a minor when he allegedly tagged along on a robbery that ended with an accomplice killing a pawnshop owner. Like Lockett, Bell wasn't directly involved in the killing, and as such shouldn't be executed, his attorneys argued. And, also like

Lockett, Bell didn't meet the mitigating standards because the Ohio statute was so narrowly written. "Only a psychotic, a moron, an imbecile, or an idiot has a chance to survive," Bell's lawyer argued before the eight U.S. Supreme Court justices.

The radio on J Block announced the news before Wiley had been processed back into Lucasville. Screams edged with joy filled the range, raw and wild. The voices crashing against the ceiling were now celebrating. Toilet paper rolls thrown from the cells twisted across the range's stale air like July Fourth rockets.[12]

Of the eight U.S. Supreme Court justices who reviewed the Lockett and Bell cases, seven ruled the law was unconstitutional under the Eighth and Fourteenth Amendments. Only Justice William Rehnquist upheld the statute. Once again, the law was blown from the books. Following procedure, each Ohio capital sentence was to be remanded to its original trial court, where the death sentence would be converted to life in prison—fifteen years inside before the possibility of parole. By the time the ruling was announced, 101 men and women were waiting to die in Ohio. The men on J Block—including Rickey and Ronnie—would be sent out into the Lucasville general population. But not Wiley. The timing of his retrial placed his current sentencing in bureaucratic limbo. Rickey and Ronnie couldn't be sure when they'd see him again. They couldn't enjoy the moment together. But the date of the decision, the day when seven strangers in Washington saved their lives with a complex bit of constitutional interpretation, had double weight for the oldest Bridgeman. The court decision was announced on the first Monday in July—the same day Wiley was scheduled to be executed.

Weeks later, Rickey was wading into life in general population at Lucasville, the adventure he'd contemplated from the isolation of death row. Here we go. It was movie night for the inmates. Turns out, they were showing one of his favorites, *Bullitt*, the Steve McQueen crime caper from '68. The car chase scene was reason enough to watch. He was excited. Just before Rickey walked into the room where the film was being shown, he darted into a bathroom, eyeing the prison guard at the door as he passed. There was an inmate standing at a urinal. His face was slack, eyes empty holes. A surgical syringe was plunged into the skin on his forearm. Rickey suddenly understood, seeing this guy shoot dope, that the adventure he was on now was no trip to the museum or hooky jaunt downtown.

They canceled movie night a few weeks later. During the last screening, one inmate shanked another as the film rolled.

# Part II

*FLAT TIME*

# 6

## MENS REA

Cleveland, 2002

SURE, HARD LIVING HAD CARVED HIM UP, NEARLY TWENTY YEARS FACE-
down in the street. The body bore the signs. Both cheeks sagging like
tents knocked down by wind, the grin strung between them a de-
feated rictus. His shoulders and joints hung at cubist angles from so
many nights sleeping in places people weren't meant to sleep in. And
when he spoke, the voice that whispered through was the scorched-
earth aftereffect of long-term pipe use. Nearly twenty years.

Yet for the homeless, the addicts, and the parolees walking through
the door of the City Mission in 2002, Ed Vernon was actually a bill-
board for the kind of lifestyle U-turn a guy could make. There he was
behind the shelter's security desk, checking IDs and signing folks
in—newly sober, committed to God, and even kicking around a healthy
flirtation with the pretty divinity student assigned to the mission. In
the bloodshot eyes of the last-chancers coming for help, here was a positive example, a survivor, a winner.

Ed wouldn't balk at the praise. He felt *good* for the first time, the
Lord knew, in twenty-seven years. But he also knew nothing could be
trusted. Sobriety didn't change that. As always, there was Ed, and
then there was everything else. No assurance bridged the two—ever.
He couldn't trust his family and friends with his real feelings. He

couldn't trust the law, of course not. He couldn't even really trust the Lord, in whom he had sought but failed to find forgiveness. And finally, most of all, he couldn't even trust himself.[1]

So yes, Ed had pulled a second act from the streets, Lord be praised; but he also knew from experience that all this hung on the weakest of threads.

And then Wiley Bridgeman walked into the City Mission.


He may not have been in a cell, but during the criminal trials in 1975, Ed Vernon felt locked up like a prisoner, stuck for three months in a hotel room at the downtown Holiday Inn. He couldn't go anywhere, per the strong words from the police detectives who were paying the room bills. But Ed was such a mess of anxiety and fear, often he'd catch himself sitting on the hotel bed, looking at the balcony, thinking about taking a kamikaze header over the railing.

All alone. His mother couldn't come down to spend the hours with him. She was wrestling through a bout of cervical cancer that kept her in diapers and made walking impossible. His father—James Cannon, a no-bullshit six-foot-five-inch, 250-pound man who never wanted his son mixed up in this criminal trial business to begin with—was working two jobs, days at Franklin Tire on St. Clair, nights at a gas station on East Fifty-fifth; he would come to the hotel for the night after his last shift ended, around 11:30 P.M. Otherwise, Ed was by himself. Only one friend from the neighborhood occasionally came down to visit. Everyone else's mother wouldn't let them. They thought he was a snitch. But the visits from his buddy kept Ed sane, the rare occasions he was allowed out of the room. Then he could be a boy again, a thirteen-year-old swimming in the pool and playing pinball in the lobby, not the state's main witness in a murder trial.

When the last guilty verdict came down in October 1975, Ed figured it was over, that he could push a reset button returning him to his old life—back delivering the morning *Plain Dealer* and pedaling his bike around with his friends. But before Ed checked out of the hotel, Detective Terpay wanted to talk. Terpay—the older white man who told Ed to call him "Gene," a bulky man who could flip from friendly to angry so quickly—informed Ed and his parents that the boy needed to go into hiding. The police, he explained, had learned the Bridgemans' brother was planning to kill Ed in retaliation for his testimony. The boy couldn't stay in Cleveland. Through tears, Ed's mom tried to explain they had heard nothing about any threats. But Terpay was adamant. Ed had to go.

The sudden escape was a heartbreaker—a boy pulled from his family after already undergoing the frightening ordeal of the criminal trials. But Ed felt it all the more because it was *him* causing all the trouble. It wasn't supposed to be like that. He was the good son. The three older Vernon daughters were always stirring up the household, especially when they got to be teenagers and started, as their mother put it, smelling them boys. But little Ed? He was polite and respectful, especially to adults. When any of the 140 daily and Sunday customers on his *Plain Dealer* route asked him to put the paper in the door slot instead of the mail chute, he did it. When his parents told him to be home before the streetlights snapped on, he was. Yet Ed was now ripping the family up right as his mother was so sick.

The only option the family had was to send the boy to live with his actual namesake, Mrs. Vernon's brother, Edward. He lived in Princeton, New Jersey, with his wife Mary, his own son Edward, and his grandson, another Edward—whenever Aunt Mary called the name, four people came running. Princeton might as well have been Mars for Ed. His uncle was one of the head chefs at the Ivy League university; the East Side Cleveland kid often found himself on the leafy, groomed campus, going to basketball and football games or whacking golf balls with his buddies. His own classroom was filled with faculty members' children, not just white boys and girls, but kids from all over the globe—Germany, France, Italy, China. Ed was in the middle of this worldwide melting pot; not everyone could speak great English, yet they could communicate enough to have fun.

Friends or no, Ed's New Jersey life was standing on lies. The police had been clear: if anyone discovered where he was now living, the Bridgemans could wreak their revenge. Ed was instructed not to tell anyone outside his family where he was really from. When he accidentally slipped, telling classmates he was from Cleveland, he quickly recovered by telling everyone it was Cleveland, Florida, not Ohio. He added a further flourish, telling his friends his father was a doctor. He didn't know whom to trust, so he trusted no one.

That strong current of fear—of being discovered, of being killed, of whatever else could be coming—was always running full speed through him; the only competing sentiment was the hard, immobile guilt that had settled in since the trials. He had *wanted* to tell the truth. He had *needed* to tell the truth. But he had not been *able* to tell the truth. Rickey, Ronnie, Wiley—he'd done those guys wrong. He had. It stayed with him. Guilt over the past, fear of the future—the two feelings hugged him so close, he felt completely paralyzed.

Cleveland kept reeling him back, homesickness outweighing everything else. In 1976, when his father died of a collapsed lung, Ed returned for the funeral. The next year, he was called back to tell his story in Wiley's retrial. Ed felt he was ready to come home for good. He was tired of hiding.

And at first, it was a good homecoming. His mother, now cancer-free, had moved to a different part of the East Side, and the family was financially steadied by the Social Security checks arriving following his father's death; after bills there was enough left over for Ed to enter a private Catholic high school at fifteen. His report card was mainly Bs. He liked school. Science, history, and math were his favorite subjects.

Ed couldn't steer completely clear of the old neighborhood. His maternal grandmother still lived on Colonial Court, and when he visited her, he ran across folks with vivid memories of the Franks murder and the trials. Everyone on the block knew Ed lied when he climbed on the witness stand. All those kids—including Kim Dickson and Tommy Hall—had been on the bus with him. Back home they wouldn't stop talking about how Ed was a liar. But the real acid behind the neighborhood's contempt was that no one understood why he'd done it. Was it for the fifty dollars? A grudge? To make nice with adults? Suck up to white cops? The familiar faces Ed saw were all stitched with anger and disgust. These run-ins only increased when his private school closed in 1979, meaning Ed had to finish up at John Hay High School, where many of the Arthur Avenue kids went as well.

Each week he still had to call Detective Terpay to check in, even though the officer had left the Cleveland police for a job at the Cuyahoga County Sheriff's Department. The check-ins always reactivated his fears. The detective reminded Ed he was still in danger and couldn't talk about the case. Ed had to carry this silently. All alone.

In his senior year he found a release—albeit a temporary one. Ed was sitting with some friends outside of the school, barely listening to the talk drifting around, his own mind kicking with the same thoughts as always—Rickey, Ronnie, and Wiley. Bottles of alcohol circulated. Wild Irish Rose. "Man," Ed announced to the surprised group. "Let me get a drink of that."

It turned out, he wasn't much of a drinker, it scrambled him up too much. But Ed's baby steps into chemical escape carried him straight to marijuana. That became his thing—it was nothing for Ed to walk around with five dime bags on him. The weed put enough mental bubble wrap around the present moment to insulate him against what had happened before and what might happen next. In this way, Ed was able to shove aside his guilt and fear and settle into a blank space—at least, until the fog thinned.

After getting his diploma in 1980, Ed had hoped to steer for college. But as he was working for tuition money, he got his girlfriend pregnant. There went college. He took an entrance exam for the U.S. Army, but decided against it. Job Corps shipped him off to Indiana, but he bailed on that, too. "What are you going to do?" his mother kept asking him. He had no answer.

Sometime in 1980, he was getting high with one of his cousins when she asked for a couple extra dollars for her own stash. When she came back with some white powder she commenced to melt down into little chalky crumbs and smoke, Ed asked for a hit. "You ain't getting this," she snapped. "You got to buy your own." Okay, he thought. That night, Ed swallowed his first blast of freebase cocaine—and waved goodbye to the world for the next two decades.

Crack cocaine socked American cities like a blizzard at the worst possible time, particularly Rust Belt areas feeling the hurt of the economic recessions running through the mid-1970s to the early 1980s. The appearance of a cheap, smokable form of cocaine diluted with baking soda would disfigure American city life as radically as the Model T or the electrical grid.

The curtain went up on the 1980s crack era in Cleveland at low volume. The drug leaked into the city early in the decade, but few in law enforcement or the city mainstream noticed. Then, in 1986, top NBA prospect Len Bias and the Cleveland Browns' own Don Rogers both suffered cocaine-related deaths within eight days of each other. Tabloid anxiety spun into national hysteria. Whether this overnight shock was the engine behind it or not, suddenly crack cocaine became a conversation piece in the national discourse; Cleveland's police began speaking publicly about a drug they had written off earlier as only a West Coast fad.

Crack's debut was fortuitously timed for the right end of the political spectrum. Ronald Reagan, like Richard Nixon, had absorbed the lesson Cleveland's pols learned in the Stokes era: law-and-order rhetoric served as a secret language for talking about race, for revving up the fears of the white mainstream against black Americans. The well-grooved financial paths between the federal government and local law enforcement had already been established by Johnson and Nixon. In October 1982, Reagan declared his own "War on Drugs," later dubbing America's drug problem a "national security threat"; crack cocaine became the perfect enemy combatant for those saber-rattling ambitions. Between 1980 and 1984, the FBI's annual antidrug budget exploded from nine million dollars to ninety-five million. In 1984 the administration pushed forward legislation that allowed departments to keep cash and assets confiscated in drug cases. Federal programs offered up military equipment to local agencies, further remaking law enforcement into a wartime enterprise. At the same time, the U.S. Supreme Court was loosening the protective grip the Fourth Amendment had on police interactions with suspects. Between 1982 and 1991, the court heard thirty cases involving narcotics and police search and seizure. The court sided with police in all but three, vastly widening police powers.

In Cleveland, law enforcement officials speculated that a local marijuana drought, combined with the increased purity of the base cocaine arriving in the U.S. from the Miami–South America pipeline, may have propelled more local users to crack cocaine around 1986.[2] Certainly it wasn't hard to find—this was the era when you could stroll into any head shop and find a freebase kit on the shelf with the bongs and black light posters. Street econ also played into it. Detroit gangs who ran cocaine figured a crack rock selling in Dexter-Davison for five to ten dollars could go for twenty-five dollars on Cleveland's Buckeye or Central. By mid-1986, one Cleveland hospital was reporting a 70 percent bounce in cocaine-related admissions.

The city was woefully unprepared for the spike. Cleveland's narcotics unit had just twenty officers, down from the all-time high of fifty-five; budget cuts had shorn the local public funding for drug treatment programs, going from $7 million in 1971 to $3.4 million in 1986.[3] By the fall of that year, Cleveland law enforcement officials were on the ground in Washington, D.C., scrambling to land some of the federal money being dished out for President Ronald Reagan's War on Drugs. "We have no money," Cuyahoga County Sheriff Gerald McFaul told a *Plain Dealer* reporter on the Capitol Hill trip. "Just tell us where we can get some more money. I didn't come to Washington to have lunch."

Throughout the middle of the decade, the local crack game was mostly a two-party system. Detroit gangs, particularly Young Boys

Inc., cornered much of the Cleveland market, often shuttling teenage drug mules on Greyhounds or in taxis from Motor City to Northeast Ohio with kilos of cocaine. Once in Cleveland, Detroit outfits became infamous for setting up beachheads in public housing facilities—once the pride of the city's liberal social justice spirit. Now, dealers were reportedly either paying single moms or elderly folks to convert their units into crack shops, or simply cocking a pistol to force their cooperation.[4] By 1988, the housing authority reported that 75 percent of their evictions were related to drug issues, and the head of the Cleveland police's drug unit told a reporter 85 percent of the crack traffic in the city was tied to Detroit operators. The Garden Valley low-rises off Kinsman, the King-Kennedy buildings in Central, Morris Black Place in Woodland—all were hot spots for Motor City drug dealers, some doing up to one hundred thousand dollars a week in sales.

The other main players in the underground were also out-of-towners: Jamaican drug gangs, mainly the Shower Posse, a trigger-happy crew tied to the warring political factions back home. With their Miami-smuggled product, the Jamaicans were running "gatehouses" up and down West Twenty-fifth, on the western lip of downtown, cashing $150,000 per kilo. The Posse was also reportedly turning those profits over to an Arab Clevelander linked to the PLO in exchange for arms or donations to Jamaican political parties back home. Police linked the Posse to five murders and seventeen shootings in a twelve-month stretch. In 1987, the local FBI office was listed eighteenth nationally in terms of drug crime; a year later, the office jumped to third.

But really the market demand was heavy enough for all comers; by the 1990s, Southern California gang members were getting in on Cleveland's trade. One memorable hustler, "L.A. Jay," was pulling $250,000 a week out of the King-Kennedy houses before his arrest in 1990; he then became a county jail legend while in lockup after paying ten thousand dollars to trade identities with a fellow prisoner about to be released. He strolled out of jail with his purchased identity. But Cleveland largely avoided the asphalt combat that bloodied so many

American cities. Eventually the Jamaican gangs left the crack rock to Motor City suppliers, focusing their business on powder cocaine. At one point, Detroit and Jamaican dealers were actually selling drugs out of the same fleabag motel in suburban Euclid, their businesses cordially chugging along only one floor apart from one another.

By far the most infamous name floating through the Cleveland drug world was "White Art." A former building contractor, Art—born Arthur Feckner—bumped around the East Side in a flashy El Camino tricked out with a drop compartment for the thirteen-kilo shipments of cocaine he regularly drove up from Miami. When the white suburbanite ran afoul of his black competition in the city, Feckner was beaten and injected with a "hot shot" of cocaine and heroin meant to stop his heart. Left for dead outside his Woodland Avenue warehouse, he was found by Cleveland police.[5]

Under pressure to make some dent in the growing local market, a group of major-crime detectives—they called themselves the A-Team—concocted a flashy plan to use Feckner to go after the Miami and Colombian suppliers selling him product. But Feckner couldn't buy any new drugs, he told the police, until he paid off what he owed to the suppliers. Eyeing the big score—and working on a timetable: The Cleveland detectives were scheduled to attend a national DEA convention in a few months and they wanted to walk in with a major bust on their record—the A-Team greenlighted Feckner to sell off enough drugs to erase his debt so the sting could march on. Feckner and a partner pumped half a million dollars of crack into the East Side while the A-Team allegedly directed other Cleveland police away from their operators.

The Cleveland cops got their bust, dramatically arresting fifteen dealers and confiscating fifty million dollars' worth of cocaine in South Florida. But the celebration was short. Feckner revealed to the FBI and DEA that he was under the protection of local police. Five internal investigations looked at the operation, all clearing the cops of knowingly sanctioning Feckner's drug operation. Yet Cuyahoga County Prosecutor John Corrigan secured indictments against five A-Team detectives on drug trafficking charges. In court, the detectives said they thought Feckner was only collecting debts from past sales. They made this claim despite hundreds of hours of police wiretap recordings catching Feckner plotting new business. The detectives simply claimed they never listened to the tapes. After the prosecution rested its case, Judge Michael J. Corrigan stunned the room—and the city—by averring that the state had failed to prove the charges; as Corrigan read the Ohio law, drug sales by law enforcement were legal if done for law enforcement purposes. The judge acquitted the five cops, and once again, Cleveland was smoking with anger from a confrontation between police and the black community.

"No decision like this could've been made to have this type of operation on the West Side of Cleveland or anywhere that's predominantly white," Louis Stokes, former mayor Carl Stokes's brother and then a U.S. congressman from the area, told the *L.A. Times*.

"They didn't do it on their own. Somebody gave approval. Somebody above those five officers made a conscious decision that this is a throwaway community."

For the seventeen years Ed Vernon was on the receiving end of this crack distribution game, you could smell him before you saw him.

Mostly he worked construction sites as a laborer for bricklayers. He'd be hauling stacks around the work area, mixing mortar, or high up on the scaffolding. All sweaty, hard effort. The other muscle on-site were union types, guys who rolled in each day in pressed, clean clothes. They would dog Ed about the stink coming off him before the shift even began. "You ain't work yet today, so you couldn't be that musty," they'd chide. Ed laughed it off. What his coworkers didn't know was that he'd often go a month without changing his clothes. He just didn't care.

Addiction stripped you bare, your normal wants, needs, and cares killed off until there was only one: getting high. Ed slid easily into the cycle. Clean clothes and hygiene weren't a priority. Food—whatever.

Sex didn't enter his head; the other guys he used with assumed he was gay because Ed never leveraged his stash to coerce favors out of junk-sick women. He passed many a night stretched out in abandoned houses on the East Side. Later his sister Darlene allowed him to crash in a car that wouldn't start anymore parked outside her house. Ed would pile into the backseat under old blankets and clothes. On nights when the temperature crawled below freezing, Darlene banged on the car window to see if Ed moved, if he was alive. Hard-core addiction also didn't leave any free space for irony, either: the busted car Ed called home was beached on Arthur Avenue, the same street Ronnie, Wiley, and Rickey all lived on before the murder.

To Ed, everyone else seemed to be chained up to the same carousel. Everybody was getting high, he thought. It spread into the very texture of the neighborhoods. Your grandmother might come to find her can opener missing, the next day her microwave gone; when she asked you about it, you'd play ignorant, even though you'd pawned it for drug money. Crack users got creative, too. Ed watched guys secretly taking out second mortgages on their mothers' houses to feed the habit. Others inherited property from their families and quickly turned the houses into drug dens, boards slapped over once-polished windows, the lawns shaggy and brown. Worse, when dealers filling their pockets with money realized they couldn't keep buying flashy cars and stay unnoticed, they bought property instead, leaving behind a trail of neglected houses and storefronts all down the way.

Ed's years puddled together in a mindless slush. Work, sleep, get high. Get high, sleep, work. But there was a hitch to his drug use. Crack might pick you clean of everything you care about, but the drug couldn't shake Ed of what he wanted to lose the most—the guilt and fear and anxiety still knotted in his stomach. They stayed around when everything else was stripped away. Usually, the feelings ganged up on him at night. Ed liked to review his day as the sun went down, going over what he did right, what he did wrong. Inevitably, like a train screaming in on time, thoughts of the trial came at him. What he did.

What he did to those three guys. Then it was time to reach for his stash again.

By the mid-1990s, Ed was sunk so deep in his addiction, beyond care or concern, he was talked into a felony charge. A friend of Ed's was a drug dealer; he'd been arrested, and the cops were pressing him to offer up his supplier. This friend, as Ed would later explain, was looking for a patsy: you play like a big-time dealer; you sell to an undercover cop; the law thinks they've snagged a big player while the real operation continues unabated. The friend told Ed that because he didn't have a previous drug charge, he might not even go to jail. But Ed was barely listening. All he focused on was the money—half now, half after the arrest. He agreed, pocketed his share, and ran for the nearest dealer.

But out on the street, Ed, crack-dizzy and careless, hadn't considered two things. The first was the 1996 Federal Crime Bill, a provision that hammered into place tougher sentencing guidelines for drug felonies. The amount he was busted with was four times the felony max; he was looking at a thirty-year stretch. The Cuyahoga County judge, however, looked over his record and showed mercy. Ed received a four-year prison term. He was lucky. But looking at four years inside, Ed slammed against the second thought he'd failed to consider: *I'm going to run into those boys and they are going to kill me.*

Ed Vernon arrived at Grafton Correctional Institute, whittled skinny like a dying tree, his head a box of terror. He didn't know what Rickey, Ronnie, or Wiley looked like now. They could be anyone. As soon as possible, he shipped a kite, a prison note, to the warden, explaining his situation. The administration decided to put him in protective custody while they verified the three inmates' whereabouts. Isolated for twenty-three of every twenty-four hours, without drugs to gag his guilt, Ed again was thinking about killing himself, be done with it. Why not? I can cut my wrists and call it a day, he thought as he searched his cell for a Bic to do the job. He called out to the guard, asking for a razor so he could shave. The prison staffer knew why Ed wanted the sharp blade.

"Shave what?" the guard told the inmate, indicating his boyish cheeks. "You don't have anything to shave."

Ed served two years, mostly in isolation, on suicide watch. He was released in 1999. Got high the same day. Sleep, work, get high. All over again.

In March 2000, Ed's maternal grandmother passed away. He went to the funeral with the last traces of a crack hit still running around his system. A cousin, an ex-addict now clean and sober, came up to Ed after the burial. "Don't let me be a pallbearer at your funeral," he cautioned.

The warning stuck in Ed's thoughts, like a song refrain you can't shake. The next time he got high, his heart started frantically rocking his chest so badly, he thought he was dying. Only a close call, but Ed was startled.

Later in the day he was back out on the streets, no place to sleep, nowhere to get a meal. His sister wasn't letting him back into her house. Ed was exhausted, his tank empty; still, he managed to walk fifty blocks or so west to the City Mission. Any self-respecting drug fiend knew which shelters were open when, where you could crib a free meal or a month's stay in exchange for sitting through some sermons or self-help spiels. Ed queued up before the doors opened at 4:00 P.M. Shook his head when they asked if he was there for the rehab program— just looking for something to eat. That's how he found himself sitting in an evening church service at the mission the next night.

When the preacher asked if anyone was interested in rededicating their life to Christ, Ed thought on it. He'd left the church when he was twenty and hadn't looked back. But he needed something now. He was exhausted with the whole deal. Get high, sleep, work. Sleep, work, get high. Maybe he needed God.

Ed entered the City Mission's rehabilitation program, a twelve-month boot camp of soul-searching and group therapy. The counselors introduced Ed to the basics of the addiction that had scrambled his last twenty years. He learned about triggers, the anxiety and pressures that sent him reaching for the chemical outs that booze, weed, and crack provided. Ed saw right away the twin jets of fear and guilt that had been snapping at his ankles since he was a boy. That, along with placing his faith in God again, allowed Ed to hoist himself up for the first time in decades.

But there are some burdens even God can't heft for you. He knew that in his heart. It wasn't that he didn't take sobriety seriously—he did, tackling the program with headlong enthusiasm. But it was nearly impossible to solve your problems when you couldn't tell anyone about what was truly sitting at your center. What wouldn't leave. And without the cloud cover of crack and weed, those issues were exposed. He couldn't hide from them anymore. I should come forward, tell the truth. No, I'd go to jail, it's perjury. Knew enough of the law to know that. Ed was caught in a battle with himself, and he couldn't trust anyone enough to tell them. Worse, as his Christian faith moved into the central place in his life during recovery, Ed knew that it too rested on lies. God supposedly had forgiven all his sins—that promise was basically his life preserver. But Ed also knew his Ten Commandments. *Thou shalt not bear false witness against thy neighbor.* There was no fixing that. I'm going to hell, Ed thought. That's where I'm going. I'm going to die and I'm going to hell.

Ed tried to swallow it all down, keep the roaring spiritual pain from showing. Even though Ed was the star pupil of the program, the counselors could sense that something else was wrong. Grief radiated off him. "There's something more than drugs," one counselor told him. "But you just aren't going to tell me." He passed through his program anyway, secured a job at a rubber company, and eventually returned to the City Mission as a security guard working the front desk intake, all while maintaining his sobriety. He hadn't touched anything since lifting his hand in that evening church service.

But by November 2002, the balance he'd achieved almost toppled. One day he was working the desk. The mindless workflow broke when he caught a piece of a conversation near the door—a stranger was explaining he'd just paroled out after twenty-seven years for a 1975 murder he didn't commit. The voice, not much more than a torn-up whisper, belonged to a round, hefty man in his late forties. He placed an ID on the desk.

Ed's eyes hurried from the man standing over him to the name printed on the card. Wiley Bridgeman. Wiley Bridgeman. Wiley Bridgeman. If the young man Ed had last seen in a courtroom twenty-seven years earlier was buried somewhere in this face now before him, he couldn't see it. An unruly Santa Claus–white beard circled the features. There was a distance in his dark eyes, as if they had trouble focusing, much less recognizing, right here, the man responsible for all the wordless pain they'd seen.

After twenty-seven years in prison, much of that time in solitary confinement, Wiley had made parole. Part of his discharge required he stay at the City Mission for the first weeks of his transition. If Wiley recognized Ed vaguely, he didn't say anything. Ed could have played dumb, ignored it. The facility employee informed his bosses of the situation, or at least he told them he'd served as a witness in the guy's 1975 murder case. "I don't want any trouble," Ed promised his supervisor. Yet he also resolved to tell Wiley. This, he felt, was an opportunity.

The next day, Ed took Wiley aside after a group therapy session. He told him who he was. The look that flashed on Wiley's face—Ed would never forget it. Soon both were crying like babies. "I'm sorry for what I did," he told Wiley.

"We've got to go to the news stations," Wiley said, when he recovered from the shock. "No no no no," Ed said. "Not yet, it's not time."

Wiley persisted, and continued to beg, cajole, threaten. Nothing moved Ed, and nothing in the following weeks changed his mind. If anything, the stress tightened the knots in his stomach more. His sobriety was so fragile then, so new; he felt the pressure from Wiley edging him closer to using again. He had a job. The flirtation with the divinity student working at the mission had blossomed into a romance. They were talking about even getting married. Ed knew that if he came forward, all that would go.

Ed conferred again with his supervisor at the City Mission. He said Wiley was bothering him about the old case. The supervisor suggested Ed just call Wiley's parole officer to complain. He did, and Wiley was moved out of the City Mission to another shelter. Within a few months, he got into an argument with his parole officer over where he was living, and he was eventually busted back to prison.

Ed married. He got another job. He joined a new church where he led Bible study. For now, it seemed like he'd been able to swallow down 1975 again. But sometimes he thought back to the meeting with Wiley, and he recalled the look on the man's face when he learned who he was talking to. That look—there was no putting that away. It was a look of pure, searing hate.

# 7

## ALHAMDULILLAH

THE CARDBOARD BOX WAS FLIMSY AND STRAINED AGAINST THE WEIGHT of all the paper inside. There wasn't a lid, so as Kwame Ajamu stepped from his apartment on a chill-shot weekday early in the new year, he had to be careful. Didn't want some subzero kick of wind making off with these transcribed pages of his past. Not today.

He was living in an efficiency on Whittier, just off East Fifty-fifth Street. There was a bus stop at the end of the block. From there, the 16 line went north, then drilled west toward downtown along Superior Avenue. Buried under a heavy coat and with a knit hat topping his round head, Kwame settled into a seat and watched the city scroll past. Anything to keep his mind away from where he was heading. He was nervous.

Kwame liked the bus. The public transit lines, their strict routes weaving a cat's cradle across the town, were an easy way to reacquaint himself with the hometown he didn't even want to live in anymore. When he was released from prison in 2003, Kwame didn't want to be like guys who got swamped by the changes outside, the ones who end up missing prison enough to slip back. So he rode the bus to familiarize himself with what the city had been up to while he was away.

The bus was also how he met LaShawn. She'd been waiting at a stop, trying to figure out how to catch a connection. Kwame didn't know her. He'd only been out a few months and was still living at a halfway house. But he approached the woman. She was rail thin and bowlegged, skin a light brown. When Kwame tried to speak, her face locked down into a hard look—just like every woman Kwame had tried talking to out here. But this time he had a slick comment ready. "Excuse me, Mrs. Buttermilk, I didn't know you'd gone sour."

LaShawn's face split with a laugh, and he'd been making her laugh ever since. Once they started seeing each other, Kwame let it be known right away he wasn't messing around. Being together meant getting married. Getting married meant he'd have to tell her about his twenty-seven years in prison. Tell her *why* he'd been in prison, as crazy as it sounded. Tell her his real name. But prison forces you to be a good judge of character, and he was right about LaShawn. She stayed. Now they had been married for nearly five years and were getting ready to move into their own house.

For twenty-eight years he had told people his story, only to watch them dismiss it as improbable. The work of an overactive, self-serving imagination. A denial of guilt. A criminal's bullshit. So after leaving prison, he stopped talking about his past. Outside, LaShawn had been the only one to know the truth. All that had recently changed. A few days earlier, he'd told a lawyer, Terry Gilbert. And now, on this January morning, Kwame was hauling this box to meet another stranger downtown. He was worried once again he wouldn't be believed.

There is a beautiful story in Islam about Bilal ibn Rabah, an early convert to the one true faith. This was in the first hard days—the Prophet Muhammad, peace and blessings be upon him, marching through the desert, tribe warring against tribe, sandstorms and persecution and bloodshed. Bilal was a slave. His master was an enemy of Islam. When he learned of Bilal's choice to follow the Prophet, he ordered the slave be whipped until he renounced the teachings. But no matter the blows he took, Bilal would only utter *ahad, ahad*. The one, the one—the one true God.

The master finally had Bilal dragged to the desert. The slave was thrown onto the scalding sand. Heavy rocks were piled upon his chest. But Bilal still refused to relent. Even though he could no longer speak, his index finger lifted—the one, the one.

That total act of defiance sang through Ronnie Bridgeman. All those years earlier, on death row, the lines from the Koran had poked a comforting light through his desperation. For a prisoner in his twenties, Bilal's story reached across thousands of years to touch him where it mattered.

Prison was not easy on Ronnie Bridgeman. Sure, Lucasville wasn't easy for anyone. Seemed like every day for the nine years Ronnie spent at the facility, a ten-inch shiv found a home in someone's belly. Blood covered the walls, dashed the ceiling, even spilled on your morning mess hall eggs. He lived inside a bubble of fear. But the violence was only part of Ronnie's unease. He also was completely at odds with his surroundings. Some of it was age. Most of the hard-timers in Lucasville were in their thirties. Ronnie was still lightly glazed with childhood innocence—he still got excited about Christmas and Thanksgiving. On the range nobody wanted to hear that holiday shit. But the displacement also ran deeper. Ronnie might get to talking to some guy one day, only to learn he'd chopped off his wife's head or was a cattle rustler—what the inmates called a serial rapist. Ronnie wasn't a criminal; he wasn't wired that way. Bessie Bridgeman didn't raise her son like that. Yet his only companions were men serving time for crimes they'd meant to commit; they had stolen, hurt people, lied. He couldn't relate.[1]

Islam, however, offered shelter. He studied the religion and found the Muslim faith was one not of compulsion but of choice. You *entered* into it, and by doing so, reached right back thousands of years. When Ronnie raised his head from the floor following the second *ruku*, his face pointed east, his lips moving around the strange words of the *tashahhud,* his index finger danced, just like Bilal's all those centuries back.

More than death row, general population was a top-down matrix of dos and don'ts. The administration told you when you woke, ate, what job you'd fill your hours with, when you'd see the sun, even when you could walk through a door. Your personhood was denied, individuality stomped out. Grafted onto this were the unwritten dictates of the population: never talk to a guard; don't snitch; when someone does you a favor, pay them back double. A prisoner's behavior, then, was penned in on all sides by someone else's ideas.

In Islam, Ronnie found individuality in structure, a system he willingly chose. There was a logic to it, sequence to the process of prayer, strict order dictating how you interfaced with the world, right down to your greetings to fellow Muslims, even what you said when you sneezed, *al-hamdu Lillaah,* or when someone sneezed near you, *Yarhamuk Allaah.* There was also elegance to how the religion's dictates tidied up the smallest corners of your life, from going to the bathroom to eating. It kept you clean, pure, as well oiled as a Cadillac, Ronnie thought. The control was empowering, he felt, like slipping on a Superman cape. This was not structure that obliterated you; these were processes linking you to a larger tradition.

Religion wasn't his only outlet. When the truth finally clicked into place—I'm not going nowhere—Ronnie decided he might as well make his life as enjoyable as he could. He started boxing, training with old pros and sparring with guys who could have been professionals had criminal charges not torpedoed their chances. School was another outlet. He went through the program to get his GED, then began working as a clerk in the facility's education department; that way he could take as many classes as he wanted. The culinary classes were a favorite; after a couple of years, Ronnie was a wizard in the kitchen, whipping up stuff from the meager ingredients. Not that he was a Boy Scout. Ronnie had a taste for weed; it was plentiful in any prison facility, as long as you didn't mind smoking something that had been smuggled in through someone's ass. Ronnie did mind it, meaning he usually had to find prison staff willing to smuggle stuff for him. Over the years, he became a PhD in bullshitting with them. He had more games than Milton Bradley, as he liked to say. But on the main, he stayed clean: prayer, helping guys get into the right GED program, and the occasional lungful of Colombia Flower Top to mellow the edges.

Ronnie also talked about his case to anyone who would listen. No one, it seemed, believed that he was an innocent man flung into prison for murder. That was hard enough. As Ronnie got older he also began to notice something in the staff and teachers he knew from the education office. They would chat and laugh together, and Ronnie would lay some of his stories on a roomful of people, build an easy camaraderie. Then he recognized the thought forming in their faces. They liked him, he saw that. But they tapped the brakes—he was a convicted murderer. They couldn't *really* like him. Just as he couldn't walk those last steps to bond with his fellow inmates, outsiders couldn't ultimately connect with him. Regardless of who he was as a man or how he acted, no matter the number of the course certificates he earned or the words per minute he could snap out on an administration type-writer or how many inmates he steered into education courses, he was still on the other side of a line in the eyes of the staffers. He was a killer.

In 1995, Ronnie decided to change his name to Kwame Ajamu. It was a final, definitive move to push free from who he had been.

It was January 2003, and the flat farmland surrounding the Richland Correctional Institute was arthritic and brown with winter. But as Kwame walked out of the building, his lungs hauling in cold breaths, the landscape glowed as if under spotlights. Green as a bright summer day, he thought. Martin Luther King Jr. was on repeat in his head: *free at last, free at last, thank God Almighty.* A cab was waiting outside the prison. "Take me to the Grey Dog," he said.

The driver shot him an awkward look. "Grey Dog?"

Kwame thought. "Grey . . . hound?" The drive to the bus station cost him ten dollars. The ticket for the eighty miles to Cleveland put him back fourteen dollars. And like that, he was home after twenty-seven years.

Kwame never wanted to go home. As far as he was concerned, it wasn't his home anymore. When he finally got word that the state was considering paroling him out, he asked to be assigned elsewhere— Columbus, Toledo, Akron, Canton. Anywhere but Cleveland. Too many ugly thoughts tied to the place. But the parole board ignored his request and placed him in a halfway house on the East Side. His return was all the more painful because there was no missing how much time had been lost. It wasn't just the city's changed face—new skyscrapers rubbing elbows with Terminal Tower; plywood filling up the windows of corner stores and shopping centers; shaggy fields sitting where blocks of houses once stood. He was also coming home to a family tree that was missing all the branches he knew. His mother had died in 1990, his sister in 2000, his brother Hawiatha in 2002. Both his siblings left behind large families, bundles of nieces and nephews; but Kwame had never met any of them. They put in the effort to get to know him, but they were still strangers.

People had also changed all over the city. The intervening decades had pounded friendliness out of them. Kwame was a talker; he was always trying to strike up conversations with folks. No one seemed interested in hearing him out. Most of the time, Kwame's banter was met with a look like he was something someone had just stepped in. In time, he began to feel crack cocaine itself had subtly altered the tone of the whole town. He'd had the interesting experience of watching the impact of the epidemic from inside the prison system. He first learned about crack in the 1990s, when he spotted old guys twisting metal clothes hangers to their boom boxes where the antennas were supposed to be. Crackhead prisoners had been stealing the metal antennas to use as makeshift pipes for the drugs they got inside. The same desperation now seemed to be driving life on the outside. After six months at the halfway house, he moved into a small place off Cedar

Avenue. Crackheads clustered outside his door. A cloud of freebase smoke lingered over the whole street.

At first, the only job he could get was working at a recycling center, six dollars an hour and a stink he couldn't get off him after work—just like the chemical smell that had stuck to his father all those years back. But Kwame had caught a serious break, *alhamdulillah*, right at the start of this whole nightmare. When he'd been taken into custody in May 1975, whoever plugged his information into the system had flubbed one digit on his Social Security number. Outside, it meant Kwame Ajamu could apply for a job with his actual government-issue ID, a number that would not be red-flagged with "prior felony conviction." Fingerprints—that would give him up. But not those nine digits. Like his new name, it was one more way to lay distance between who he had been and who he was today.

The typo also meant he could get a better-paying job without the stigma of a criminal conviction. When an acquaintance asked if Kwame would be interested in a ten-dollar-an-hour job at the Cuyahoga County Board of Elections, he applied without worry. He was assigned to the warehouse where the voting machines were stored and fixed. The gig ran 7:00 P.M. to 7:00 A.M. Kwame liked it. He became proficient at fixing the machines and started going out on calls with other board employees. The job made him feel like he was representing something important. The problem was that it was seasonal work—ramping up toward Election Day, dying off after. The board liked Kwame so much, they asked him to apply for full-time positions. But he always declined. It puzzled his coworkers, but Kwame knew that official employment would necessitate a deeper background check, including fingerprints. So despite loving the job and getting high marks from the bosses, Kwame couldn't advance.

This was just how it was going to be. Wife, job—sure. But the past would always wall him off from a truly normal life. And if he ever wanted to scale that obstacle, he'd have to get Rickey and Wiley up and over with him. He couldn't—wouldn't—leave them behind. Their shared pain was like an invisible mark. No one else could see it; they

alone knew what it meant, understood the constant maintenance required each day to keep going. The three men were stamped with what
had happened to them. Passing time could not wear it away.

Could he get them out? As Kwame's life was shaping up in Cleveland, Wiley was locked away at Lima, mostly in solitary confinement. Kwame couldn't reach him easily. Rickey, however, was in
Marion. Kwame mailed regular letters to his best friend. Rickey
sometimes would lapse into long silences, months where the letters
ceased and Kwame could tell his friend was buried under a deep depression. Kwame knew he needed help, someone who could jolt the
case back to relevance. He needed someone like Terry Gilbert.


*"Hello."*

Anyone who got Cleveland attorney Terry Gilbert on his office
phone couldn't miss it: the irascibility, like you better have a good fucking reason for phoning because you were ripping him away from more
pressing business. You probably were. For more than three decades,
Gilbert was on the front lines of nearly every controversial legal issue
in Cleveland and beyond.

He radiated the same jammed-up, short-fuse energy in person—
he was bald and short, and the smiles that made fugitive cameos
on his face were cagey; his features seemed more comfortable in an
irritated scowl, the game face he wore when tearing into police officers in court or blasting city hall on nightly television. To city attorneys and prosecutors, he was an opportunistic plaintiff's attorney at
best, a media-hungry bomb thrower at worst; to many people sitting
in the Cuyahoga County Justice Center, he was a last chance. But it
was easy to misread the brashness. Under the hard shell, Gilbert was
simply a throwback, a man who had never been disabused of the ideals born out of the 1960s counterculture.

Law or radical politics weren't in Gilbert's DNA. From Cleveland
Heights, the Gilberts were comfortably working class; Dad was a sales-

man for a snack company, Mom a housewife.[2] Gilbert grew up boxed in by the *Leave It to Beaver* conservatism of 1950s America. He turned up for his freshman year of college at Miami University in 1966 as a blue-blazered, penny-loafered, pipe-smoking square. By the time he graduated, he was a shaggy-haired conscientious objector who'd attended Woodstock and been tear-gassed marching on his own campus.

It was a well-trod path for a generation. These were white middle-class kids nursed on Eisenhower, hypnotized by the images from the South of the civil rights struggle, and liberated by the escalation of the war in Vietnam. Social justice, voting rights, equality, unencumbered sex, freedom—this was a wave of young people who felt they'd rearrange the world along those lines. And for a true believer like Gilbert, this wasn't just hippie shit. These beliefs were convictions running deep as church dogma. But by the time Gilbert got out of college in the 1970s, the movements were running on fumes. Optimism was yellowing at the edges. King, Malcolm X, the Kennedys were dead. The war seemed unending. The Black Power movement turned inward. If you were socially conscious, keyed up to change the world, suddenly the world seemed less friendly to progress. The legal system—which, along with the rest of the country, was undergoing its own radical alteration—provided an unlikely opportunity for remaking the system from within. "There were enough of us that were conscious of the idea that there was something more law could do," Gilbert would later say.

In part, he was inspired after watching the Chicago Seven trial on television. Courtroom proceedings as absurdist theater, the trial featured Abbie Hoffman, Jerry Rubin, Tom Hayden, and other antiwar-movement figureheads fending off government charges following the police billy-club crackdown at the 1968 Democratic National Convention in Chicago. Gilbert was hooked by the group's lawyer, a wild-haired New York lefty named William Kunstler. Using the trial less as an opportunity to defend his clients than as a platform for questioning the entire American system, Kunstler saved the defendants from serious prison time. Terry Gilbert's direction was fixed.

Gilbert started law school in the fall of 1971. The Cleveland State University Marshall College of Law was not the scene of high-minded activist jurisprudence. It was an assembly line for anyone interested in practicing downtown at the courthouse—nearly every lawyer or judge walking the hallways was an alumnus. But Gilbert found that many of the students he matriculated with were hotwired with the same mission. "This wasn't about career, it wasn't about making money," he would later say. "This was about struggle and the movement for social change."

The young law students quickly bucked against the administration. They felt that the curriculum focused too much on property and business law, with no classes on equality and employment, the First Amendment, or poverty law. Gilbert, along with his fellow students, boycotted superfluous courses while turning out an alternative student newspaper, *The Trade School News* (the name was a dig at the law school's commercial leanings). Similar convulsions were shaking up other law schools, and a cord of activist zeal connected like-minded students coast to coast. An informal network developed under the umbrella of liberal legal groups like the National Lawyers Guild and the ACLU. Through federal work-study programs, Gilbert and his fellow CSU students could volunteer for attorneys who were defending farmers against the federal government, or working with antiwar protestors facing criminal charges. Gilbert himself volunteered for the attorneys defending the prisoners involved in the bloody 1971 riots at Attica Correctional Facility in New York State. He also traveled west to work with Native American tribes fighting government incursion, and later played a role in the defense for the men arrested after the 1973 Wounded Knee shooting that left two FBI agents dead. When Gilbert graduated law school, he already had serious legal experience on the vanguard of civil rights litigation.

But it was hard paying bills with these cases. In 1974, Gilbert took an office with a crusty old communist lawyer in the Leder Building downtown. From there he began picking up cases at the Cuyahoga County Courthouse. There he found that the marble hallways were as grounded in the old school as CSU. It was a political scene—not the politics of the new left, but the backslap variety. Defense lawyers did little prep work for their cases; often they just winged it. Postconviction appeals were pretty much nonexistent. Prosecutors took the word of police officers without questioning the facts. Judges were buddy-buddy with the lawyers, who turned out their pockets to fund judicial campaigns. Most afternoons you could find attorneys and judges boozing in the padded leather circular booths of the Theatrical Grille, a favorite haunt of Cleveland's mob elite, like Shondor Birns and Danny Greene.

Gilbert—with his long bushy hair, blue jeans, and perpetual pot cloud clinging to his person—was a natural outsider. But it went beyond dress code. His generation was bringing something new to the practice of American law. The toolbox had greatly expanded under the U.S. Supreme Court of Chief Justice Earl Warren. In fact, three cases tied to Cleveland police misconduct had helped change criminal procedure across the country. In 1961, the court heard a case involving a Cleveland woman whose house was illegally searched by police looking for evidence of a gambling operation; the Supreme Court ruled that no, evidence seized without a warrant could not be used in a criminal prosecution. Three years later, the justices heard a case involving Cleveland police pulling over a man without probable cause, but finding gambling slips on his person; again, the court ruled that no, you could not use evidence in a prosecution if it had been obtained illegally. In 1968, Cleveland police again were the topic when the Supreme Court discussed whether officers could randomly search suspects on the street; no, the court concluded, not unless there was "reasonable suspicion."

These Supreme Court decisions opened new legal possibilities; attorneys like Gilbert could push to have cases tossed before trial. The decisions shifted the spotlight away from what a defendant might or might not have done and pointed it at the actions of police. The new breed of activist attorneys was also straddling the line between criminal law and civil rights actions, seeing the two areas not as separate specialties but inevitably linked. If police beat your client when he was arrested, why not file a civil rights lawsuit? If your client was sent to prison and the conditions were terrible, why not take the matter to federal court? Gilbert's generation was the first to steer their practice on both courses.

In court, this meant Gilbert was operating from a different playbook. Courtroom vets often brushed off voir dire, or jury selection. "Just give me the first twelve damn people in the box," he'd hear. But the younger generation of lawyers used voir dire to question possible jurors for bias, including tapping behavioral analysis to detect how a juror might lean. Similarly, Gilbert might try to have cases dismissed based on an unequal protection argument—going big picture and systemic even in the smallest cases.

Gilbert's earliest years in Cleveland also dropped him in the middle of the tension between law enforcement and the black community. One of his first clients was Black Unity House, an East Side Black Power organization that also used government grants to run a drug treatment program. In 1973 Cleveland police raided the group's headquarters, roughing up residents and confiscating guns the group had legally acquired for protection. Gilbert was tasked with getting the firearms back. He also filed a federal harassment lawsuit against the department on behalf of the group. He dropped the complaint after the U.S. Attorney's Office publicly admitted they had been surveilling the group. For Gilbert, it was a victory—a bullying government admitting it was harassing citizen activists.

These were the thoughts and ambitions shuttling around the young lawyer's head each night as he drove home to Cleveland Heights. The commute took him past the black neighborhoods where many of his clients lived. Eventually, he would turn up Fairhill Boulevard to get to the Heights, and as his car climbed the incline out of the city, Gilbert would often shoot a glance to his right. A corner store sat at Petrarca. That's where the white guy was killed, Gilbert would think. He must have picked up the information from the news. He didn't know anything else about the murder, or even if anyone had ever been arrested.

But each night, the young lawyer drove by the store noting: *a white guy had been killed right there.*

That memory—the neighborhood corner store where the white man died—rushed back at Gilbert thirty-six years later as he listened to the voice on the other end of his office phone in early 2011.

As Kwame Ajamu unwrapped the details of his story, the attorney recognized it was the same killing. Shit, he thought, I remember that.

Kwame hadn't just yanked Gilbert's name randomly out of the phone book. He called him because of Sam Sheppard.

Sam Sheppard was prison-yard famous in the Ohio correctional system. Ghetto African American or white hilljack, young buck or grizzled lifer—everyone knew the case. The story had mesmerized America: the dashing young doctor accused of bludgeoning his beautiful wife to death in their bed in suburban Cleveland; Sheppard's story of being knocked unconscious by an intruder before his wife's death; the media circus and trial ending in conviction; his ten-year fight for innocence that inspired a hit TV show (*The Fugitive*) and ended in 1966 with an acquittal at retrial. But Sheppard's legend in jail was even larger. Uncharacteristically for a white suburbanite doctor, Sheppard fought whomever he had to fight inside and didn't take shit from anyone. He also provided medical care for prisoners because the institution's own was often careless or terrible. And ultimately, Sheppard fought the law and won. So as Kwame began researching Sheppard's case, he read up on a 1999 civil suit by the doctor's son charging the state of Ohio with wrongful imprisonment. Although Sheppard's son was ultimately unsuccessful, Kwame noted the name of the attorney representing America's most famous wrongfully convicted man: Terry Gilbert.

Kwame's hunch was spot-on. Gilbert's legal career had naturally tracked with issues of innocence. In fact, the attorney had been there when DNA changed legal history.

In February 1988, a music store clerk named David Hartlaub was shot inside his van in Sandusky, Ohio. Police later learned the murder was a botched hit conducted by three Cleveland-area members of the Hell's Angels motorcycle gang. The men—Steven Wayne Yee, Mark Verdi, and John Ray Bonds—had mistaken Hartlaub for a member of a rival bike crew, the Outlaws.

Prosecutors would later allege Bonds had hidden in Hartlaub's car, waiting for the target to climb inside before pulling the trigger. One of the shots seemed to have ricocheted back, striking the shooter's arm. His blood was left inside the vehicle. And although no physical evidence or witnesses linked the suspects to the crime, the FBI used a new technique to match the DNA from the blood spatter to Bonds.

At the time, the forensic technique behind DNA matching was still in its infancy. The science had been used in a few criminal cases, but its reliability was questionable. DNA matching had also never been used in a federal case before. The Ohio Hell's Angels case became the legal test for whether this new groundbreaking forensic approach would be admissible in American courtrooms.

"It is scary because arguably the only concrete piece of evidence is DNA and [Bonds'] life and death in these cases depends on science," Gilbert, an attorney for the defendants, told the *Plain Dealer* at the time.[3] But he also recognized the wider legal consequences in play. An admissibility hearing on the FBI's DNA evidence attracted attention from across the country. Gilbert's courtroom hero, William Kunstler, was brought on for the defense, as well as two young New York City attorneys who had begun studying DNA forensics, Barry Scheck and Peter Neufeld. At the two-month hearing, the pair argued against the admissibility by critiquing the bureau's procedure and the probability of their findings. The judged ruled for the state, swinging courtroom doors open for DNA forensics. The Hell's Angels were convicted in 1991. But the new science also had application for the other side. A year later, Scheck and Neufeld started the Innocence Project at Cardozo School of Law, an effort to leverage DNA to help the wrongfully convicted.[4]

Gilbert's early tour of duty in what would eventually be known as the Innocence Movement meant Gilbert was regularly snowed under with piles of jailhouse letters from men and women claiming they'd been wrongfully convicted. But in his first phone call with Kwame, something told the attorney this was different. A twelve-year-old boy was the only witness? Doesn't sound right, he thought. Gilbert was also struck that Kwame wasn't calling about his own case—he was free but pushing forward because of Rickey and Wiley. But Gilbert also realized Kwame was bringing absolutely nothing to the case—no new evidence, no new witnesses, no new information. The attorney was basically a one-man operation, he explained. He didn't have the time or resources to dive into the situation.

But he had an idea.

Gilbert suggested that Kwame get a journalist interested in the story, do some digging, create public interest. The attorney said he had someone in mind; he had worked with a reporter before who could do the case justice. Not from the *Plain Dealer* or TV stations; they wouldn't and couldn't give a story like this the time it needed.


The Starbucks downtown was a busy hive. When Kwame thought reporter, he was expecting someone like you see on the news each night: granite anchor jaw, gray at the temples, a smoke-cured baritone with authoritative boom. His eyes roamed the morning-busy Starbucks, hoping to spot his man.

Kwame had called the writer right away at Gilbert's suggestion. It wasn't much of a conversation. The guy asked Kwame to meet him the same day at this coffee place. Before hanging up, he'd asked if Kwame had any documentation. Oh, did he. Kwame had his trial transcript, about a thousand pages recording the State of Ohio's bid to take his then seventeen-year-old life. His files stacked in the flimsy cardboard box at his side, Kwame sat in the busy coffee shop and eyed the room, looking for the newsman. He was nervous. *Here we go again.* Spilling his story, his secret, and hoping some stranger believed.

That's when I walked through the door.

# 8

## THE MALES ARE FROM THE NEIGHBORHOOD

Cleveland, January 2011

*"SEE," KWAME TOLD ME, HIS HANDS RESTING CALMLY ON THE TABLE,* "this was a neighborhood thing. What happened was a robbery-homicide at the Fairmount Cut-Rate store. Myself, my brother, and our close family friend, Rickey Jackson, were the three individuals subsequently charged and convicted."

Quietly, in sentences stripped of emotion, Kwame relayed his story. The foot traffic inside the Starbucks we were sitting in was heavy, businessmen and -women shaking snow from overcoats, squeezing past our table. Kwame's attention stayed stuck on his story; he only made eye contact with me at times to emphasize a point: Arthur Avenue. Ed Vernon. Death row. Twenty-eight years. Rickey. Wiley.

If he was feeling any disappointment—he'd probably expected a veteran news hard-ass, a trench-coated Peter Jennings—it didn't show on his face. At this point I was used to starting interviews by parrying questions about whether I was an actual reporter or an intern. But little feeling at all broke through as Kwame spoke. If this man had been wrongfully convicted, his entire life stolen, he was playing against type. I assumed a man like this would be emptied of everything save rage and injury. Yet Kwame was cool and calm.

"If you read these transcripts," he said, waving a finger at the cardboard box brimming with pages, "you'll see that at one point the judge even says he doesn't believe Edward. To my mind, how can a judge let that case go forward then?"

My mind built a case against Kwame. I was ignorant of the statistics, but wrongful convictions had to be rare; I reasoned that the basic chutes and ladders of the court system and appeal process were enough of a safety net to keep them from happening. Even when a bad conviction slipped through, I assumed the postconviction process would flag and overturn those cases within, what, a decade, tops—right? Innocent men wouldn't be abandoned in prison for thirty-six years. But whatever argument I came up with to dispute the likelihood of Kwame's tale was easily dismantled by something else. Kwame's demeanor, his words, his face. Most people I interacted with for my job offered up their deepest feelings and memories in a confused gush, just happy to have an interested listener. As Kwame spoke, it was clear he had thought carefully about what he was saying. These were thoughts minted over a lifetime, not testimony he delivered lightly.

I ran the numbers—the crime had occurred thirty-six years before, in 1975, ten years before I was born. Pop culture and historical fact assisted with the picture. Gerald Ford in the White House. The official end to the Vietnam War. *Jaws. One Flew Over the Cuckoo's Nest. Blood on the Tracks.* The details put weight on the story. But they also pushed the events Kwame was describing further into the past. It was hard to compute. I began to seriously consider that if this man was telling the truth, if a boyhood lie from a twelve-year-old's mouth had ruined so much, the human toll was inestimable. The size of that hurt—the emotional mileage and pain and despair—was too big to properly think through. I really couldn't. But I really didn't need to. I was a reporter at a weekly paper brought low by tough times but still chasing its past relevance. The small staff was overtaxed, underpaid, waiting out the fresh layoffs constantly in the offing. Every month I was tasked with filing a five-thousand-word cover story, and I was a few months behind coming up with ideas. So although I heard Kwame's story, up front it didn't really sink any deeper than a story idea, a news item, five sections, some heavy anecdotes up front, mix in national statistics, maybe grab some good timepiece photos from the library archives. My understanding remained professional.

I agreed to look into the case. Kwame pushed the cardboard box over the table to me. "My mind is now: Get Rickey out. Get Rickey out. Then maybe we can clean up our names. But get that man out of there."

Before we parted, Kwame said something that shifted the way I looked at his tale, as if a sharper camera lens had clicked into place. As he'd been talking through his situation, my mind had been staging it as history, grainy footage from the 1970s, a closed chapter. But Kwame brought me into the present. "We are now in a society that beats the little guys down," he told me. His shoulders shrugged as if he was inviting me to acknowledge what I should have already known. "If they get you, they get you."

About three months after I first met Kwame, I was standing on the edge of a weed-spewing lot on East Ninety-second Street. The street was a quick two-block run of houses north of St. Clair in Glenville. The buildings still standing were bled dry from neglect. Porches melted into overgrown lawns. Graffiti-striped cardboard covered many windows. The power lines stitching the houses together overhead dripped like old shoelaces.

I was the only white person within sight, likely the only white person in a two-mile radius. Young black men in dreads and sweatpants were tossing hard eyefucks in my general direction, but no one spoke to me. If the sight of a twenty-five-year-old paleface geek with a notebook in his hand was usually enough to draw curiosity on this block, today it was losing out to what was happening in the field.

A circle of black women, their ages running from teens to late sixties, held hands in a circle, screaming into the mild afternoon. Each pair of arms flung up and down with no concern about syncing with their neighbor, as if a different electrical bolt jerked each limb. Rick

Ross charged out of the stereo speakers of a parked car, laying an in-congruous Miami-booty-bass backdrop against hard grief pooling in the dead field.

On paper this was a protest. Until a month ago, a thirty-six-year-old black man named Jamelle had lived with his girlfriend and five kids a few houses away. He'd grown up nearby, and like many guys in the neighborhood, he was trailed by a handful of felony drug convictions. Recently he'd been trying to stay straight. One evening in April, he got into a fight with a neighbor. Over what, stories shifted. But the conflict ended with the neighbor unloading eighteen bullets into Jamelle. Cleveland police arrested the shooter. The Cuyahoga County Prosecutor's Office filed murder charges. But just when it seemed as if the societal machinery designed to right a criminal wrong was work-ing smoothly, the Cuyahoga County Prosecutor's Office dropped the charges. The shooter walked. The reason: the Castle Doctrine, a stand-your-ground-style law cooked up by the National Rifle Association and spoon-fed to the Republican-controlled state legislature, part of the national creep to expand gun laws. Ohio had embraced the stat-ute; because Jamelle had technically fallen in the shooter's house, the state felt there was no grounds for prosecution. Case closed.[1]

This was understandably shocking to the victim's family. They couldn't arrange their grief in a way to provide for such an unexpected curveball, and it soon grew into flabbergasted rage. To draw attention to the case, the dead man's bereaved family had asked friends and neighbors to come out for a show of outrage this afternoon. But the political theater quickly ran off elsewhere.

From the brief conversations I had before the circle formed up, I learned that most of these women—and only women came—had seen random violence sweep away pieces of their lives. The uniform chorus of chants that started the rally soon splintered into a berserk heartbreak babel, each woman shouting her own plea to Jesus or naming a lost loved one or stuffing her personal anguish into a wordless cry.

I couldn't decode this, neither the words nor the names being flung about. But I understood that the downtown world responsible for the ruling on this case—not to mention the world of buddy-buddy hay-seed legislators and gun lobbyists—did not stretch out to St. Clair and East Ninety-second. Here and there—between them sat a massive dissonance. Later I thought of Thoreau's line from the close of "Civil Disobedience," after the writer has spent a night in jail and escaped to the woods, away from town: "then the state was nowhere to be seen." Take that sentence, hose off the romantic self-assertion, and you could easily, sadly, find Jamelle's neighborhood—a place the state had left behind.

By 2011, you ran smack into the dissonance all around the city. Whatever connections once linked Cleveland together seemed to have been unplugged. The longer I spent in the city, the more I realized that the recent civic dysfunction was tied to a shifting power struggle that had pitted the region against itself. It was a cresting wave, years in the making, now breaking across town. Everything—from the ignored grief of East Ninety-second Street to Kwame's story—was wrapped up in it.

Downtown was a glass castle of condo projects rising above retrofitted brick warehouses and other antique pieces from the last century saved from bulldozers. But this wash-and-scrub only went for about twenty blocks in either direction from Public Square. After that, the neighborhoods—or what was left of them—began. Between its population high point in 1950 and 2000, Cleveland had lost around 436,000 people. The ruined infrastructure and vacant housing left behind looked less like the result of demographic shifts than what remains after floodwaters slurp back to the sea. Just over the city line but still in Cuyahoga County, the fifty-eight suburbs were engaged in an ongoing cold war, undercutting one another for retail projects and corporate headquarters in an effort to block the deleterious influence of the urban core's tailspin.

To say race—or at least the leftover tensions from the sixties and seventies—was the reason Cleveland was in such disarray was to risk a sarcastic *no shit* from anyone who knew the score. But that was also to undersell the complicated realities.

By the 1990s, the power structure of the city was firmly in the hands of second-generation black politicians who owed their footing to Carl Stokes's vision. Yet Stokes's legacy also did not succumb to easy analysis. After he left office, Cleveland didn't elect another black mayor until 1990. The black political scene was dominated by George Forbes, the city council president between 1974 and 1989. Forbes was a bombastic presence, a hulking man who threw reporters out of council chambers and once even swung a chair at a council member. Forbes cozied up to business interests, worked alongside Republicans, and survived a bribery trial with an acquittal. The question of his legacy was whether the power he held was used in the service of civic goals or for its own preservation. And the same question can be raised with respect to those who followed him. His protégé, Mike White, was mayor for three terms between 1990 and 2002; these years not only saw the city's manufacturing base and population dwindle, but gave rise to persistent whispers about corruption at city hall. Eventually, two of White's closest advisers went to prison for pay-to-play schemes involving city contracts. White himself never faced charges. The ostensible inheritor of White's political machine is the current mayor, Frank Jackson. But while White was an operator, it does not appear that Jackson has inherited his forcefulness, certainly not enough to maintain the power of the black community.

For decades, the city's clout had been positioned against the leadership of Cuyahoga County, until 2009 controlled by a three-person panel of commissioners. Countywide elections were controlled by the Democratic Party, the late-stage iteration of the white ethnic voting bloc from the last century, now relocated to inner-ring suburbs like Parma, Euclid, and Lakewood. Any urban studies professor worth tenure will tell you that from a governance standpoint, a regional, countywide authority is the best political structure for handling the civic challenges presented by postindustrial America—the challenges aimed directly at Northeast Ohio's head. A regional government can rule based on the interests of the entire region, rather than the narrower goals and needs specific to cities. But the Cleveland area had fended off any political rethink because of the détente between county and city—between white and black. Cleveland was left to black politicians. The county stayed with white suburbanites. Any strong regional government would dilute the sway of the former and dump urban problems on the latter. It was a mutually beneficial balancing act.

Then the 2008 political scandal erupted, forty federal indictments, the entire county government ripped up by the roots. Into that disarray, savvy suburbanites—including suburban Republicans who had little regional power under the status quo—made a hard sell on a voter referendum that reorganized the government under a regional eleven-person council and executive drawn from the entire county. It passed. The city—meaning Cleveland's black political class—watched its regional influence slip to the suburbs.

This sudden senescence left black political might sidelined in Cleveland. But if Carl Stokes's political offspring were surprised, they shouldn't have been. The county's wrenching power from the city was the last stage in a fait accompli that was decades in the making, less a masterminded plot than the gradual but complete isolation of this corner of urban black America. It was the feeling I bumped against on East Ninety-second Street.

In Cleveland, the housing statistics told the story. Beginning in the late 1980s, sociologists Douglas Massey and Nancy Denton proposed that the skeleton key to understanding the country's racial inequality was residential housing segregation, a legacy of federal redlining, discriminatory banking practices, and racist suburban pushback that created the modern urban ghetto. Cleveland was front and center in this thesis. In 1930, there were only two American cities where the average African American was likely to live in a neighborhood where their fellow residents were also exclusively black—Chicago and Cleveland. By 1970, blacks in every major northern American city lived in segregated neighborhoods. Five cities, however, had a higher segregation index than the others, meaning that the city's black population was crammed into a particularly confined area: Chicago, Newark, St. Louis, Philadelphia, and Cleveland. This condition—which Massey and Denton termed *hypersegregation*—still held in Cleveland.

Massey and Denton's research showed that extreme neighborhood segregation concentrated poverty and increased the impact of economic downturns, leaving black neighborhoods more vulnerable to any twitch in the economy or bad news out of Wall Street. After decades and generations, this created at the century's end a community apart, separate, and unequal. "People growing up in such an environment have little direct experience with the culture, norms, and behaviors of the rest of American society and few social contacts with other racial groups," the two wrote in their 1993 book, *American Apartheid*. "Ironically, within a large, diverse, and highly mobile post-industrial society such as the United States, blacks living in the heart of the ghetto are among the most isolated people on earth."[2]

Public records were always dicey in Cleveland. When future archeologists finally dust off the ruins of our Rust Belt hub, I would not be surprised should they uncover a bunker under Public Square containing the whole stash of civic records, every memo, police report, employee review, and letterhead missive spelling out our history. Or—they might just find a room full of ash. Every reporter in town understood that when you made a legal request for documentation from the city, you were about as likely to be ignored or stymied as helped.

"Open investigation," "unable to find," and radio silence were among the usual responses. I don't know whether this was the product of an Orwellian memory hole or just the indifference of city workers punching the clock in the records department. Ohio has a good public records law. The city was required to comply. But you likely had fifty-fifty odds of dragging to light the requested documentation from the city and county.

Not long after meeting Kwame, I went to the county clerk's office to see what court filings related to the three trials were still in the building. One of the women staffing the desk showed me to the microfilm, but cautioned that much of the material hadn't made the jump from paper to film. "A lot of that stuff is just gone," she told me. Sure enough, most of the court filings and motions were missing.

We were lucky with the trial transcripts. The appeals process basically ensures that the stenographic play-by-play of criminal cases is kept. Still, three decades is a long time for documents to sit on a shelf without being misplaced or damaged. It took an afternoon of leapfrogging from one county department to another before I tracked them down. In Ohio City, a Cleveland neighborhood just over the river from downtown, the county owned a stately Victorian mansion that had been converted into an archive. Here, in dusty rooms that once hosted the soirees and chatter of Cleveland's big money, were stacked boxes filled with birth certificates, land deeds, and court paperwork. The whole mothballed predigital legacy.

The individual court transcripts for each trial were in leather-bound books. Unfortunately, the place wasn't a lending library; I'd have to copy the material—time consuming to anyone interested in a large number of documents. Plus, the pages were so brittle—as delicate as insect wings—that you couldn't just load a stack of pages into the Xerox or else they'd jam up the machine. Each page of testimony, over three thousand sheets, had to be individually copied. It was tedious enough work that I flirted with the idea of giving up.

It took a little over three weeks to copy everything. I ran over to the archive on my lunch hour, carved a half hour free from my daily schedule when I could. I recognized right away that portions of the transcripts were missing—a page or two here, larger sections in a few places. Wiley's first trial lacked all record of the opening and closing statements. When I finally had as complete a record as possible of the four trials, leaning Pisa towers of papers stacked on my bedroom floor, I sat down to pore through the pages.

On a first push through, the material outlined the general shape of the proceedings. Ed's credibility was easily the main issue driving the trials. The central inconsistencies in his story—the wild departures between Ed's written police statement and his testimony; the differences between Karen Smith's eyewitness account and Ed's own—blared from the pages. But as I reread, I began catching tiny cracks and chips in his story, double-backs and errors and miscues. I got a helpful assist here from an unknown hand: tucked into the material from the court was a typewritten list tracking inconsistencies in the transcripts, a list prepared, I assumed, for a doomed appeals bid.

Often these discrepancies appeared in the same trial. For example, in Ronnie's trial, Ed initially testified he'd left school after his ninth-period class. Later in his testimony, he told the court he'd left before his eighth-period class. In the same round of testimony, the witness claimed he'd never seen the green-colored drop-top Wiley was driving before the crime. Yet later, in the same trial, Ed told the court he'd actually seen the car before "in front of their house." When Ed was asked during Wiley's trial if he saw Mr. Loper that day as he disembarked the city bus, the boy told the jury no. In Wiley's retrial, he said the exact opposite. "Yes," Ed testified. "I waved."

Then there was the flowered shirt. Anna Robinson had told the court she noticed one of the killers wearing it. In his statement, Ed told police Rickey was wearing the distinctive shirt. But in Wiley's trial, Ed said it was Wiley wearing the shirt. There emerged questions about what Ed claimed he saw when. Throughout his trials, he testified he could only recognize Wiley behind the wheel of the car as the boy spotted them from the city bus. But when Ed gave his written statement, he clearly stated that he could identify all the passengers in the car: "I saw buddy [sic] driving the car with Vincent and Rickey in the car with them and I waved to them."

Ed's story also changed in terms of where he was when he viewed the crime. In some testimony, the boy told jurors he was walking down Fairhill toward the corner of Petrarca when he witnessed Franks doused and struck with a stick; he claimed he then turned around and ran back to the bus stop, where he hid behind the shelter's wall. From there, he testified, he saw Rickey shoot Franks twice, then turn the gun on Mrs. Robinson. But Ed also testified he saw the first two shots up close near the corner, then ran back to the bus shelter, where he watched the third shot fired.

Teasing out Loper's own testimony yielded another crop of inconsistencies. First, the old man had testified he watched the boy get off the bus and walk up Fairhill, crossing in front of Loper's house. His house was connected to the store, so had Vernon crossed the lawn, he would have been steps away from in front door of the Cut-Rate. But Vernon testified he didn't get so close. Loper also told the court he'd heard three shots, then saw Franks fall to the ground. But according to all other accounts—including the medical examiner's report—Franks was thrown onto the ground, *then* shot.

One or two inconsistencies could be explained away. Your mind misfires, recollection sputters like a bad engine. But taken together, they showed that the foundation of the state's case wasn't firm but constantly shifting, details jockeying into new position. I realized that it would have been impossible for a juror to catch many of these errors in real time.

My understanding of the case deepened significantly when I got access to the police file. Again, this was a bit of a miracle. In my reporting career in Cleveland, I'd never been given access to a complete investigative record—mostly because the cases I was writing about were fresh. So when my office phone buzzed one afternoon with a call from city hall relaying that my public records request was ready, I literally gagged on my coffee. Waiting for me at the records department was a thick folder with 101 pages of notes, photos, and duplicate reports, the tick-tock of the police investigation into Harry Franks's death.

At the time of the murder, cases were assigned to two main detectives, but the entire homicide squad worked each killing on different shifts. The daily reports from detectives not only detailed daily findings, they also communicated messages from one shift to another about what new routes needed to be explored.

On the day of the crime, May 19, the lead detectives, Eugene Terpay and James T. Farmer, logged five pages of careful notes sketching the outlines of the murder. The write-up was exhaustive, covering everything from what eyewitnesses reported to how much money Franks had in his billfold when he died. My radar pinged here. None of the witnesses in the early case notes—including Loper—mentioned Ed's presence at the scene.

In fact, Ed doesn't turn up in the file until the next day, but only after a suspect is named. On May 20, the day-shift detectives on the case, John Staimpel and Frank Stoiker, reported that they'd made contact with a woman from the neighborhood named Doris Gardenhire who "feels that her son, PAUL, may be involved in this crime." The mother told the detectives Paul had been at her house with a gun.

The afternoon-shift detectives—Terpay and Farmer—showed a photo of Paul Gardenhire to Karen Smith. She identified "this male someone she has seen but not one of the suspects," the detectives wrote. In the same report, the detectives stated that after speaking with Robert Robinson they "were able to locate a young citizen" who revealed he'd seen the killing.

"THIS INFORMANT DEFINITELY STATED THAT HE CAN'T IDENTIFY BECAUSE HE DIDN'T GET A LOOK AT THE FACES AND APPEARS TO BE VERY SCARED," the detectives wrote in attention-snagging all-caps. "WE COULD ONLY GET THIS INFORMATION AFTER PROMISING THE SUBJECT THAT HIS NAME WOULD NOT BE USED." The detectives did not mention the informant's name. "WE ALSO FEEL THAT HE KNOWS MORE AND WILL MAKE ARRANGEMENTS TO TALK WITH HIM ON OUR NEXT TOUR."

A surprise arrived for the detectives the next day gift-wrapped from the local FBI: a message from a local field agent about possible suspects. The unnamed agent relayed that "several of his informants" believed the Franks murder was the work of a robbery crew headed by brothers Willie Joe "Skip" King and Arthur Lee "Railroad" King. Both men had past arrests for armed robbery and also were suspects in a 1969 murder, the note stated.

The same shift yielded another possible avenue. Detectives learned from Franks's employer that it was not common for the victim to be carrying so much cash. The reason: the stop before the Robinsons' store, the Maxwell Cut-Rate, had paid Franks $429.12 in bills. "This is very unusual since the owner has done business with them for eight years and always pays with bank receipts." Detectives also learned the store's owner, Earl Rogers, had three young daughters "and it is rumored that these girls consort with shady characters." When Terpay and Farmer talked with Rogers "he appeared very nervous and evasive." The officers concluded someone could easily have followed Franks from the Maxwell location.

The notes from May 22 and May 23 are where the written record got even more interesting. On a write-up dated May 23, Rickey made his first appearance. According to the afternoon recap filed by Terpay and Farmer, at 10:45 P.M. the detectives met with their informant again. The informant identified one of the suspects as "Rickey." He rode in a car with detectives that night, pointing out Rickey's house as well as the house of another suspect on Arthur—Wiley. An afternoon report from the same detectives dated May 24 started off with "SUSPECTS," and went on to list Wiley and Rickey's full names and birth dates. Yet the homicide file I'd been given had two copies of this report. One copy looked normal. But in the second duplicate set, the dates had been scribbled out by hand; *May 23* was crossed out and *May 22* was written beneath. The second copy of May 24 report was similarly backdated one day by hand to read *May 23*.

My radar was screaming now—why were these reports altered? Was it an honest mistake? Or were they backdated in order to make it look like the investigators closed in on Rickey and Wiley a full day before they actually did? Throughout the trials, the defense attorneys repeatedly dug into both Ed and the detectives about when the boy first made allegations against the defendants. It was a moving target in all three trials, and this paperwork only sank the issue in more fog.

Another suspect also emerged in the May 22/May 23 space. Detectives interviewed a witness who claimed he'd spotted the green auto fleeing the scene. The man provided a license plate number, which led back to a 1965 Buick owned by Ishmael Hixson. This hit was big news.

Hixson's record included robbery and arson arrests, among others. By 3:30 P.M. on May 24, detectives were waiting outside the suspect's house, where he was arrested for the Franks murder.

Despite taking Hixson into custody, detectives, with their informant driving the investigation, pushed forward on Wiley and Rickey. At 5:45 A.M. on May 25, police banged on the Bridgemans' door on Arthur Avenue. The follow-up report from the raid contained the first mention of Ed Vernon's name. The paperwork noted that Ed did not pick anyone out of the lineup, but later made a statement to police. Hixson was also among the seven men with Rickey and Wiley during the lineup. Neither Ed nor Karen Smith identified the suspect, and he was apparently let go. Rickey, Wiley, and Ronnie—the younger Bridgeman's name never appeared in the case file until after the May 25 arrest— went on to face formal murder charges.

But the detective work didn't stop there. In the days following the arrests, the homicide squad was contacted by a woman from the neighborhood who reported that the actual killers "were still in the area and are operating a pea green convertible." In early June, detectives wrote up a report about a separate tip from Edward Garrett, a neighborhood guy with his own past record for armed robbery. Garrett told police the Bridgemans and Rickey Jackson "had nothing to do with the crime." Paul Gardenhire, the same teenager whose mother had contacted police the day after Franks's death, was the actual killer, Garrett claimed. The tipster also told police Gardenhire was driving a green convertible Oldsmobile and brandishing a .38 revolver he'd stolen from his grandfather. Police thought enough of Garrett's information to actually go looking for the car, locating it parked where Garrett said it would be. The write-up noted officers should keep an eye open for the car on the street so the driver could be questioned and the vehicle searched. But the file didn't mention any follow-ups.

None of these other suspects were mentioned in the trials. I wondered whether the defense teams actually knew if they existed. From what scraps of the law I knew, I understood that in 1975 police and prosecutors had less incentive to turn over their case files. On the defense side, alternative suspects were not part of the strategy to secure Ronnie, Wiley, and Rickey's freedom. Curious, I plugged the names into the court system. Less than six months after being picked up in the Franks murder, Ishmael Hixson was charged with eighteen counts of aggravated robbery in a separate case. In 1978, Gardenhire was sent to prison for his part in another brutal robbery-homicide.

I'll be honest: I would not jump out at you as a natural chronicler of the African American urban experience. I'm white and suburban, my stats chart vanilla and marked by socioeconomic stability. Growing up, my two-parent household pitched around the middle class, some years good, others spotty, but I was never in material want.

Home was an exurb nowhere, on the southeastern edge of the county, farmland that had been plowed under by interlocking grids of residential developments, the houses all copy-paste replays of one another. It was nice and uneventful. Some people like to graft depth to such neighborhoods by claiming the banal front hides weirdness and ennui. In my experience, it was a boring a place to grow up.

Despite that background, as a reporter, my work has always zeroed in on race and class and their impact site, the U.S. criminal justice system. I was drawn to stories that looked at inequality. Not to go deep-sea Freudian fishing, but I believe this has a lot to do with growing up alone and oddball, and being from the Cleveland area. The first quality is textbook: we moved a lot growing up, so I was usually edged out of the social norms. I was also awkward, acne-marked, speech-impeded, and wired with an ADHD streak that instead of shooting me out into the world had me obsessively tunneling into my own head. By the time I was a teenager, I was so used to being harassed and picked on, I developed a standard skate punk underdog ethos. I used a lot of four-letter words, dyed my hair red my senior year, and had a surly attitude toward most everything. Being a news reporter—a paid professional agitator—was a natural fit.

Then there was Cleveland. The American city is nothing if not a hard-knuckle demolition derby of interest and muscle pitted against one another, and I enjoyed reporting on the places where those scores were fought in the open. Although I grew up a thirty-minute drive from the city proper, my dad worked on Public Square, and our family was in Cleveland nearly every weekend. Race was there in Cleveland, a surface play, its energy aboveground, not neatly channeled into dog whistles or innuendo. People discussed it openly. I came to appreciate that honesty, but the familiarity also put me in a self-congratulatory bind. I grew up believing that because I was from a diverse city where race relations were an open battle, I had somehow soaked up an enlightened stance on the topic.

I was knocked out of that mind-set in college. I went to a leafy liberal arts school in rural Ohio, isolated as a desert island. The student body was overwhelmingly white and upper middle class, yet a hefty slice of the curriculum was devoted to issues of race and diversity and the worldwide legacies of imperialism and American bigotry. There were a lot of -isms and deconstructions and heady theories jumping in the air. The coursework, however, never seemed to touch the actual problems infecting urban areas. And my own feelings on race weren't altered by high-minded theory or historical analysis, but by an American literature class. Go figure. I was a junior. The course was taught by a small but intimidating southern man. We were reading Twain's *The Adventures of Huckleberry Finn*. It wasn't a book I enjoyed too much. In the final lecture, the professor brought up a test we'd taken earlier in the week: the essay prompt was to explain the character arc of one of the main figures in the novel. No one in the class, he told us, had chosen to write about Jim, the runaway slave who spends the final chapters locked in a cell, believing he'll soon be returned to his plantation. The professor waited a few beats, then pointed out that none of us—fifty academically savvy, progressive young Americans—seemed to have considered that during the whole last act of the novel, Tom Sawyer knows Jim has already been freed. Yet, instead of sharing the good news with Jim, Tom keeps it to himself so he and Huck can go on with their "adventures." Two southern boys getting their fun in while a grown man sits in a cell, his thoughts no doubt nailed to the brutality waiting for him back home. "In my experience," the professor said, "racism isn't just institutional, or even outright, blatant expressions of bigotry. It is a lack of empathy."

It's tidy to think you have the correct opinions on equality and civil rights and the systemic predations on African Americans—especially when you're doing it from a place of relative privilege, as I was. What that professor had exposed was the failure of some fifty highly educated Americans to think beyond themselves, to sink a connection outside their own borders, and that lack of empathy to me was a deep moral failing.

Fast-forward to 2011: the cold slap of the same revelation hit me while I sat on my apartment floor in Cleveland, the towers of transcripts now scattered in piles, nicked with margin notes and exclamation points. Days earlier, I'd stood on the street corner with Kwame, watching the bus make the turn that shifted my thoughts on the case. Now the documents at my knees blurted the same message: the men who had been imprisoned were innocent, they had been wrongfully convicted. I'd gone into Kwame's case as a reporter looking for a possible story. I'd worked on it as a side project I tinkered with when I had the time. Journalism required such compartmentalization. But that professional detachment was as comfy as my socially correct opinions had been in college—an easy perch to stand on, but with little action required on my part. I finally also realized my initial inability to empathize was exactly because of my background. I had been suspicious that the justice system could jail the wrong men because I had never been on the wrong end of the justice system. No one I was close to had ever even been arrested. It was easy from my perspective to let those jailhouse letters pile up in a desk drawer.

There is responsibility in our perspectives. We're accountable for what we see in the world, and more importantly, we're responsible for what we don't see. At some point in reading through those transcripts, I had stepped from the safe enclosure of journalism. This was real life. Three lives. It was all much more important than just another story.

# 9

## WHAT THE BOY SAW

ONE MORNING IN APRIL, I CLIMBED INTO MY CAR, THE GHOST OF A dead fifty-four-year-old salesman riding shotgun. I was making a copycat run of Harry Franks's last drive, scraping my Buick down roads that were now buckled like storm-wild surf.

In spring, Cleveland explodes with vegetation, an overnight express delivery of green. I drove east, away from downtown. Fresh bushes and shrubs were already spilling from lots. The sidewalks were parted by tufts of grass like liquid bubbling from below. The sudden splashes of color were a shock after so many months of gray, but the vivid contrast was greatest in the neighborhoods where abandoned buildings, weatherbeaten to a kind of noncolor, marked the streetscape. Spring polished up the city. A weak sun was doing its best to push through tissue-paper cloud cover. People were on the streets, walking and gliding on bikes.

Franks's weekly run went right through the main vein of black Cleveland—then and now. Pulling south onto East Fifty-fifth took you past Central, the city's first black neighborhood. The domed and stone eminences of powerful black churches ran along the strip, from Shiloh Baptist to St. Paul's Zion. Nearby stretched the cherry-brick Outhwaite Homes, the first public housing development to break ground in the U.S., dating from 1935, when the idea of government housing was a radical New Deal proposal. East on Quincy Avenue drilled you deeper into the Fairfax area; Woodland Cemetery, the final resting place of Cleveland's nineteenth-century elite, including two former Ohio governors, broke the monotony of empty fields, tow yards, and scrap outfits tucked along the base of the heights. Dip south a few blocks and you hit Buckeye Avenue, which climbed the heights to towering, well-kept mid-century homes dwarfed under huge oaks. South and east a little more brought Kinsman: fast-food grease pits, off-brand cell phone stores, beauty supply stores. Circling back south, east, and up, the route continued along Cedar Avenue, where the Maxwell Cut-Rate still sat on the first floor of a three-story apartment building, a blue neon Colt .45 sign humming behind the grated front windows. A bunker-looking strip club—the Wolf's Den—perched across the street. Almost all the other stores on Franks's regular route were gone—either physically obliterated, covered in boards, or under new ownership. Yet in the 1970s, these were properties like the Robinsons' store, black-owned neighborhood anchors. Harry Franks, I saw, had friendly business with blacks every day of his workweek. How many white suburbanites in 1970s Cleveland could say the same?

I rolled the Buick to a stop on Arthur Avenue, the street near Cedar where Kwame, Wiley, and Rickey had all lived. The passing years had taken a sledgehammer to most of the lots here as well. On foot, I saw that many of the two-story homes were gone, some re-placed with belt-high grass while elsewhere foundations, piping, and chimneys still stood, as if the homes had been airlifted away in a hasty evacuation—picked like flowers. Skyscraping maples dropped a checkered sunlight from above, laying a gloomy magic-hour tint on the street regardless of the time.

I was striking out on a shoe-leather hunt for old witnesses or anyone else who remembered the murder. No one answered my door knocks. Occasionally a curtain flickered with movement. Meanwhile, Kwame worked his own paths. He brought back the name he had cast off in prison, stepping into it again like old clothes. He contacted friends, family, and neighbor folks; each one had the same frozen beat of silence after he said, *Hello, you might not remember me, this is Ronnie,* the mental time machine darting back three decades plus, and then *Ohhhhh,* the voice warm with recognition.

By panning his old life, Kwame picked up bits of rumors, names, rusted shrapnel off old stories; he would relay the information back to me, and I'd plow ahead, often smacking against walls. One rumor had it that a neighborhood woman once overheard guys boasting at a party of pulling off the Cut-Rate murder. Another story told of a career stickup artist confessing to the killing on his deathbed. Nothing could be confirmed.

These trips down memory lane took a toll on Kwame. As we spent more hours together, the businesslike tone of our first conversation had smoothed out; Kwame was friendly and funny, his big personality rolling out of him in belly laughs and jokes. We got along; our talks strayed all over the place, from the inner politics of his job at the Board of Elections to pro boxing. But the smile would be chased off his face and his baritone starch up when we discussed the case—particularly when we talked about the old neighborhood.

"I'm more of an analytical person," he explained. "I like to think things out. And I've come to the conclusion that I really don't want to trust anybody from the neighborhood. It seems to me that someone knew, or a lot of people knew. And for some reason, they wouldn't do the right thing."

"Right," I said. "They could have spoken up, gone to the police. Something."

"Exactly. And they let all this destroy my life, my brother's life, and Rickey's life." But he had to keep stepping back into his old name because we needed Ed.

Alternative weeklies everywhere have institutionalized a bratty know-it-all attitude in their pages. At *Cleveland Scene,* we were constantly knocking the mainstream television stations and the *Plain Dealer,* outfits mostly staffed with out-of-towners brought in by corporate ownership.

We'd make sport when they missed context, bungled East Side for West Side, or didn't know the historical backstory. An alt-weekly editor once told me our papers—comically short-staffed, floating tenuously, finance-wise, on the bar and strip club ads at the paper's end—could only compete with daily newsrooms if we were quicker, more detailed, and smarter. We may not have always covered the first two, but we over-compensated by thinking we were smarter—if only because we knew Cleveland.

Most of that institutional knowledge came from one primary source. I would say Michael D. Roberts was the dean of local journalism, but he would probably roll his eyes behind his red Coke-bottle glasses and tell me to go to hell. So let's say he was more like the cranky uncle of Cleveland journalism, a longtime vet who was expertly positioned to hear the historic legacy running beneath current events. Cleveland born and raised, he was a cub reporter at the *Plain Dealer* on the streets of Hough during the '66 riots. Later in the decade, he embedded with grunts in Vietnam and covered the Nixon White House. After lead-ing the paper's city desk, he became the editor of *Cleveland Magazine* in the 1970s, when city magazine journalism had real teeth. He ran an award-winning staff comprised of the best journalists in town. Re-tired, he still penned columns for publication; more importantly, he served as a mentor to dozens of young reporters, shaping their views of the city. I counted myself among them.

Often I'd cut out on work early, meeting Mike in a downtown bar off Public Square where he posted up most days, a half-finished glass of white wine on the bar top. In between rapping with down-town lawyers or business heavyweights, he'd unroll stories about his reporting days or stew on the latest gossip. Inevitably, he'd ask me what I was working on. That spring of 2011, I kept him updated on Kwame's case—a story that I could tell didn't punch his buttons too much (not overtly political enough). But he was encouraging. There in the honey-colored murk of the dive, Roberts would raise his wineglass, squint his eyes, and say what he always said, the same question he believed you had to point at any Cleveland story. "You gotta ask yourself," the news vet said to me, "what's it say about the town?"

I initially felt wrongful convictions were rare, a feeling based on little more than gut conjecture. Until relatively recently, the same sentiment echoed off the highest peak of the U.S. court system. "Our society has a high degree of confidence in its criminal trials," Supreme Court Justice Sandra Day O'Connor bragged in a 1993 majority opinion, "in no small part because the Constitution offers unparalleled protections against convicting the innocent."[1] In a 2006 opinion Justice Antonin Scalia stated that the American criminal system had an "error rate of .027 percent."[2]

Such comfy assumptions, however, have been systematically undercut over the last thirty years. But rather than occasion a game-changing reevaluation of our justice system, much of the legal world has resisted the implications. Spend time around studies tackling the topic, and you'll see we haven't recalibrated our ideas or policies. We might never be able to. There is a fundamental resistance there. People don't want to admit the criminal justice system is capable of such a serious mistake.

DNA testing is what originally dynamited the unquestioned reliability of the legal process. Beginning in the mid-1980s, lab tests began to prove—beyond a reasonable doubt—the innocence of felony defendants. These were men (overwhelmingly men) who had been served punishment through the standard mechanics of American courts—police testimony, eyewitness evidence, confessions, and guilty verdicts. Yet science upended everything: here, science was saying the law had failed. By the start of 2012 the National Registry of Exonerations, a tag-team effort by the University of Michigan Law School and the Center on Wrongful Convictions at Northwestern University School of Law, determined that between 1989 and 2012, American courts saw 873 exonerations. These innocent men and women spent an average of eleven years in prison while waiting for the truth to emerge.[3]

Combing through these cases, experts have filed down the factors common to false convictions. This "catalog of errors" includes missteps and bad acts along each step of an investigation and trial: eyewitness misidentification, false confession, perjury, official misconduct, and false or misleading forensic evidence. Yet each case represented its own unique mix. That's why much of the research on false convictions is more speculative than systemic—each case study resists classification.[4]

Cuyahoga County had its own record of wrongful conviction. By 2011, the county had seen nine exonerations since 1989; that figure did not include a number of high-profile cases that were then currently being fought out in the courts and regularly featured in the news cycle. And true to local style, these fights were dirty—enough to question the reliability of cornerstones of the local legal process.

For example, in 2000, David Ayers, an African American security officer at a Cleveland public housing project, was arrested and convicted of the murder and rape of a seventy-six-year-old woman. Detectives initially zeroed in on Ayers not because of concrete evidence but because he appeared "gay-like"—an observation the officers were stupid enough to put in their notes. Despite no physical evidence, detectives arrested Ayers after lying in affidavits, forcing a witness to make a statement implicating Ayers (the witness later retracted), and illegally using a jailhouse snitch as a witness against the defendant. Eleven years later, Ayers was still in prison and trying to get DNA evidence from the victim tested—tests that would eventually clear him.[5]

Official misconduct had also shipped Joe D'Ambrosio off to death row. In 1989, the Clevelander and another man were separately tried and convicted of the murder of a nineteen-year-old acquaintance on the testimony of a third defendant who cut a deal with Cuyahoga County prosecutors. Thanks to a Catholic priest D'Ambrosio met while awaiting his execution, the case was reopened; D'Ambrosio's attorneys discovered that a prosecutor named Carmen Marino had withheld key evidence pointing away from their client. In 2009, D'Ambrosio was released from prison, but the county continued to push to retry the defendant. In 2010, a judge granted a motion blocking a retrial—but in

2011, the county appealed that decision. Prosecutors still wanted another chance at D'Ambrosio.[6]

Bad DNA evidence was behind Wally Zimmer and Tom Siller's hellish experience. In 1998, the two men—sometime neighborhood handymen who also used crack—were convicted of the murder of a seventy-four-year-old woman who was beaten and robbed in her Slavic Village home. Police found the fingerprints of both men at the victim's house—they regularly did work for her. Prints of a twenty-eight-year-old con named Jason Smith also turned up. When police arrested Smith, they found what appeared to be a bloody pair of pants in his possession. Smith, however, told police he'd seen Zimmer and Siller kill the woman and had only come in later to ransack the house. A county lab expert named Joseph Serowik testified that Smith's pants were not bloody; prosecutors told the jury at Siller and Zimmer's trial that the lack of blood pointed to Smith's truthfulness. The two were given thirty years to life. However, in 2001, Serowik came under fire when a Cleveland man convicted of rape was exonerated by new testing. A review of Serowik's lab work showed rampant errors and fabrication. When Smith's pants were retested, the lab discovered more than twenty bloodstains, including both the victim's and Smith's blood. But the county continued to fight motions for Zimmer and Siller's release, and by 2011, the two were mulling over whether to take a deal on a theft charge in exchange for immediate release. They'd already been in prison for thirteen years.[7]

So, as recent Cleveland history attests, there's no one weak spot in the armor: the fatal errors behind a wrongful conviction can come at any point in the process—from misguided detectives to belligerent prosecutors to lying experts on the government payroll.

But what really drives you into Kafka territory is that we still can't say with any clarity how large a problem wrongful incarceration is in the United States. That's the great knockout punch of false conviction scholarship—it's guesswork. Yes, we can tally the number of cases we've caught. But the actual number of innocent Americans imprisoned for something they didn't do is unknowable. Some experts have estimated that as many as five thousand to ten thousand wrongful convictions occur each year. Another group posits that 1 to 5 percent of annual felony convictions may be erroneous. Still a separate camp has cited surveys with judges who said they believe the jury got it wrong in 10 percent of the trials they oversaw.[8] This moving target actually handicaps the movement. It's hard to wrap systemic research around a loose data set. It also hands ammo to critics: there's no institutional wrongful conviction problem, they can say, these are just one-off situations, random mistakes instead of endemic issues.

So I didn't have an answer ready for Michael Roberts when he asked me what the Jackson and Bridgeman case said about the town. That would take time. But I had already begun to see that it wasn't just a Cleveland story.

Karen Smith, the neighborhood teen who walked into the Cut-Rate just as the 1975 robbery was unfolding, was key. She had both seen the actual stickup men as she entered the store and also maintained neither was Rickey or Ronnie.

I was excited to learn Smith was still around. After graduating high school, Smith went on to Oberlin College and later earned a master's degree at Ohio State. When I got her on the phone, the warm voice on the other end explained that she currently was still in the Columbus area, working with developmentally challenged children.

May 19, 1975, was still clear in her memory. "Oh, yes," she said, stretching the words into a singsong. Her account matched what she had told the juries in 1975: the men outside the store as she walked by were not Ronnie and Rickey. But she went further and filled in what happened after the arrest of the three men. She was taken to the police station and urged by police to make an ID during the lineup; the cops asked her how she would feel if her mother had been the dead victim. Later that day, she remembered, police brought Ed snacks at the station house. She was treated with frosty indifference. Smith also recounted how investigators plied her with additional details of the crime, information she would not have known from her own vantage point, such as how acid had been used in the attack, or that the culprits got away in a green car.

The courage of a sixteen-year-old girl to keep facts straight under that full-court press must have been considerable. Then to go to trial, telling her story while trying to fend off hostile assaults and embarrassing innuendo ("Do you go on many dates, Karen?") from prosecutors—the kind woman I was speaking with had shown serious resolve as a teenager. "Over the years, it's kind of bothered me that people didn't take my word to be the truth," she admitted to me. "That is something I live with."

Some spelunking through online databases brought me a phone number for Ivan Tanksley, another neighborhood kid, who was ten at the time of the killing. Now living in South Florida, Ivan also remembered the day, and brought my heartbeat up to a gallop when he casually mentioned he'd seen the murder.[9]

"What?" I said.

"I had a paper route," he said, explaining he'd been walking by a nearby gas station when he heard the shots. "I seen the guys going to the car, and then they went up Fairhill." It wasn't Rickey, Ronnie, or Wiley. "I knew them. Especially Rickey Jackson and his brother, Ernest. I could tell them from the back, especially back then, and if it *was* them, I would have known. It wasn't them."

"Did you ever get interviewed by police?"

"I don't remember being interviewed by police."

Ivan also recalled seeing Ed around the neighborhood after the trials, after everyone knew he'd lied and sent three innocent guys to prison. "Did you ever ask Ed about it?"

"No," Ivan answered. "One of my brothers has kids by Ed's sister. If I were to talk to him about it, it would have gotten out of hand. *Something* would have happened. So I just left it alone." Before hanging up, Ivan offered a last thought. "That's crazy they've been in jail for all this time for something they didn't do."

Kwame was able to track down a phone number for Valerie Aber-nathy.[10] Eighteen in 1975, she fit another piece into the emerging pic-ture. "At the time when this was supposed to take place," she told me, groping around her memory, "if I'm not mistaken, that day me and Buddy were together. We were just hanging out. His friend was my boyfriend at the time. I'm just wondering with all of that going on, why nobody ever called me." Valerie went on to explain that around Arthur, no one believed Ed was telling the truth. "Edward Vernon's eyesight is terrible," she said. "How did he see anybody?"

By far, the most interesting conversation I had was with Lynn Gar-rett. Kwame again found his phone number. Lynn had, as Kwame would later relate, been as close to him growing up as Rickey Jackson was right before their arrests—as tight as friends could be. But Lynn, unlike his buddies, had stayed in school, graduated, and earned a foot-ball scholarship to Bowling Green State University. Lynn was a tailor in Cleveland now. He was also—and this was just the first of many surprises Lynn would have—the father of two kids with Ed Vernon's other sister, Darlene.[11]

Lynn, then, wasn't just a witness—he was a connection to Ed. I wasn't sure what to expect when I got him on the phone, where his loyalties were parked after all these years. But out of the gate, Lynn understood why I was calling. "It was a great injustice," he told me. "To this day, it's unbelievable. Rickey, Wiley, and Ronnie—we grew up together. If they were the kind of guys who robbed stores, I would never have been around them."

His next statement also sent my pen furiously scribbling notes: ac-cording to Lynn, he remembered the day of the Franks murder clearly—because he'd been with Ronnie and Rickey that afternoon when they were supposedly committing the crime. Lynn told me about hanging out in the street with them when a neighborhood girl told them about the shooting.

After our first conversation, I spoke to Lynn a number of times through the late spring. He seemed to genuinely want to help his old friends; but I also sensed he felt I was not getting the right angle on Ed. Lynn didn't defend him so much as try to defuse any hostility I might have by placing the situation in perspective. "Who knows what's in a kid's mind or heart," he told me one day, the deep baritone quaking a bit. "I can't answer why he would have done something like this."

One afternoon while we were on the phone, Lynn put me on hold. When his voice jumped back on the line, it took me a moment to understand he was talking to someone else, a third party he'd looped into the call. ". . . Edward, that court thing, he really didn't see the murder, did he?"

"Oh no," a woman's voice, rusty with age, said. "See, [Ed's father] Cannon didn't want him to testify. But by then it was too late."

"Right, too late," Lynn answered. This, I suddenly realized, was Darlene. Before I could introduce myself, Darlene rang off, leaving Lynn and me on the phone. He seemed happy that, whether Darlene knew it or not, she had helped explain Ed's situation.

The initial revelation I had on the street corner watching the bus with Kwame—*this guy is actually innocent*—had been bolstered by the mess of contradictions in the transcripts and police documents. Now these new interviews, by adding different pieces to the case, supported the contention that in 1975 three innocent men had been sent to prison for a murder they didn't commit. Ivan claimed he saw the actual killers. Valerie was a possible alibi for Wiley. Lynn did the same for Rickey and Ronnie. None of these individuals had been interviewed before, yet their stories could have seriously altered the flow of the investigation or at least added more building blocks to a case for reasonable doubt at trial.

I was excited to share the news with Kwame. One afternoon we met on a bench in an Asia Town strip mall, not far from his job at the Board of Elections warehouse on the near East Side. Spinning with the new finds, I babbled out the developments, only to watch Kwame step back inside whatever headspace he'd outfitted to handle this. Tight lips curling into a bemused smile and wincing eyes dammed up any words or feelings. After prodding, Kwame finally explained he was surprised. "All those people remember the case?"

I could see what he was thinking: If the neighborhood consensus was that they were innocent and the young eyewitness was lying, why didn't anyone come forward? It would have been easier for Kwame if the whole neighborhood had written him off as guilty—but for all these people to know the truth, and ignore it, and let three boys go to prison was a terrible thing for him to comprehend. More so now: staying tight-lipped as a child was understandable. *But as an adult?*

"It just baffles me," he said quietly. "You were young and knew the truth. And you grew old and still knew the truth."


Ed Vernon had checked into my head and wasn't going anywhere. Lynn Garrett was right to try to lower the heat on my feelings about him. As the details in my notebooks began stacking up into a full picture of the case, Ed's part—as a villain—loomed large. My editor had scheduled me for a June publication date. The closer to deadline, the more desperate I was to find the witness.

Ed held the answers: you couldn't properly fit the story into a coherent sequence without him. I knew the facts. I understood the inconsistencies. I could spotlight the errors. But something had sparked this whole situation—a choice on the part of a little boy. Was this witness misidentification a colossal fuck-up on Ed's part? The altered documents suggested official misconduct—was this an ugly plot on the part of the cops? But why would officers go to such lengths for a relatively low-profile robbery-homicide? Did the Robinson family pressure Ed? Had the Bridgemans or Rickey done something to him? Was this revenge? The possibilities circled around the case. I had spent six months working on this story, yet the only answers I could cough up were all conjecture. Ed—the squinty-eyed, scared-shitless paperboy who couldn't spell and didn't know how many inches were in a foot—could tell me.

But Ed was MIA. No one in the neighborhood knew where he now

lived; the best intel Kwame and I received was that he was somewhere near East Fifty-fifth and Superior, a heavy-traffic intersection
surrounded by dozens of buildings. He no longer worked at the City
Mission, and no one on staff would provide me with any information
about the former employee. Only Valerie Abernathy volunteered an
idea. "You need to get to the church," she said, explaining that Ed regularly bowed his head with a congregation off Superior in the east eighties.

The Emmanuel Christian Center was a beige pitch-roofed building on the north bank of Superior. Despite apparently being one of the
rare steady pulses of life in the surrounding gutted blocks, the church
was empty when I stopped by on a weekday morning. There was, however, a phone number listed on the sign. There in the chain-link parking lot, I rang up and left a message for Pastor Anthony Singleton
explaining who I was, that I was trying to get in touch with a man
named Ed Vernon who might worship at the church, and if he did,
could the pastor please pass along my contact information. I didn't go
into the specifics on why I was calling.

I heard nothing for days. My time was draining away, only a week
from publication. I called the church again and left a second message.
Within an hour, my office phone rang. The pastor was returning my
call. "Yeah, I just wanted to let you know that I passed your first message on to Ed," Singleton said. The pastor was friendly, but his tone
was heavy with question marks; he left plenty of wide silences for me
to fill in with the reason I was interested in his parishioner. As we vol-
leyed around small talk, the pastor's interest got to be too much—he
just asked point-blank. "What do you want with Ed?"

"Honestly, I probably have to keep that between me and him," I said.

"Ah," Singleton responded. "Okay."

"But it's really important that I talk with him."

As I hung up, Kwame suddenly swung into my thoughts. I realized
that if I ever did confront Ed, I was as likely to ask him questions about
the case as scream. Reporting edges close to obsession. Three men here
had suffered an incredible injury; Kwame was a living reminder of the
damage done. Ed was center stage in my imagination—the prime

perpetrator of this wrong. The man to blame. I was so distracted thinking of what I'd say if we spoke, I almost didn't realize the phone was ringing again.

The first words from his mouth melted down that anger, at least for the moment. The voice on the other end was cracked and raspy, all frayed wires and quick-trigger fear. "Hello, sir," he began, as if he was reading from a written statement. "My name is Edward Vernon. I understand that you have been trying to get in touch with me."

Here was the showdown I'd been thinking on for six months. Somehow I was calm; I explained I was writing an article on the 1975 Franks murder at the Fairmount Cut-Rate. "I don't want my name in any article," Ed snapped.

"Well, the article is coming out," I said, trying to muffle the hot spike of emotion rising through me. "Your name is in the public record, so your name is going to be in there. But look, I really need to ask you questions about the case. You know, there are still inconsistencies in a lot of your testimony—"

Ed cut me off before I could finish. "I'm not even going to talk about it," he said. "As far as I'm concerned, it's a done deal." A dial tone droned in my ear.

There's every reason to believe the number of innocent men and women sitting in American prisons is far larger than we suspect. This has everything to do not only with how our legal system has developed over the last sixty years, but how American culture itself has shifted—changes legible in Cleveland's own story.

The biggest factor prepping the stage for wrongful convictions is—in an irony of ironies—the body of legal safeguards installed to make the system more fair and just. The U.S. Supreme Court under Chief Justice Earl Warren is credited with completely rewiring the American legal system between 1953 and 1969. Responding to the dramatic, violent tug-of-war between civil rights activists and southern states, the Warren Court extended the Bill of Rights to state courts through decisions—like the famous Miranda case or the three Cleveland cases previously cited—governing due process. This meant the rights of the accused and proper evidence collection and warrant execution were, for the first time, topics fought over in the courtroom; previously, the manner by which the accused ended up in trial wasn't even questioned much—not by lawyers, judges, or juries.

Some argue that this diverted the court's attention away from the facts of any given case. In his 2011 book *The Collapse of American Criminal Justice*, the late Harvard legal scholar William J. Stuntz wrote that it was a grave mistake "to tie the law of criminal procedure to the federal Bill of Rights instead of using that body of law to advance some coherent vision of fair and equal criminal justice." The laser focus on due process created a situation where "the chief subject of criminal litigation became the definition of procedures based on the Bill of Rights," or the "process by which the defendant was arrested, tried, and convicted"; this siphons "the time of attorneys and judges away from the question of the defendant's guilt or innocence." All this laid the foundation for a "less accurate system of criminal adjudication."[12]

Procedure-geared litigation also was time consuming, and therefore costly. The jury trial—the purported centerpiece of fact finding—became less common. Today, around 95 percent of all felony convictions are the result of plea deals, and many legal scholars argue with that much of the court's traffic flowing through without reaching a jury, there are likely to be a significant number of innocent defendants caught up in the daily waterworks without the means or will to fight their charges—*why not just plead guilty?*

These internal changes in the court system ran parallel with two major shifts in society. The first was the politicization of crime to an unprecedented degree occasioned by the War on Crime and later War on Drugs. One of the lasting effects of the federal government's entrance into local law enforcement was a new emphasis on data—numbers tallied up, reported to Washington, D.C., shared with other departments. In local departments across the country, this opened the gates to a stats-driven culture favoring high arrest numbers over slow, laborious investigations—a culture of speed over accuracy. Cue a rise in arrests and prosecutions: nationally, between 1976 and 1989, arrests per officer rose by one-third; between 1974 and 1990, felony prosecutions per prosecutor doubled.[13] But this increase in numbers threatened quality assurance. Speed came at the expense of accuracy.

During this period a growing body of tough-on-crime politicians assisted police and prosecutors. Riding the national anxiety churned up by the upheavals of the 1960s and early 1970s, politicians began mouthing a political rhetoric that pushed forward a strong agenda on crime. These politicians expanded the law into new areas—for example, toughening up statutes against minors and banks and moneylenders. Later, this same momentum resulted in legislation for uniform sentencing requirements. Legislatures were deciding and defining laws, not the courts. The huffing-and-puffing discourse in state capitals and the U.S. Congress meant there was more law, and the law was tougher.

The unforgiving nature of the evolving American justice system is likely tied to the second major culture shift. Stuntz calls this nothing less than a failure of democracy itself. The professor argues that during the late 1800s and early 1900s, the criminal justice system was "lenient and modestly egalitarian."[14] This was because crime was a local issue. Judges and prosecutors depended on working-class city dwellers for votes, the same demographic that had the most direct contact with crime. Urban police forces were drawn from this same slice of the population, as were juries ruling on guilt or innocence.

This intimacy disappeared by the mid-twentieth century. White flight out of the suburbs shifted the political power away from the cities; the main actors in the criminal justice system—the judges, the prosecutors involved in daily court business, the legislatures sculpting the process—were now elected primarily by voters in suburban counties, voters with little experience or stake in the criminal justice system that most often dealt with urban crime, voters who rarely saw a courtroom that wasn't on television. The people involved in the criminal justice system and most affected by that system were no longer the ones with the power over it.

The Cleveland I knew had been completely shaped by this second force of suburban voters. The city Kwame grew up in had been fashioned by the first force. A politicized, tough-on-crime rhetoric was what ejected Carl Stokes from office; the rhetoric, weaponized with federal dollars, was what emboldened and allowed a reactionary police force to stomp through Cleveland with little check or pushback; and it was what made significant police reform politically impossible. My Cleveland was marked by a division that had culminated in a black urban population completely isolated from the levers of power. The two moments were more than just points on a shared time line: both had molded the criminal justice process to a point where its reliability was now frighteningly suspect.

So I did eventually have an answer for my buddy Roberts's question, the one you had to ask about every Cleveland story: *What's the story say about the town?* I never told him, but by the time I was finished writing my piece on Kwame's case, I had an answer. *What's the story say about the town?* Everything you need to know.

From the moment I learned the outline of Kwame's story, one question crowded in on me. I held off from asking; I didn't want to come off as cynical or cold. But really, my question was about the prerogative of survival, how much a person has left to give when so much has already been taken. As we were prepping the story for publication, I asked.

Was he ever tempted, I needed to know, to make a final break from his past life? Because the horrific hand life had dealt him in some ways had been partly offset through a twist of circumstance: thanks to that typo, he didn't have to live with a convicted felon's Social Security number. This let Kwame build a life for himself beyond Ronnie Bridgeman. You could understand how someone in his place might be tempted to pull up the drawbridge for good. *Ronnie who?*

"I've thought about that a few times," Kwame admitted. He seemed to have already seen the question coming. He shrugged his large shoulders, a hand slowly raking his beard. "But the reason that I can't is because of Rickey. It's not that I'm carrying him, but he's carrying me." Rickey was fingered as the triggerman, that's why his parole was constantly rejected, Kwame explained. But Ed could just as easily have told the courtroom that Ronnie Bridgeman fired the shots. Then it would be Rickey on the outside now while Kwame was sitting in a cell. "Here's this guy, he didn't get the same break that I got. He's still in that little bitty place. But he's just as innocent as my brother."

Kwame stopped, seemed to gather the right words. "I've been able to get out, get a job, buy a house, get a new life. I've been able to get on with my life. But I'm living a lie still."

My story was published in the *Cleveland Scene* the first week of June 2011. My editor came up with the story's headline, a slam dunk: "What the Boy Saw."

As a journalist, I felt this was as good as I could get. The story exhaustively tackled the murder investigation and subsequent trials, spearing the state's case against Kwame, Wiley, and Rickey with the inconsistencies of their own chief witness. The piece also outlined the new evidence of the old neighborhood friends who had been around during the crime—potential new witnesses and alibis for the wrongfully convicted men. Outside of an outright retraction from Ed himself, I didn't think the piece could have been more sturdy or bulletproof.

More importantly, Kwame was pleased. "My man, that is a great piece of work," Kwame wrote me in an email on the day the article went live. "I will be getting back with Mr. Gilbert in a few days and am more than hopeful of good results." He signed off, "Thank you for believing and caring enough to help me get the ball rolling toward justice."

But my confidence in the story quickly evaporated. The piece, I began to feel, was a belly flop. In some corner of my mind, I had laid my hopes on a best-case scenario. I don't know if I expected gavels to slam at the courthouse or cell doors to clang open. We didn't have an editorial board at my paper to issue a stern call for justice. But I did feel that an airtight instance of injustice would attract wider attention. The outraged fire sawing through my guts—I wanted that to light in anyone who picked up the paper. Yet outside of a few emails, *hey great job, keep it up,* the response was nil.

This was not vanity, like a playwright seeing his would-be smash charbroiled by critics; I also wasn't possessed by some white-savior complex. There was real-world heft to this: two men were sitting in prison cells, a third was adrift between a past he was powerless to escape and a present he couldn't comfortably embrace. To say I was depressed doesn't really describe the mine shaft I spilled down. I was overloaded with a heavy sense of futility. Either I wasn't good enough, or journalism wasn't good enough, to right a real wrong here.

Channeling my frustration in either of those directions wouldn't help much (and wouldn't help me pay the bills as a reporter). Eventually, my anger swung around on the city. Cleveland: my hometown, the smokestack metropolis on the great rolling American in-between, twentieth-century whiz kid of the republic stumbling through the twenty-first like a drunk uncle, a throwback upset by its own backstory and memory-looped mistakes, a mean motherfucker. Fifty years of social upheaval and economic pain had left behind scar tissue; the resulting apathy was so thick that the story of three young black men snatched from the streets by the violent reactionary arm of unchecked government power couldn't break through. I placed this frustration on top of all the other tragedies I saw around me: schools blowing state tests, murdered black women stinking in a serial killer's backyard, graft powering the business of government, white suburbs sandbagging black urban citizens, the police department running wild. Good stuff, if you are a reporter; not so much if you are trying to live in the city. I recall sitting in my car one morning on my way to work, deadline approaching for a story about the police shooting an unarmed guy in Parma, my age exactly. "Fuck this," I announced to no one and everyone. For me, that said everything you needed to know.

Years later, I would be able to place a more articulate frame around the feeling. City life begs questions, but city life also expects an exchange. The big brains of the Enlightenment called this the "social contract"; we've all cosigned, inked our names on the dotted line of civic responsibility, whether we realize it or not, simply by living here. Cleveland wasn't holding up its end for Kwame and Rickey and Wiley and so many others.

The legal historian James Q. Whitman has argued that murder is the core of the social contract. When the modern state emerged in Europe after the Dark Ages, law was the key binding in these new, fragile social arrangements; before the state, one murder was avenged with another, often spawning an endless back-and-forth of violence, leaving the whole region unstable. The modern state placed murder and punishment in the hands of a central authority for the sake of stability. Whitman says that when a murder is committed and the state arrests and prosecutes the perpetrator, there's a sense of restoration of the social order.[15] If that's true, then an innocent person going down for a crime he or she didn't commit hands us a false sense of restoration. A bad conviction lays false bedrock. There's a bad stitch in the weave. What was more Cleveland than the justice system sitting smugly on a false sense of accomplishment?

Kwame was what really had me heartsick. Without ever quite saying it, we had both hoped this article would be the needed jump start to his exoneration. That didn't seem to be the case. And every time my caller ID lit up with his name in the weeks and months after the story was published, I felt slugged by guilt. Could I have done more? Tried harder? What could have worked?

My frustration with Cleveland pushed me out the door. I moved away about a year and a half later for another reporting job. I picked the least Cleveland place on the map. I pulled a LeBron. I moved to Miami Beach.

# Part III

*NOT YOUR TOWN ANYMORE*

# 10

## SUPER FLOP

*THE RULING CAUGHT HIM LIKE A SUCKER PUNCH—TOTAL SURPRISE. THE* parole board decided Rickey Jackson, Grafton Correctional prisoner #143953, aggravated murder, would have his sentence extended for another ten years. Ten years. He was thirty-eight. Wouldn't see a parole board again until he was just shy of fifty. Might not even be *alive* in ten years.

Really, he *should* have seen it coming, he realized later. Been happening to enough guys. When Rickey was first locked up, parole was easy to make. If you had served the minimum of your sentence, the board signed off on your release with the stipulation that if you landed back in prison, you'd have to serve out the remainder on top of whatever new sentence you were saddled with. But ever since the early 1990s, new sentencing guidelines—tougher, stronger—had come into play, cutting down the board's discretion. Now, for heavy felony offenders or former death row inmates like Rickey, they were handing out ten years or more of additional time. Ten years. The prisoners called them "super flops."

The change at the board fit with the shift Rickey could read across the whole system. Prison once sent a message: if you wanted to, and weren't too much of a knucklehead, you could straighten out, do the

programs and classes, and go home better than you came in. Reha-
bilitated. Now that philosophy no longer existed. The classes were
bullshit. Parole was impossible to get. And the guys who did get out
seemed to boomerang right back. Rickey saw clearly: it was a revolving
door in here.

His sense of the shift was correct. The War on Crime and the
War on Drugs had acted as they were designed, funneling generations of the urban poor into the prison system. Mandatory minimum
sentences and three-strike laws kept those prisoners inside for longer
and increased their likelihood of reoffending. Between 1980 and 2000,
the country's prison and jail population exploded from 300,000 to
2 million.[1]

Rickey knew his own situation was a dead end under the new
hard-edged penal approach. No matter if it was 1995 or 2005 or even
2015, every time he sat across a table from three members of the parole
board, they'd want to hear the same words from him: tell us about
what happened, about Mr. Franks and Mrs. Robinson. And Rickey
wouldn't, couldn't, deliver: *I can't tell you what happened 'cause I wasn't
there*, he'd always tell them.

Within a few days of the 1995 decision, Rickey thawed out, thoughts
and feelings rolling through him again. Ten years. That's like a whole
'nother prison sentence, he thought. I'll go crazy in here. To hell with
working out, going to the job, or mentally checking out with science
fiction novels. To hell with trying just to get along.

He needed to bend all he had toward being released, Rickey decided. Got to do something.

The American criminal justice system isn't wired for claims of innocence. The mechanisms just aren't there, and the reasons why run deep.
Much of it lies in the basic decentralized setup: each of the fifty states
has its own criminal justice system; the federal courts run parallel to
the local judiciary. Together, this creates a mess of overlapping juris-
dictions and crisscrossing legal avenues, counter-case law and prece-

dent and political leanings—a lot of white noise often drowning out real pleas for help.

The post-trial plumbing is further marked by one fact: from the moment a case reaches their docket, the higher appellate courts assume the trial judge or jury made the right call on guilt or innocence. The upper courts aren't interested in rehashing the facts unless something new enters the frame, and then do so only with the utmost suspicion.

The first shot at an appeal is a new trial motion. These are submitted back to the court where the original trial occurred. The thrust of the filing must be new evidence. This is material that has not previously come to light, and it must be forceful enough to convince the judge a retrial would end in acquittal. Time limits, however, are a significant roadblock to new trial motions; they range from one month to three years after the original sentencing, depending on the state. These calendar restrictions were passed in response to the flood of appeals filed following the advances of the Warren court. They are kept in place due to the high case volume in American law. If everyone could file for a new trial, the thinking runs, the courts would be overwhelmed. But even if you file within the window and can produce evidence meeting the criteria, a new trial motion is still a long shot. The filing lands back on the desk of the judge who just finished trying the case. He or she might not be open to more of the same, tired of the whole thing. And a judge can reject the motion without holding an evidentiary hearing or even issuing a written explanation.

The next open lane for postconviction relief is a direct appeal to a higher court. But again this panel is uninterested in claims of innocence. The appellate level is tasked only with looking at procedural errors. These issues include government evidence that should not have been allowed at trial or misleading instructions to the jury or prosecutorial misconduct. None of these issues can be flagged in an appeal unless the defense counsel objected during the original trial. Otherwise, in the eyes of the law, the issues are not preserved. Often, even if a defendant is able to spotlight procedural mistakes, the court still won't upset the trial verdict; sure, the courts may admit in these instances that there were procedural missteps in the trial—but they reason the verdict would still have been the same. The U.S. Supreme Court has dubbed this the "harmless error test." It is "notoriously flexible," in the words of one expert.

The final state opportunity for review is called postconviction relief. This motion, filed again with the original trial court, represents a completely new challenge to the conviction. You could, for example, argue for ineffectiveness of counsel. The bar for proof, however, is usually incredibly high—yes, the court may say, you might have had a bad lawyer, but can you prove conclusively the bad lawyer was the reason you were convicted? This level of the appellate layer cake is further complicated by the fact that most state law doesn't provide an inmate with an attorney for postconviction review. State statutes also often do not provide attorneys for a prisoner's final shot at the federal level. This final Hail Mary, a habeas petition, must argue on the grounds of a constitutional rights violation.

Although it seems there are a number of options, in truth, there is little reason to think the courts regularly correct their own mistakes through the postconviction channels. Studies have borne out the terrible odds of the system. In 2011, a law professor named Brandon L. Garrett published a detailed excavation of the first 250 exonerations achieved through DNA testing. Part of the examination looked at the success rate of postconviction appeals on behalf of the exonerees *before* DNA testing incontrovertibly proved their innocence. Ninety percent of the high court appeals failed to help these innocent men and women. Without science, they would likely still be guilty in the eyes of the law.

Worse, the access these innocent men and women had to the appeals process dwindled the further they drilled into the process. Of the first 250 DNA exonerations, Garrett was only able to obtain written appellate decisions for 165 prisoners. All 165 applied for direct appeal; by the postconviction level, only seventy-one filed; thirty-five filed federal habeas petitions; thirty-eight filed directly with the U.S.

Supreme Court; the high bench only agreed to hear one case—which was then turned down.[2]

The existing decisions also show that invariably the courts lean toward the original trial verdict. Of the 165 records Garrett pored through, in seventy-eight cases the ruling judges affirmed the petitioners' guilt based on the strength of the prosecution's cases; in sixteen, the judges referred to the "overwhelming" guilt of the petitioner. Remember: these are men and women later *proven* innocent by science. Yet the human intellect on the judicial bench could not reach the same conclusion through the law.[3]

Even the most promising situations can roller-coaster through the courts to a tragic finish. The case of Troy Davis may be the most shameful example. Convicted of murdering an off-duty police officer in 1991, the Georgia man maintained his innocence from death row, where he awaited execution. He immediately filed for a new trial with the same judge within the state-mandated thirty days. It was denied. A direct appeal was also shot down—the presiding judges emphasized the jury's verdict. Davis next filed a federal habeas claim, arguing that prosecutorial misconduct and ineffective counsel at his trial were constitutional violations. Both the federal district court and appeals circuit denied his motion while noting they wouldn't touch his innocence claims.

Davis launched another motion for a new trial in the Georgia state courts. This time he had considerable evidence on his side: seven of the nine witnesses who originally identified Davis as the murderer had recanted their statements. Key to their reversals was not that they'd been mistaken, but rather were pressured by police to name Davis. But this motion was also denied; again, the decision noted the weight of the original verdict. No evidentiary hearing was even granted to hear from the recanting witnesses.

Davis again filed with the federal court on the basis of actual innocence. Here his prospects seemed to turn. The U.S. Supreme Court granted his petition in August 2009—the first time the country's highest court had granted such a petition in fifty years. The court directed the lower district judges to reexamine the case to see "whether evidence that could not have been obtained at the time of trial clearly establishes petitioner's innocence." Troy Davis was finally going to get his day.

But the district court was not sympathetic to Davis's pleas. This court decided the "new evidence casts some additional, minimal doubt on his conviction" but was largely "smoke and mirrors." The court—once again—deferred to the original jury: a "federal court simply cannot interpose itself and set aside the jury verdict in this case absent a truly persuasive showing of innocence." To do so, the decision noted in an argument grounded more in housekeeping than justice, would set a precedent that could wreak "complete havoc on the criminal justice system."[4]

His options were done. Davis was executed by lethal injection on September 21, 2011.

Rickey tried to tell the kid, but he wouldn't listen. Walter was a younger guy on his range, serving out a minor sentence. He was constantly stealing stuff from other Lucasville inmates. Rickey told him to quit. Wasn't worth the risk, especially if he was going home so soon. Then one day Rickey watched in the dayroom as one of the guys Walter had stolen from walked up to him and killed him right there. Rickey's heart broke to see a guy so young killed, but he didn't say a word. It was one of three killings he would personally witness at Lucasville.

Rickey's game plan for surviving prison was to unplug. Prison wasn't the place for a sensitive, perceptive man. Too much of what you saw stuck to you, and if you let your emotion spill out, you were only marked as weak. The next victim. So you parked your emotions as far away as possible. Some small part remained, nagging away. But you ignored it. As his years inside added up, Rickey learned to stack as much as he could between himself and his surroundings.[5]

In the early years, sports and athletics were a good buffer. He worked out, played basketball. Tired muscles and straining lungs were an easy distraction. At Lucasville he got a job handing out recreation equipment in the rec room, and work became another outlet. But even a heavy schedule didn't completely fence off the brutal reality of prison life. One day when Rickey was cleaning up the gym, he walked around a corner. A group of big inmates had a smaller, screaming man in a headlock. They were taking turns raping him. Rickey was terrified if he said something, he'd be the next one on the ground. He carried the shame for years.

After he was transferred to Lebanon in 1987, he continued throwing himself into employment opportunities. Rickey ran a printing press, worked a shoe-stitching machine, and later landed in the kitchen.

He didn't gamble, didn't seek out drugs. He fought when he had to, but was able to steer clear of the gang beefs responsible for most of the bloodshed inside the penitentiary. Keeping to himself also meant zipping shut about his case. Kwame might have told anyone who wanted to chat about how he did not commit the crime he was inside for; Rickey barely shared the details of his charges, much less his innocence. By his way of thinking, every pair of ears belonged to a possible snitch, some fucker looking to spin information into an advantage. You might confide in someone, only to see the same face at your next parole hearing.

There wasn't much peace behind the barricades Rickey erected. How could there be? He was left with blazing hate. As years passed, the floating anger narrowed down to a thin blade pointing at one person: Ed Vernon. Rickey stewed over the kid, endlessly working over how he could have done what he did. He kept it going like a furnace.

But it all changed in 1995, after the parole board gave him ten more years. Rickey was determined to do something about his case. He had no idea what, but he guessed where to start. After his shifts in the kitchen he would wash the food stink off, then head for the law library. Inside there were always guys bent over law books, trying to squeeze sense from the thick language as it pertained to their bit. Rickey learned he needed to obtain his trial transcript. He requested the documents, and after months of waiting a thick stack arrived from the Cuyahoga Court clerk. Now Rickey had to relive his courtroom ordeal, or live through it for the first time—so much had shot over his head during the trial. He ordered the Bridgemans' 1975 trials as well, and soon he was spending hours flipping through the files. *I've been mad at the wrong person,* Rickey realized. *It was all there in the record.* His hot anger swung away from Ed Vernon, fixing now on the police, prosecutors, and judges who let this whole mess go down. *Ed did his part, but he couldn't have done it without the cooperation of the whole system,* Rickey saw. *They basically kidnapped this boy from his parents. Ed was powerless, too.*

Rickey began taking detailed notes on the transcripts, jotting down when Ed's testimony contradicted other statements in the record. He would later hop on a typewriter, carefully pecking out the errors and missteps from the legal proceeding.

Armed with this information, he returned to the law library, asking about nonprofits or organizations willing to work pro bono for prisoners. From there he wrote Centurion Ministries, the Innocence Project in New York City, every elected official he could think of in Ohio and Cuyahoga County, every newspaper and television station—anyone who might be able to help. He made a promise to himself: send out one letter a day, five days a week. He saved his state pay up for stamps, stuffed his typed-up pleas for help into envelopes, and mailed them off like SOSs in bottles.

Replies rarely came. When they did, the responses might be encouraging but promised no action. The case was too old. There wasn't enough evidence. Everyone was overworked. Rickey also saw that he wasn't bringing much to the situation. *I can't really give them anything,* he told himself, *other than Ed Vernon.*

DNA evidence splashed into the American mainstream in 1995. For ten months, Americans binged on the daily legal maneuvers inside a California courtroom as former NFL superstar O.J. Simpson fought off charges that he had brutally murdered his ex-wife. The trial unfolded under a harsh tabloid glare; undercurrents of race and fame fed the drama. But probably the most consequential figure for Simpson's defense was a lowkey New Yorker talking science.

Barry Scheck, assisted by Peter Neufeld, was arguably the key figure in Simpson's "Dream Team" defense. Day after day, the attorneys meticulously picked apart the Los Angeles Police Department's handling of forensic evidence. By the time of Simpson's trial, the legal issues involving DNA were largely settled. But Scheck and Neufeld's work in LA was central to the evolving narrative of wrongful conviction. The pair introduced the science to the world beyond the legal community. They also advanced the idea that sloppy police work can jeopardize a slam-dunk criminal case.

The general population has never absorbed the full implications of wrongful convictions, even though the issue has been pitched by reformers as a public policy crisis for most of the twentieth century.

Today, many experts and lawyers consider Edwin Borchard's 1932 book, *Convicting the Innocent*, the Big Bang moment for exoneration studies. A three-hundred-page run-through of sixty-five instances of men and women convicted for crimes they didn't commit, the book also contained one of the first diagnostics of wrongful conviction "causes." Borchard, a progressive liberal and comparative law professor at Yale University, wrote the book in order to push ahead federal legislation providing financial compensation for exonerees—legislation that was signed into law by President Franklin Roosevelt in 1938. Borchard's efforts to get similar laws on state statutes failed, however, and the cause never led to a brushfire of public outcry. Erle Stanley Gardner, the creator of iconic fictional attorney Perry Mason, was similarly stymied. Between 1948 and 1958, the lawyer turned author wrote a column called Court of Last Resort featuring wrongful conviction stories.[6] Gardner was credited with exonerating at least eighteen individuals. But a true-crime television show based on the concept flopped after a single season. Gardner's efforts to spark a wider awareness and conversation also failed to take.

In the 1980s, while the legal system increasingly evolved along a hard-line punitive trajectory, the main interest in wrongful conviction came from academics. As Robert J. Norris outlined in his book *Exonerated: A History of the Innocence Movement*, early in the decade philosopher Hugo Adam Bedau and sociologist Michael Radelet began examining capital cases as part of their opposition to the death penalty. The results, published in 1987 in the *Stanford Law Review*, presented three hundred and fifty cases which Bedau and Radelet believed were wrongful convictions. The authors also argued that in twenty-three of those cases, innocent men and women had been put to death.

The publication set off tempers at the highest level of government. President Ronald Reagan's Department of Justice was overseeing a War on Drugs and an explosion in incarceration. Realizing Bedau and Radelet's work questioned the very integrity of the whole criminal justice system, U.S. Attorney General Edwin Meese III tasked two Justice Department attorneys with penning an attack on the study. Published the next year in the same journal, the DOJ response blasted Bedau and Radelet's methods and bias. The academics responded with their own attack, calling the DOJ's reaction "an effort to protect the myth of systemic infallibility."[7]

DNA was what sprung wrongful conviction out of partisan gridlock. The irony is that this game changer for criminal defense never would have entered American courtrooms if it hadn't originally been devised as a tool for prosecutors. Beginning in the mid-1980s, the government started tying defendants to crime scenes by matching blood samples (cases such as the motorcycle gang murders Cleveland attorney Terry Gilbert worked on). The earliest form of forensic DNA was a rough, approximate science called DQ-alpha. The testing, however, was limited, focusing only on eight genetic markers that could place a suspect in the general genetic neighborhood. The early 1990s saw the development of restriction fragment length polymorphism (RFSP) lab work; highly effective at singling out the owner of genetic material, the testing required large amounts of undamaged material—rare in a criminal setting. By the late 1990s, however, scientists broke ground on testing that sewed up these holes; short tandem repeat (STR) was both accurate and only required minimal DNA—a few cells—for testing. STR's appearance on the stage directly fed into the creation of national DNA databases, where genetic material from crime scenes could be collected and compared to track repeat offenders.

Like Gilbert, Scheck and Neufeld came to the law energized by the social activism of the 1960s. Both men worked as public defenders for indigent clients in New York, bolstering their experience with defendants caught up in the new machinery of an aggressive punitive legal system. "When I was a public defender, 1976 to 1977, I handled cases of people who had been sort of pressured or coerced into pleading guilty to crimes they didn't commit, and I reopened their cases," Neufeld told Norris. "So I was very much aware of wrongful convictions in that sense years before [Scheck and I] ever did anything."

In early cases like the Ohio Hell's Angels trial and later the O.J. Simpson case, Scheck and Neufeld targeted the sloppy application of DNA forensics. But both men early on recognized the powerful potential of the new science. DNA could provide bulletproof, scientifically stamped evidence of innocence. As Scheck testified before Congress in 1991, the technique could be "an amazing tool to revisit old cases where people had been dragged out of the courtroom screaming, 'I'm innocent! I'm innocent! I'm innocent!'"[8]

In 1992 Scheck and Neufeld launched an organization geared to using the new science to free wrongfully convicted prisoners. Named the Innocence Project, the organization was a clinic run out of Cardozo School of Law at Yeshiva University. Any outfit working on behalf of the wrongfully convicted faces logistical uphills: little funding, poor clients, more cases for review than available eyeballs. Scheck and Neufeld met those problems by grounding their assault on the justice system in an educational setting. Students handled the legal grunt work and drafted motions; staff attorneys supervised the progress and represented clients in the actual courtroom. DNA was the cornerstone of the work, and the Innocence Project tended toward rape, murder, and sexual assault cases where physical evidence was in abundance.

The group achieved headline-snatching success. By the 2010s, the

Innocence Project had secured the release of more than three hundred wrongfully convicted prisoners. Scheck and Neufeld's largest impact, however, was inspiring similar clinics at other law schools. Within a decade there were innocence projects operating as campus clinics in every state. By placing wrongful conviction in the spotlight, the movement has sparked a significant change within the legal community, with advocates going as far as calling Scheck and Neufeld's revolution a "new civil rights movement" and the "most dramatic development in the criminal justice world since the Warren Court's due process revolution of the 1960s."[9]

Yet the law itself—so poorly designed to address postconviction pleas of innocence to begin with—has dragged behind the steady flow of exonerations. By the early years of the new century, most states had passed legislation granting convicted felons access to DNA evidence for retroactive testing. But red tape still straitjackets the process: some states, such as Florida, demand a "preliminary showing of innocence" before testing gets the green light; others bar access to prisoners who pleaded guilty.

Even when the testing does go forward, both courts and prosecutors have often been stubbornly resistant to the results. Darryl Hunt was convicted in 1984 of a North Carolina murder. In 1994, DNA testing proved a sample found on the victim did not match Hunt; his appeals, however, were rejected—the court ruled the findings didn't conclusively prove his innocence. Hunt wasn't exonerated until 2005, when a DNA database matched the evidence from the crime scene to another culprit.[10] Similarly, Chicagoan Ronald Jones went down for a 1985 rape-murder; in 1997 testing cleared him of the crime, and the Illinois Supreme Court ordered a new trial. But prosecutors let Jones languish in prison for two more years—two years after he was scientifically cleared—before deciding not to retry.[11]

The courts' reluctance to acknowledge wrongful convictions hasn't stopped exonerations. Despite regular news about exonerees winning freedom, there has not been a fuller conversation or call for reforms. There are two possible reasons why. On a large scale, there is a very distinct difference between the way experts and academics talk about wrongful conviction and mainstream media accounts. In the former, wrongful conviction is a symptom of a greater sickness woven through the entire criminal justice system, a network of depredations and historical injustices rotting every working piece. Media versions, on the other hand, almost always frame wrongful convictions as stand-alone travesties, the wronged man suffering through hellish circumstances, random bad shit visited upon a poor-luck sucker. A larger context is almost always missing.

Partly the systemic issues are muted in the myriad factors involved in each individual wrongful conviction, often down to the very genetics. But DNA testing is arguably also preventing a larger outcry. When Scheck and Neufeld started the first Innocence Project, they consciously decided to only tackle DNA cases. Their vision was larger than case-by-case exonerations. The pair instead hoped to fundamentally change public policy. That mission required the kind of irrefutable evidence of innocence only DNA can provide, facts detractors could not refute. Each DNA exoneration also provided "a learning moment for the criminal justice system," Scheck told Norris.[12] After innocence is established, attorneys and researches can reverse-engineer each wrongful conviction, decoding what exactly went wrong in each scenario. Concrete policy suggestions—such as recording interrogations, changing eyewitness identification policies, freeing up access to DNA testing— are born out of such research.

But the emphasis on DNA partially overshadowed cases without forensics. And much of the state law written in the wake of exonerations requires a high burden of proof, such as the unimpeachable "actual innocence" only DNA can provide. Under this statute test, for the law to acknowledge that a prisoner has been wrongfully convicted, DNA is often necessary—sometimes DNA evidence and additional proof of innocence. The law has also severely squeezed the federal court's power. In 1996, Congress passed the Antiterrorism and Effective Death Penalty Act (AEDPA); the legislation clamped down on federal habeas review with time limits and other procedural restrictions while also forcing federal courts to respect original trial verdicts. So as the law currently sits, and as cases like Troy Davis's illustrate, without scientific backing, it is extremely hard to prove you didn't do it.

And Rickey Jackson didn't have any DNA evidence.


In 2004, a prisoner at Grafton tried to rape Rickey. The guy was big, 230 pounds or so, and he sprang when Rickey was walking back from the shower in a robe. He tried to fight out of the headlock, but it was useless. Luckily Rickey made enough noise that a CO intervened before anything happened.

The near rape shook him, but not in the usual way—that's what shook him. Something so traumatic would terrify a normal person. Rickey responded on autopilot, his emotions stuffed so far away, he wasn't even sure if he could feel anything anymore. It was scary. He'd spent his whole adult life in prison, operating like a machine. Survival exacted a price. He was running out of time to be a normal person again.

A lifeline finally came. In September 2006, Rickey opened a letter from the Ohio Innocence Project (OIP). The newly formed organization expressed interest in his case and outlined the conditions for its involvement. First and foremost: you had to be completely innocent. No problem there, Rickey thought.

Ohio's own branch was opened in 2003 at the University of Cincinnati's school of law; Mark Godsey, a former New York City federal prosecutor, took the helm of the nascent outfit modeled on Scheck and Neufeld's clinic. Within three years, OIP had already freed three Ohio men from incarnation. Gary Reece was a Cleveland man who was released from prison after twenty-five years following an OIP investigation that turned up a history of fabrication and mental illness on the part of the victim. Chris Bennett, an Akron man serving a sentence for causing a deadly traffic accident, was freed after the organization proved he wasn't responsible for the crash.[13]

The group's most dramatic early success, however, was Clarence El-kins. An Akron-area father of two, Elkins was convicted in 1998 of raping and murdering his mother-in-law and raping his six-year-old niece. Elkins was charged based on the identification of the young victim. The girl wavered before the trial, but was pressured into tes-tifying against Elkins by the prosecutor, Maureen O'Connor (who later would be appointed as the chief justice of the Ohio Supreme Court). Elkins was convicted and received two life sentences for the crimes. But Elkins and his wife continued to investigate after his sen-tencing, eventually focusing on a convicted rapist named Earl Mann. Coincidentally, the suspect was then serving a prison sentence in Mansfield Correctional—the same prison holding Elkins. The wrong-fully convicted inmate surreptitiously picked up cigarette butts be-longing to Mann and turned them over to OIP. DNA testing matched the swabs to the '98 murder. The prosecutor, however, still refused to release Elkins. The office only caved after Ohio Attorney General Jim Petro intervened in the case and publicly pressed for Elkins's freedom. Elkins was released in 2005. Mann pleaded guilty to the murder and rapes.

For OIP, publicized success meant more cases to investigate. For Rickey, unfortunately, that translated into more waiting. Hope even-tually curdled into frustration. The students assigned to his file were Rickey's main points of contact with OIP. But it seemed that once he'd get the students up to speed, they would move on and his file would end up in the hands of another set of students—and the new ones would be asking the exact same questions. He got pissed and stopped writing the group back.

At OIP, Rickey's case passed through a number of staff attorneys— usually falling to the bottom of the stack as more pressing cases with better evidence nudged to the top of the pile. But in February 2010, a new attorney joined the organization, inheriting Rickey's file along with hundreds of others. Carrie Wood was a graduate of the Univer-sity of Cincinnati law school who later worked as a public defender in the Bronx. Returning to her alma mater, she brought a big-city rigor to the work waiting for her at OIP.[14] Since the organization had taken on the case, numerous law students had worked the file, nosing down a number of possible avenues. Could the money orders be traced? Was the acid cup found at the crime scene still available for DNA testing? Was the victim's briefcase ever located?

The student Wood was supervising on Rickey's case was coming to the work from the other side of the courtroom. Scott Crowley had been a criminal justice major as an undergrad. He'd originally wanted to be a police officer, but eventually shifted his ambition to the prosecutor's office.[15] He interned with the Cincinnati state's attorney, an experience that gave him a unique insight when he started working with OIP as a law student in 2008. Crowley went in with no hard opinions on Rickey's case. But two aspects of the conviction stood out. First, the entire case was based on Ed. There was no other evidence save the boy's testimony. Crowley found a phone number for the witness and made a call. Ed hung up.

The second intriguing part of the case for Crowley was Kwame. Almost immediately he began fielding phone calls from Rickey's codefendant. "Kwame was relentless about the case," Crowley told me later. "That stood out because he was done, he was out. But he wouldn't let this go. That made sense—if they were innocent."

Despite the lack of evidence, Crowley told his supervisor that OIP should keep the case open. Rickey was just a name on a file to Wood; yet she also realized there was something more here. "For a capital murder case, there are teenage romance novels that have more paperwork," she would later tell me. As Wood was talking with students about the case, one of the fellows told her he truly believed Rickey was innocent. But—no new evidence. The case had languished with the organization for so long, Wood considered closing out the file—essentially telling Rickey there was nothing OIP could do. "But in my mind, if a prosecutor had come up to me and said I think that guy is probably innocent, as a public defender, I'm not going to take his word. I want to know that I've left no stone unturned," Wood explained later. "If we're going to send a closing letter, I don't want to have the nagging feeling that there's something else I should have looked at."

Wood kept Rickey's file active, passing the work along to another set of students, hoping for a break.

I never met Rickey while I was working on the article about his case. Through six months of reporting and writing, I submitted requests with the state corrections department for the opportunity to interview both Wiley and Rickey. All the petitions were shot down. If I was ever given an official reason, it wasn't meaningful enough to remember.

What I knew then about Rickey, I picked up from the few letters we swapped. The man who reached up out of the neatly typed pages—brushed here and there with pencil marks correcting small typos—was warm, articulate, serious, and friendly; he never forgot to ask me how I was doing, what was new with my life. These pleasantries, I came to see, were far from empty politesse, but important—vital, even—points of human exchange for a man well into his third decade of incarceration.

He was a full-on science fiction nerd, from *Star Trek* to the weighty philosophical novels of Robert Heinlein. He worked in the greenhouse at prison, a job where he was mostly left alone with his plants. It was quiet there, and he didn't get hassled by other prisoners or guards. Could even catch a quick rule-breaking cigarette out among the growing plant life, turn the big garden fans on to blow the smoke out. The COs never noticed or, if they did, didn't care. Rickey Jackson wasn't giving them a hard time. He was fifty-four years old.

Not long after the publication of my article on the case, I got a letter from Rickey asking me to send a copy of the *Cleveland Scene* story to him at Grafton. He hadn't seen it yet. "My apologies for the long delay in correspondence," he wrote. "Kwame has, however, kept me abreast of your activities." Closing out the letter, he again asked about my well-being. "How has life been treating you of late?" he wrote. "Me personally, what can I say? Just trying to stay positive and keep hope alive, which isn't always an easy thing to do under these circumstances. But continue to hope I must, because I can't even begin to contemplate the alternative."

We lost contact soon after and eventually I moved out of state. I never learned his reaction to the story. But the piece actually had more of an impact than I could have then realized. Seeing his name in print, reading the details of his case, watching the story, *his* story, crawl out of the intervening decades of silence—it shocked him like a bolt of energy. So much so, he threw off the self-imposed omertà he'd clamped over his own story. For the first time Rickey started professing his innocence inside, showing off the *Scene* article to cellmates and coworkers, even handing the newsprint over to friendly COs. Equal doses of pride and hope blitzed him. Pride at what he'd endured. Hope that he finally could be heading home.

Rickey's excitement was woven with a practical element. He knew most of the folks from the old neighborhood were still living back in the city. The *Scene* story would make the gossip. Ed Vernon knew the story had been published. It would be hard to hide from that newsprint.

"For the most part, Edward had suppressed it to the point where he could live with it," Rickey would later tell me. "But when that story popped? Uh-oh. The closet is getting too full for all those skeletons."

# 11

# HYPERTENSION

THERE WERE USUALLY TEARS. THAT WAS THE POINT OF THE ALL-nighters, where men prayed and reflected from dusk to dawn in the church's sanctuary as Christian songs and gospel murmured gently from the speakers. It was one-on-one time with the Lord, spiritual traffic between sinner and savior uncongested by daily demands. Pastor Anthony Singleton knew many of the brothers in the room had dark patches in their history. Pastor had them himself. Here, the world wasn't around to distract you from who you really were. So you expected to see red, swollen eyes among the men at Emmanuel Christian's shut-ins.

But this was different. Tonight, the usual sniffles were overpowered by something much louder. The cries scraping the sanctuary's pitched roof were pained, ear-busting. Pastor Singleton noticed that all that noise was coming out of Brother Ed. Something's wrong, the preacher reasoned.[1]

Cleveland—city of churches. East Side, West Side, the whole spectrum: fish-fry-Friday Catholics and suburban megachurch holy rollers, lukewarm Protestants and Greek Orthodox. You've got quarry-rock cathedrals haunting corners of Ohio City. Old World cupolas and onion domes marking the skyline in Tremont. Beautiful stone wrecks patched with graffitied plywood lining East Fifty-fifth. And down on Public Square was the Old Stone Church, two modest granite bell towers dark with 150 years of soot, the oldest standing structure in town.

Emmanuel Christian is just one of a dozen houses of the holy running up Superior on the East Side. It holds neither the political clout through mobilized voters nor the deep pastoral lineage of other black religious powerhouses in town. But a faithful two hundred or so regular worshippers bow their heads there each Sunday, hearing the Word delivered by Pastor Anthony Singleton. Pulled-taffy gangly and given to dapper, screaming-loud suits, Singleton has a commanding patter and confident stage prowl that give him the veneer of a showman. But preaching wasn't exactly the road Singleton had originally planned to walk. The opposite, actually. "By the time I got to twenty-two years old, I had done everything but kill somebody, sleep with a man, and shoot heroin," Singleton would boast later, a Cheshire-cat smile on his lips. "We grew up in the projects, not having a father. So I engaged in a lot of stuff."

Crime? "Little petty theft." Drugs? "We had our weed and our beer and wine. Crack wasn't out then, and we couldn't afford cocaine, that was for rich people." Women? "Girls was my thing. If I had one girlfriend, I wanted two. If I had two girlfriends, I wanted three."

But at twenty-two, a niece dragged Singleton by the arm to a church service. The words storming out of the preachers made little sense to the young street hustler. "I knew a Mark, but I didn't know the Mark of the Bible. I knew a John, didn't know a Matthew. Didn't know nobody named Luke. I just thought, What's he talking about?"

When the preacher asked for all the sinners present to march to the pulpit to be baptized, Singleton's niece urged him up. He didn't care much for the ritual, but something had shifted: the urge to chase girls and get high—they were gone now. His brush with the Lord reconfigured Singleton. This was the launchpad for a preaching career that eventually stopped at Emmanuel Christian. In his new life behind the pulpit, Singleton didn't ignore his past—most of the brothers and sisters filling the pews had suffered their own hard knocks, many self-inflicted. Singleton was a walking, talking example of the righteous path.

That was certainly the case with Ed Vernon. In 2007, Emmanuel Christian started receiving vanloads of City Mission residents for Sunday service. The congregation became so popular with the recovering addicts and homeless residents that drivers had to make two trips to the mission to collect them all. Singleton stopped by the shelter to give small group talks, which is where he met one of the staffers, a little guy with midnight-dark skin and thick glasses. "I've heard a lot about you," Ed told the pastor. "I'm going to come to your church." He joined the congregation on the first Sunday he attended.

Here was a humble man with high-voltage faith, Singleton thought, looking over his new parishioner. Drink, smoke, and vulgarity never passed Brother Ed's lips. He knew his scriptures front to back. He threw himself into the church's business, participating in services and ministering to sick members at home who couldn't make it to weekly church service. Every Sunday, he was a bouncing, laughing presence in the congregation.

As dedicated as Ed was to his scriptures, bad luck dogged him. He started hitting up Singleton for loans, and when it came time to pay them back, a teary-eyed Ed would apologize for not having the money. He's working, and he's still broke, the pastor thought. He often let Ed forget about the debt. The pastor picked up that Ed was infatuated with a woman who wasn't interested in him—most of his money was going to her.

When Ed lost his job at the City Mission, his situation became dire. One Sunday while the congregation was in service a repo man came right up on Superior and snatched Ed's van away for missed payments. The next job he got was working security at a mental health center. The one rule: don't touch the patients. Not long after starting, however, a patient fell on Ed during an incident. He pleaded, but no luck. They fired him.

But Ed started dating a woman from the congregation and his prospects brightened. A new job worked out at a dry cleaner's. And— amazingly—a fat check arrived in his mailbox from the IRS, a lump sum owed from a tax snafu involving his ex-wife, the former divinity student at the Mission. Ed was suddenly eight thousand dollars richer. He presented his new love interest with an expensive engagement ring.

However, the run of luck didn't stick. His girlfriend, he would later say, relapsed into a drug habit, siphoning money away from Ed and hocking her engagement ring. He lost his job again, then quickly fell behind on the payments for a new car he'd bought with his IRS check. Once again, the repo guy took the vehicle. By that point, Ed was out three jobs and two cars in a stretch of twelve months. Whatever it was—karma or his spiritual balance—it was all wrong with Ed, Singleton thought. And then there were those intense crying jags during the all-night shut-ins. It was as if a black cloud clung to Ed at all times.

In 2011 Singleton started to gather clues about what was going on with Ed. When a reporter—me—and then attorneys began filling up his office answering machine looking for Brother Ed, the parishioner swatted it off, telling the pastor the calls were about some business back at the City Mission—old story, he claimed. But then Singleton found himself flipping through *Scene,* reading about an Ed Vernon who had testified against three neighbors in a 1975 murder case. Fireworks went off inside Singleton's head.

"Honey!" Singleton yelled to his wife, bent over the family computer one night, searching online for more details of the case. "This is it! This is what's wrong with Ed." His wife wasn't convinced. "You can't go by what that newspaper says," she said. "That's one of them free newspapers."

Singleton went as far as heading downtown to the public library, hunting for old newspaper articles on the crime and trials. Armed with the information, one day he risked mentioning it to Ed when the two were driving together to Bible study. The preacher casually asked why a *Scene* magazine reporter was looking to speak with him.

"No, Pastor," Ed said. "That's something about the City Mission." Singleton, though, had already read the story. He *knew* why the reporter had called. But here Ed was, lying to him still. Singleton was in a bind. If Ed didn't want to go there, he couldn't push him. But the pastor also couldn't leave it alone.

Not much later, Ed disappeared. Poof, gone. He stopped showing up for Bible study, wasn't in the pews for Sunday service. When Singleton called, Ed's cell cut right to voice mail.

Down in Cincinnati, Sierra Merida's brain was also stuck on Ed Vernon. After inheriting Rickey's case from the last round of OIP interns, the second-year law student looked at the recaps of available leads and information.[2] Clearly nothing so far had inched the case forward. There was only one serious option: talking to Ed.

When she walked into her first year of law school, Merida, like Crowley, had every intention of sitting at the other table in the courtroom as a prosecutor. OIP, however, offered a great opportunity at real-world legal work, so she showed up for an informational meeting. After a spiel about the program from staff, Dean Gillispie spoke. A burly white man from the Dayton area, he had been convicted of three rapes in 1991 despite passing numerous polygraph tests and providing a bulletproof alibi for the window of time when the crimes took place—he wasn't even in Ohio. Still, Gillispie spent twenty years in a cell before OIP obtained a reversal of his conviction in 2011. The story hit Merida where it counted; she put her name down for OIP.

The law student picked up parallels between Gillispie's nightmare and Rickey's own. No physical evidence was presented at either trial. The convictions were sealed with eyewitness testimony. Both Gillespie and Rickey had clean records before their arrests. Merida could only imagine what it must have been like—sitting in a courtroom, scared, indecipherable legalese flying over your head, and feeling like no one was fighting for you. Reading the 1975 court transcripts, she was shocked by how transparent Ed's lies had been. Even the judges didn't seem convinced, at least from the comments in the record. And the state presented no other evidence. The case was so thin. In her mental snapshot of Ed, the thirteen-year-old transformed into a villain. How can someone say something like that? How could he lie? And now, how could be still remain silent? Yet Ed was the only answer to Rickey's predicament.

OIP's Carrie Wood shared Merida's feelings. Ed was the only path left for mounting Rickey's case. Pastor Singleton was the only gateway to the witness. Together, Merida and her OIP partner practiced what they'd say on the phone, then punched in the numbers.

Singleton wasn't even supposed to be in the office. But instead of letting the call slip to his voice mail, the pastor's long arm grabbed the braying receiver. A beat or two, that's all it took for him to connect the woman's voice on the phone, the nervous practice rap, with what had been sitting like a rock in the back of his mind for weeks.

"This must be the Lord," Singleton told the young women. The pastor explained he'd read the *Scene* piece and done his own fact-finding on the case. "I believe one hundred percent these guys were innocent."

"Well, Pastor," Sierra ventured, "we believe one hundred fifty percent." The law students explained that they needed Ed to retract his testimony for Rickey to get a shot at release. The pastor explained that Ed wasn't ready now. He'd try to work on him. They'd wait and check back, the women said. Singleton neglected to tell them Ed was off-grid, no one knew where he was—not a lie, exactly. If OIP thought Ed wasn't going to surface again, Singleton worried they'd shrug and move on to the next case.

But the Lord, Singleton liked to say, comes through. A few days later, Singleton was back in his office at Emmanuel Christian. Once more, the office phone rang. It was the woman who had been engaged to Brother Ed on the line. "Guess who was just here?"

It was Ed. "I need you to do something for me," the pastor explained. "I need you to keep him around."

"Why?" the woman blurted back. "I don't like him like that anymore."

The pastor said she needed to keep Ed close anyway. It was important. "Just be his friend then."

Ed was in his kitchen futzing with a can of beans when his fingers went AWOL on him. The can. The opener. One moment he felt the weight, his hands in action. The next, nothing. The wiring between his mind and parts was cut. Then the light quit his eyes.

He woke up four days later strapped to a hospital bed. A stroke, triggered by sky-high blood pressure. This was in June 2012, and what followed was a medical mystery: the doctors couldn't herd his systolic and diastolic numbers to a safe level. Drugs, diet, therapy—the man's system remained dangerously unstable. For the next year he was in and out of the hospital for treatment.

His condition caused wild attacks of hypertension. His body would swell, the inflation starting in his feet and creeping up as pain pounded through him. Often, lying in a hospital bed, barely able to breathe due to the fluid buildup, it felt like each of his cells would explode. Ed wished for death. Lord, just take me home, he'd pray. I don't want to keep suffering like this. No relief came. He consoled himself by figuring God had other plans for him.

Pastor Singleton made regular visits whenever Ed was in treatment. He was convinced his friend's health was so bad, he might die before anyone got the opportunity to pull the truth from him. The preacher chose a Sunday in early 2013 to finally confront Ed. He brought Ed's old girlfriend along. He was still sweet on her. Maybe Ed would see the moment as a way to prove himself. Singleton couldn't promise Ed how this would all play out, if he might land in legal trouble or even jail. All he could do was appeal to his friend. When they arrived in Ed's room, the patient was in good spirits—giddy, even. Tomorrow he was being discharged. The preacher wasted little time. "I have something to talk to you about," Singleton said. "I've been praying about it and watching you." Singleton told Ed he'd read the *Scene* story. Knew about 1975. Ed's body went rigid. Behind his glasses, tension glazed his dark eyes. Ed's head started swinging from side to side, *no no no.* "I want to know if you're ready to talk about it," the pastor said. "I think you should tell the truth."

Ed was suddenly out of the bed. Arms wrapped around Singleton, the IV tubing nearly yanked out of the machines. A weeping face soaked his shoulder. Half-heard words tumbled out.

"Listen here, this is fitting to be over," the pastor told his sobbing friend. "I've been in touch with the Innocence Project, this girl named Sierra. They are ready for my phone call."

They met at the church. The pastor let them have the sanctuary to talk. It was a safe space, the same room where Ed's sealed-up anguish had sprung a leak during those shut-ins. A frostbitten April morning pressed in against the building. Behind the altar, tapestries with Bible verses hung from the baby-blue walls. Hebrews, chapter 11, verse 1: NOW FAITH IS THE SUBSTANCE OF THINGS HOPED FOR, THE EVIDENCE OF THINGS NOT SEEN.

The four sat by the altar—Carrie Wood, Sierra Merida, another OIP student, and Ed. The visitors from Cincinnati weren't sure what to expect. Ed might stick to his story, or force them to cat-and-mouse with him until he was cornered. He might get angry. He could scream. But when Ed opened his mouth, the man simply started talking in a voice that steadied the more he spoke.

One hour fell into the next. Then another. A question from the others occasionally interrupted Ed, but mostly he spoke. It was rare for Wood to take an actual written affidavit on a first meeting. But Ed was on such a roll, the attorney handed him a pen and legal pad.

"My name is Edward Vernon," he lettered at the top of the page. "I live in the city of Cleveland. My date of birth is 6.10.62. I testified in the trails of Rickey Jackson, Wiley Bridgeman, Ronnie Bridgeman. The testimony I gave was False. I am writing this to tell the truth about what happened that day."

Thoughts he'd never before wrapped into actual words popped into his head faster than his hand could put them down. His tight scrawl covered three pages. "I swear or affirm that the contents of this affidavit are true to the best of my knowledge," he inked in closing before the hurried dash of his signature.

Six hours after first walking through the door of Emmanuel Christian, Wood and her law students left the church gunning for a notary to sign off on the affidavit, certifying its legal value. And as far as Sierra Merida was concerned, Ed Vernon had stepped out of the villain role.

# 12

## WE CAN FIX THIS

*I THUMBED KWAME'S NUMBER INTO MY CELL PHONE, A SLIGHT BUCK OF* excitement forcing me to bungle the digits at first. When the line connected, I slipped into an empty office at the newsroom in Miami.

"Hey, Kyle," Kwame said, a little confusion edging into his voice, puzzled no doubt why I was reaching out from twelve hundred miles away. We hadn't spoken in six months.

It came tumbling out of me in a clumsy rush. Ed. The affidavit. The Ohio Innocence Project. Motion for new trial. The upshot cradled there in my babbling: Ed Vernon had recanted his 1975 testimony. He'd admitted he'd lied. Lawyers had just filed motions on behalf of Rickey for his release. It was finally happening.

"That's beautiful," Kwame said in his slow-rolling voice. "That's beautiful," he repeated. I plowed ahead, talking until I realized there was only dead air on the other end. "Kyle," a woman's soft voice came on. "This is Kwame's wife. He can't talk right now. He's . . . he's too emotional. He's crying now."

I'd known what was in the works for months before my call to Kwame. One afternoon in Miami in the fall of 2013 my cell phone pinged with a number from the Cincinnati area. I almost let it kick to voice mail—wasn't interested in anything coming from Ohio—but answered at the last moment. The caller, young but armed with a commanding old-man-river baritone, introduced himself as Brian Howe. He was an attorney with the Ohio Innocence Project.

It wasn't the first time I'd heard from OIP since moving to Florida. Usually, it was a student, asking for another copy of the police reports or the trial records. These were touch-and-go exchanges: I'd mail off the files again and hear nothing back. After leaving Cleveland, I was not hopeful OIP or anyone else could really help Kwame, Rickey, and Wiley. "Off the record," Howe told me about a minute into our call, "Ed has recanted."

Everything I knew and felt about the situation was suddenly rearranged. My thoughts jumped to Kwame, but Howe cut me off. "We don't want Kwame or Wiley or anyone else spooking Ed at this point." He asked me to wait to share the news until they actually filed the motion for Rickey's new trial on the basis of the recantation sometime next year, in spring 2014. He shared little else about the developing case.

Howe rarely let his poker face slip in our early conversations. Later I learned Ed had recanted his 1975 testimony in spring 2013, before Howe came on at OIP. Then in early thirties, he was polite and formal, a reserve that camouflaged a tenacious attorney who fought zealously for his clients. He was a true believer in the work, a dedication born out of his own time as an OIP intern while in law school. A philosophy undergraduate major, he was drawn to the law by the power it had to force an outcome outside the courtroom. As a law student working OIP cases, he had seen this up close: it was Howe who had gone to Mansfield Correctional to pick up the cigarette butts Clarence Elkins had surreptitiously grabbed to secure his release. After working a few years handling tenant issues with the Legal Aid Society after law school, Howe returned to OIP when Carrie Wood left for the Ohio Public Defender's Office. He later told me the *Scene* story was the first thing he'd read when he was handed Rickey's case. Like

Wood, he understood that Ed was the key to dismantling the convictions. If they could overturn Rickey's conviction, Wiley and Kwame's cases would follow.

Ed's affidavit both confirmed my conjectures and contained surprises. He drastically altered his account of May 19, 1975. Ed stated he actually had been on the school bus that day, not alone on the city bus, as he'd told the court. Along with the other children from the neighborhood, Ed heard the gunshots from the Cut-Rate robbery. "I couldn't see anything from the bus," the affidavit read. "When we got to the store, we saw the white man lying on the ground gasping for breath. This is the only thing I saw that day regarding the crime."

A lot of joking and talk was spinning among the neighborhood kids at the scene. When the police asked if anyone knew anything, Ed volunteered. "I think I just wanted to be helpful," he wrote in his affidavit. "You have to understand I was twelve years old at the time. I thought I was doing the right thing." By then it was too late: the police thought they had a witness.

The boy believed he could easily back out. His plan was to go into the lineup, not identify anyone, and then leave. But once he failed to pick Rickey and Wiley out at the police station, Ed's time with the police didn't end. "At that point, a detective took me into this other room," he wrote. "As far as I can remember, it was just the two of us in this room. He got really loud and angry and started yelling at me and calling me a liar. He was slamming his hands on the table, and pushing things around, calling me this and that. I was frightened and crying. You know it's a scary thing for someone that young." The affidavit continued: "The detective said that I was too young to go to jail, but he would arrest my parents for perjury because I was backing out. My mom was sick at that time, and that really scared me. I didn't want my parents to get in trouble over this.

"When I was crying, the detective said 'Don't worry about it, we can fix this.'"

According to Ed, the detective then concocted a statement for the boy implicating Rickey and Wiley—and later Ronnie—in the murder.

"I just kept meeting with police to go over my story," he wrote. "Some parts I just made up. . . . The more we would talk about it, the more details they would hand me. Like they would bring up acid in a cup or a description of a green car, and I would take that information and add it into the story."

In July 2014, Northeast Ohio's own LeBron James announced in *Sports Illustrated* that he was leaving the Miami Heat to play for the Cleveland Cavaliers again—the prodigal son boomeranging back home.

The move was a headscratcher for the sports establishment—*Cleveland instead of Miami?*—but it made sense on the Lake Erie shoreline. This was the pop culture crescendo of momentum you could feel all around town in 2014, the gears shifting on the narrative. A new vitality had rushed into the city for the first time in decades, as if Cleveland was sliding into a different era, leaving behind civic decline and starting a new postindustrial phase.

The evidence was both concrete and subtle. I picked up on something all the way down in South Florida. It seemed that every day I saw a Facebook post about another friend or expat Clevelander packing up in Brooklyn or Boston or Chicago and heading home, for budget rents and empty lofts and house parties and cheap beer and the burgeoning food scene. They were settling not in the suburban ring but in Tremont, Ohio City, the Detroit Shoreway, Gordon Square—back to the city proper. On my trips home, the new bars and restaurants filling once-barren street corners were choked with tattooed arms and beards and Day-Glo hair and other social markers of the gentrifying wave. Once I almost gagged on my beer when a bartender told me she'd moved from San Diego to Cleveland in the middle of a winter where the thermostat rarely made it above twenty degrees. At times, the enthusiasm felt to me like the focus-grouped pap of a chamber of commerce ad. But the energy was definitely there.

More noticeably, the physical face of Cleveland was also changing. For all my life, downtown had been rough-and-tumble, a business district by day, dicey ghost town after hours. Now development money was being shoveled into the core, an architectural nip-and-tuck that dramatically altered the setting. The East Bank of the Flats, the abandoned bottomland running along the Cuyahoga River, was the site of a new $750 million mixed-use development at the river's mouth. A $200 million project turned an empty Brutalist tower on East Ninth called the Ameritrust Building into a stack of fancy condos favored by pro athletes. Another $200 million was planned for a project between the baseball and basketball stadiums. Construction started on a new $271 million county-owned high-rise Hyatt to go with a new convention center. Monolithic nineteenth-century office buildings were being retrofitted into boutique hotels and retirement digs for empty-nesters. Even Public Square was gifted its own $32 million face-lift, a plan to magic-wand a homeless and drug pastureland into modern green space. The transformation pulled in the desired national gaze. *The New York Times* labeled Cleveland one of the "52 Places to Go in 2015."[1]

Yet as much as city power brokers liked the image of a Rust Belt city rehabbed for the twenty-first century, Cleveland was still haunted by the unresolved legacies of the last fifty years, realities that threatened to undercut any rosy forecast for the region's future. The signs were also in the headlines, below the cosmetic news of ribbon-cuttings. And Ed Vernon's new revelations also reached out from the dark spots of the city's history that investment capital and new breweries couldn't fix.

The year 2014 started with Citigroup, one of the largest sources of the subprime loans that decimated the city's housing stock, paying a seven-billion-dollar fine to the federal government; none of that money, however, landed in Cleveland, where the physical aftermath of the crisis still bombarded the eye.[2] Housing woes leaked into other aspects of city life. A study found that since 2010, Cleveland had lost around sixty-seven hundred residents. Cleveland public schools' enrollment had dropped by eight hundred students from the previous year; twenty-one million dollars was hacked from the district's budget. Citywide, the poverty rate remained at 36.9 percent, second nationally to Detroit. Cleveland also took second to Motor City for children living in poverty, at 54 percent.[3] The city's infrastructure continued to be an outdated and poorly maintained punch line—in March a city fire truck was swallowed whole by a pothole on the East Side.[4]

And yet no facet of city life seemed mired in the past more than the Cleveland Division of Police. The years leading up to 2014 were filled with discrediting episodes for local law enforcement. In 2012, six Cleveland officers set off on a high-speed chase involving an unarmed black couple, Timothy Russell and Malissa Williams, who refused to pull over for a traffic stop. The frantic debacle ended in the parking lot of an elementary school, where police unloaded a total of 137 rounds into the car, killing both passengers. One officer, Michael Brelo, climbed onto the hood of his cruiser, pouring rounds into the couple's car. Investigators later determined Brelo alone fired forty-nine shots.[5] The officer was criminally charged for the shooting. The incident arrived in the middle of a fresh barrage of coverage on the division's policies and practices. Much of the best work was done by two *Plain Dealer* reporters (and friends of mine), Henry J. Gomez and Gabriel Baird. Their reporting painstakingly wormed behind the blue wall, revealing systemic issues. The department's internal review process nearly always justified uses of force—both deadly and non-deadly—even when witnesses and evidence contradicted the accounts of the officers involved. The rubberstamping included incidents involving Tasers: between 2005 and 2011, division brass had cleared all but five of the 969 uses of the shock weapon. Citizen complaints were also regularly ignored or abandoned in administrative limbo.

For all the complaints about his leadership, Mayor Frank Jackson was sharp to the historic distrust polluting the relationship between black Clevelanders and their police. Law enforcement misconduct was also an unattractive stain on the image of a resurgent modern city. At the mayor's request, the Department of Justice's Civil Rights Division was invited to investigate. But Michael McGrath, the police chief presiding over all this institutional dysfunction, was not removed from office but promoted to safety director.

Nationally, the Innocence Movement was having a groundbreaking year. By the close of 2014, 125 men and women would be exonerated in twenty-seven states as well as Washington, D.C. The number, according to the National Registry of Exonerations, was a new annual record, representing a 37 percent increase over 2013, which saw ninety-one exonerations. Significantly, there was reason to believe the movement had finally established a stable beachhead within the legal system. Of the 125 exonerations, 104 were not DNA related, signaling courts might no longer be as hostile toward innocence cases missing a DNA component.[6]

Attorneys and experts tied the growing number of exonerations— DNA and non-DNA—to a shifting trend within the most powerful part of the criminal judicial system: the prosecutor's office.

Of the two parties wielding state power in the criminal justice process, the police and prosecutors, experts have argued that the latter have proven to be more resistant to change than the former. A police force today, this line of argument runs, is fundamentally very different from its predecessors fifty years back. Some of this is modernization and developing tactics. But modern law enforcement has also been shaped by outside pressure. Departments have been forced to adapt to complaints, scandals, lawsuits, and the intrusion of the federal courts, not to mention aggressive press coverage. Critics may blast departments for being slow or unwilling to fully embrace reform, but it's hard not to concede that the police officer asking for your license and registration today has been trained more thoroughly and is subject to more policies and paperwork than an officer fifty years ago (whether those policies are followed is a whole different issue).

This isn't the case with the government's arm inside a courtroom. Prosecutors' offices tend to be much more insular and, as such, inoculated against change or reform. In terms of day-to-day operation, today's prosecutor's office is much the same as it was fifty years ago—fed by local law schools; staffed by career attorneys; and susceptible to local political winds and power struggles. The major shift in the culture has been the increase in pressure following the War on Drugs—more cases, and more incentive to win at all cost or else risk political repercussions. And when it comes to a postconviction claim of innocence, prosecutors have traditionally been unwilling to concede that their own actions may have put the wrong person in prison.

But this may be slowly changing. Beginning in the 2000s, prosecutors in different corners of the nation began establishing what came to be known as conviction integrity units (CIUs). The essential idea, as formulated by early practitioners at the Dallas County District Attorney's Office in 2007, was to form a unit inside the prosecutor's office to examine postconviction claims of innocence—kick the tires, basically, on earlier convictions won by the office. Over the next seven years, the Dallas unit would quarterback twenty-five exonerations while becoming the national model for proactive government response to wrongful conviction. By 2014, fifteen units were up and running in the U.S. Together, between 2003 and 2014, the CIUs combined pushed ninety exonerations, including forty-nine in 2014 alone.[7] The increase was seen among members of the Innocence Movement as the tacit acknowledgment among prosecutors that not all convictions are perfect. And in 2014, Cleveland's Cuyahoga County was among the offices boasting a unit.

The CIU in Cleveland was the result of regime change. In 2012, Tim McGinty, a lifelong presence in the downtown courthouse, stepped down from his position as a common pleas judge to campaign for and win the office of Cuyahoga County prosecutor. The tenure of the previous county prosecutor, Bill Mason, had been tainted by his close association with a number of local Democratic party officials brought down by the county corruption scandal, and his office's failure to sniff out the corruption in the first place. McGinty was elected by promising an office soul-cleansing.

McGinty didn't come without his own heavy baggage, and he was by no means an outsider. Throughout the 1980s, he cut his teeth as an assistant county prosecutor under longtime head John Corrigan. McGinty had a reputation for being fierce in the courtroom, outworking every other attorney there and doing whatever it took to win. He was no silent grinder. Short and squat, McGinty was propelled by a flamboyant zeal. He had no problem punching at the status quo as both an attorney and judge. In trials McGinty slashed and burned, presenting defendants as morally repugnant and splashing their defense attorneys with similar scorn. Once, while facing off against Ronnie Bridgeman's former attorney Thomas Shaughnessy, the prosecutor told the judge the defense attorney stank of booze and should be given a sobriety test. Shaughnessy shot back that he'd take a sobriety test—if McGinty took an IQ test. While on the bench, McGinty blasted other judges for funneling cases to defense attorneys who funded their campaigns. He even sparked a feud with shock jock Howard Stern after a courtroom rant about the radio personality made it back to New York. Stern later called on-air for McGinty to lose his judicial reelection that year.[8]

The judge's bantam-cock combativeness earned him enemies—and official censure. As a prosecutor, McGinty was cited eight times for prosecutorial misconduct, mostly for using excessive and prejudicial language in court. A few of the black marks on his record went further, including withholding details of a sweetheart deal cut with a snitch in a murder case, and possibly failing to hand over exculpatory information that might have helped the case of a suspected child rapist. But McGinty's most critical courtroom error came in 1988. The case that landed on the then-prosecutor's desk was particularly gruesome. A female patient dying of cancer had been robbed and raped at the Cleveland Clinic. From a photo lineup, the victim identified a former hospital employee named Anthony Michael Green. No additional evidence—physical or otherwise—tethered the suspect to the crime. McGinty made the best with what he had, battering Green before the jury as "a fraud, a phony, and a liar." The defendant was found guilty and sentenced to ten to twenty-five years.

Green, however, maintained that he was not guilty, eventually contacting the Innocence Project in New York City about his case. In 2001, DNA testing led to his exoneration. McGinty had been wrong. "The worst thought ever is to think you put an innocent man in jail," McGinty told my old paper the *Cleveland Scene* in 2006.[9] "I feel so bad about that case."

McGinty, forced to confront errors within the system—"Mistakes can happen," he told *Cleveland Magazine* in December 2012.[10] "We've always got to look out for them"—established a CIU early in his tenure at the Cuyahoga County Prosecutor's Office. And although his intent appeared genuine, and his gesture was in line with the acceptance growing in similar offices around the country, there was still reason to be cautious. There is always reason to be cautious, experts will tell you. Although CIUs are popular, they can also be an empty gesture—ultimately ineffective window dressing. Of the fifteen CIUs open in 2014, only seven had produced exonerations. The other eight had yet to overturn convictions, including Cuyahoga County's unit.

It soon became clear Rickey Jackson's case was not going to be the local CIU's first case. After months of delays and extensions, the prosecutor's office filed a motion opposing the petition for postconviction relief in September 2014. "Vernon's claims are not credible," the filing stated. "His affidavit should not be accepted as true." The state argued that Ed had already identified Rickey and the Bridgemans as the assailants before he was allegedly threatened by police. "Nothing has been provided to demonstrate Vernon's affidavit sets forth sufficient *facts* to establish relief."

The challenge teed up an evidentiary hearing over the validity of Rickey's petition; OIP and the Cuyahoga County Prosecutor's Office would face off before a judge, battling over whether Ed Vernon was telling the truth. The date was set for November 17. I arranged with the editors at *Scene* and my bosses in Miami to be in town for the hearing. I'd write a follow-up piece for the Cleveland paper. There was no way I could miss it.

———————

Time was a slow-motion crawl in the months following the initial fil-ing. I felt out of the action down in Florida, and every week I was ring-ing up Ohio for more news about the case. Brian Howe and I spoke regularly, and although he was extremely careful every time we talked, picking his words with tweezers to make sure he didn't jeopardize the evidence he was hoping to present to a judge, I began to see the situa-tion was legally quite precarious.

Ed's words were not simply going to throw the cell doors open. Courts don't like witness recantations. Case law in Ohio and beyond instructs judges to treat a witness's reversal with the utmost suspicion. Why, the thinking runs, are you changing your story now? Is it because of guilt? You feel bad these people have been in prison so long? If you are saying you lied at trial, why should we believe you now? This atti-tude persists even with growing scientific evidence on the unreliabil-ity of eyewitness accounts. In Brandon L. Garrett's study of the first 250 DNA exonerations, 190 involved eyewitnesses.[11] In six of those cases, witnesses later came forward to recant, but judges in none of the six reversed the original conviction on the basis of the new testimony. A recantation on its own is not enough.

So Howe and the other attorneys at OIP had to couch Ed's new version of events in a legal argument. When they filed Rickey's case in March 2014, the document submitted to the court was a petition for postconviction relief. In Ohio, this legal channel is only open for up to 180 days after the conviction, unless new evidence turns up that wasn't available at trial. Ed's recantation was this new evidence, the corner-stone of the new petition. The legal strength of the petition did not just lie with the witness's new account, but what the witness said in the new account: Ed now claimed he was pressured and threatened by police to testify against Rickey, Wiley, and Ronnie. Howe wrote his petition arguing that the police coercion was exculpatory evidence that should have been handed over to the defense at trial; even if prosecutors didn't know the police had pressured the witness, the information should still have been disclosed. It wasn't, however, meaning Rickey's constitutional rights had been violated. This was the thrust of OIP's argument.

When allegations of official misconduct land in a courtroom, judges tend to sit up, numerous attorneys would later explain to me. Again, this is more of a recent sea change in the legal world than traditional practice. A 2012 study by the National Registry of Exonerations found allegations of police and prosecutorial misconduct in 42 percent of nearly nine hundred exonerations studied, and in 56 percent of homicide cases.[12] But the same report noted these numbers are likely low; unless journalists or attorneys later uncover misconduct, it likely goes unnoticed. But the prospect of civil litigation is exactly why judges are more apt today to pay attention: if the allegations are borne out and an exoneration results, a lawsuit on behalf of the exoneree is likely on deck. Whether that suit ends in a settlement or civil judgment, the city—or its insurer—will foot the bill. And nothing is more political in twenty-first-century urban life than court judgments that reach into a city's coffers.

From my conversations with Howe, I also picked up the feeling that OIP was still digging for as much information as possible to buttress Ed's claims. The city hadn't responded—or even acknowledged—OIP's public records request for the homicide files on the case, Howe told me. The copies they were working from were the ones I'd given them. The attorneys were also still sending groups of students up to Cleveland on the weekends, hoping to locate new witnesses or information.

On my own, from Florida, I began scouting around for more information on the police officers involved in the case. Per the contract with the police union, the city scraps all disciplinary reports tied to officers a few years after they've left the department. But the city still maintained the full personnel files, and through public records requests and newspaper clips I was able to pull together some picture of the men involved. Overall, these were former military men, guys who'd seen real action in World War II and Korea. The job of policing Cleveland's streets was both violent and underpaid. Nearly all of the files I examined included requests for secondary employment. Each file also contained numerous instances of officers using their service weapons on the job.

The main detective working the Franks murder was Eugene Terpay. His name was inked on the majority of the police file reports; he testified in each trial, carrying the weight of the police case in the courtroom. He was on the Cleveland police force from 1949 to 1977, when he left to take a job as a lieutenant with the Cuyahoga County Sheriff's Office. A former corporal in the U.S. Army, Terpay spent the majority of his career in the detective bureau, and his time in the city wasn't dull. His file and old newspaper reports contained at least three instances of gunfire between Terpay and suspects. In 1957 he stopped a fleeing fifteen-year-old black suspect by putting a bullet through his heel; in 1964, the detective unloaded five bullets into a luncheonette robber. This was only a few months after stopping a car of teenage car thieves by shooting the driver in the arm. Department higher-ups cleared all the shootings. In his later career with the sheriff's office, Terpay was the point man on a couple of high-profile murder cases, landing his picture in the newspaper. In these photos from the late 1970s he was a solid-looking man in late middle age, stray hairs lying across a bald head, gravity and age pulling his face into a bulldog grimace.

The detective's file was mostly routine paperwork, but there were signs pointing to possible misconduct. In 1971, Terpay was personally named along with the department, East Cleveland Police, the county sheriff, and the Ohio Penitentiary's warden in a federal lawsuit snapped out on a prison typewriter by an inmate named Marion H. Williams. The personnel file not only contained a copy of the complaint, but a memo from the officer to the legal department asking for representation. The rambling lawsuit documented the abuse Williams claimed he had suffered since going down on an apartment robbery in 1967; the complaint mainly focused on abuses within the prison. But Williams also claimed "One Cleveland Detective Eugene Trepay [sic] made false statements at Plaintiffs [sic] trial" and "also this Detective was the sole reason why Plaintiff was indicted." Whatever happened with the lawsuit—or to Marion H. Williams—wasn't clear.

The file contained another surprise: a letter dated November 25, 1975, from the desk of Stanley E. Tolliver. One of the first well-known black attorneys in town, Tolliver was a civil rights and political activist. Later he served as the president of Cleveland's school board. But here he was writing directly to the chief of police about a client, George Clayton, a young black man involved in the murder of a suburban police officer. Clayton was the subject of a heated citywide manhunt, and the suspect eventually turned himself in alongside his attorney. "I advised the Police that no statements, were to be asked of the defendant, unless I was present," Tolliver wrote in his letter, explaining what he had told officers at the handoff. "I was later called on the same day by Detective Gene Terpay," Tolliver wrote. The detective told the attorney "'Clayton, had changed his mind,' and was willing to give a written statement, but only would sign it with" Tolliver present. "On consultation with Clayton, I learned that he had not 'changed his mind', but was beaten by the Police, one of which was Terpay," the attorney wrote. Tolliver demanded an investigation into the beatings. No evidence was turned up.

There was one more surprise link between Terpay and the Bridgeman-Jackson case. Months later I was rifling through the archives of the *Call and Post*. An article in a December 1975 issue discussed the trials; the piece noted an "irregularity": "[a] juror in Wiley Bridgeman's trial, during the questioning of jurors, admitted to being the niece of Detective Terpay." Nobody blew the whistle on the conflict, or thought to note it in the official court record.

"In the joint it's a little harder than playing out there," Kwame told me, a big smile sitting easy on his face. "They trying to really hurt you. The guys got their arms taped up with batteries."

"Batteries?" I asked. "Like you'd put in a flashlight or something?"

"Up to here," Kwame said, running a finger from wrist to elbow, his eyes glowing with the jailhouse memories. We were talking football, or at least what passed for pigskin action inside prison, where all the inmates' anger and resentment was channeled into the yard games, with blockers kitted out with extra armor.

It was spring, about six weeks after the postconviction relief filing on Rickey's behalf. I was in Cleveland for a wedding, and I made sure to see Kwame. We were sitting at the same Starbucks where we had first met. The man on the other side of the table hadn't changed much in the last three years—only a little more dirty snow in his beard, a few pounds slimmer. When I was writing my article two years earlier, I had been so focused on discrediting Ed's testimony, I'd spent little time looking at the other possible suspects. But Rickey's new filing triggered the logical follow-up: if Rickey, Kwame, and Wiley were innocent, then who actually killed Franks? My attention swung to Paul Gardenhire.

This was a sloping curveball Kwame didn't see coming. Paul was a year younger than Kwame and had grown up with the Bridgemans; their family trees tangled together at some distant point. Kwame told me Paul was wired bad from the beginning, starting his criminal career off before he was even old enough to drive. Kwame recalled hearing about Paul breaking into houses and businesses as a baby-faced preteen. It was a short path from there to stickups and murder—which is exactly how the two reconnected in 1978, when Paul went down on a robbery-murder and ended up in Lucasville with Kwame. The two neighborhood friends stayed close inside. Kwame explained to me that even though Paul was younger, he took an almost paternal interest in Kwame, making sure he had money in his pocket and stayed clear of trouble. But Kwame never knew that at the time of the murder Paul's mother had turned police onto her son for the Cut-Rate robbery, or that police fielded another tip connecting Paul with a two-toned green car like the one seen at the scene. It wasn't until OIP filed Rickey's motion, tagging pages of the police reports to the paperwork as exhibits, that Kwame had the opportunity to read the documents and see Paul's name down as a suspect. "And Paul's mother sat in the court-room every day of my trial," Kwame told me.

The new information scrambled all those feelings. He was clearly trying to fit the image of his friend with the man possibly responsible for derailing his life. And what of Paul's friendship and support in-side? It all could have been driven by the deep guilt of seeing his child-hood friends go down for a murder Paul himself committed or was involved with.

"So you really think he did it?" I asked.

"I've mulled that over," Kwame said, explaining he and Rickey had recently talked it through on the phone. "We went back and forth. I think Paul knows someone who had something to do with it. I really do. And I say that because of how forceful he has been over the years saying, 'I know you had nothing to do with it. I know you had noth-ing to do with it.'"

But Kwame never knew Paul had any possible connection to his own case while they were incarcerated together. "If I had known it then," Kwame said, the smile back on his face, "I probably would have beat his ass."

Kwame was actually still in touch with Paul. He was back in prison after another murder charge. They had just recently spoken, Kwame said. Paul called him up asking if he knew a lawyer named Brian Howe. Paul had received a letter from the OIP attorney asking if he knew any-thing about the Franks case. "I told him, 'If you have anything to tell him, you should tell him,'" Kwame told me. *"Anything."*

But Paul wasn't the only name from the police file jumping out at Kwame. Two brothers, Skip and Railroad King, had been identified by the FBI as the possible robbers. Kwame remembered them from the neighborhood. "Them cats was real maggots, man," Kwame recalled. "You ain't supposed to say anything about the dead, but them guys, they were the type of guys, they had a reputation in the city that if they got somebody to go with them on a caper, they would rob *them* after the caper."

That street rep seemed to have caught up with both King brothers.

In November 1979 Railroad King's body was discovered in some bushes on Kennedy Avenue. Four years later, Skip King was driving a car down Beulah Avenue when a passenger shot and killed him.

In August, with both sides prepping for the showdown in November, Rickey's lawyers visited him in Grafton and threw down a hypothetical: What if Rickey could leave prison right now, no problem? the OIP team told him. All he had to do was sign some papers absolving the state of future legal and financial liability. The word "free" set Rickey's head and heart stampeding. But after a moment, he saw it was a no-go. "I knew there was no way in hell I could seriously contemplate any deal that did not include my (our) complete exoneration in the death of Mr. Franks," Rickey wrote to me in a letter a few weeks later, recounting the offer. "I'm an innocent man, Kyle, and my stance on that isn't open for negotiation. Not now, not ever. The way I look at it, man, I don't have too much more to lose and I'm pretty much bottomed out as it is. There isn't a whole lot more they can do to me. I know I don't want to die with Mr. Franks' blood on my hands. That's not how I want to be remembered."

Rickey's resolve to push his innocence didn't seem to spring just from stubbornness or a desire for a civil suit payday down the line. All he had was his innocence. Giving up was giving in, a way of debasing what had been stolen. "Honestly, though, I doubt this will ever be over entirely," he wrote. "How do you shake off something that has been a part of your life for so long? As much as I might long for some semblance of a 'Normal life,' there are certain realities that I have experienced throughout this whole ordeal that have so profoundly changed the way I look at everything and everybody. I simply have to accept the fact that I will never be happy or completely whole again. They broke something inside of me, Kyle."

———

They came to get him in November, piling Rickey and eleven other Grafton inmates into a Department of Rehabilitation and Corrections van meant to seat eight. Rickey didn't care about the tight squeeze. Two feelings were bumper-to-bumper in his head. The first: he'd be back to Grafton. Brian Howe and everyone else at OIP had made that clear, kept the temperature realistically low on his expectations. This was just a court date to see if he'd get another court date, as Rickey understood it. Grafton would see him soon enough.

But Rickey was also consumed by excitement. The prison van rolled up onto the highway heading north for Cleveland. It was thrilling. Even the smell, country air stained with the van's exhaust, had him almost giddy. Rickey was pinched against the window, his shackled hands together. Through the tiny mesh wiring covering the glass, he watched farmland bunch up into neighborhoods, houses and strip malls veined with trees spangled with fall's gold and brown and red. It was the first time in thirty-nine years he'd been out on the open road heading for Cleveland. Man, he thought. I don't want to go back the other way.

When the van arrived in the city, Rickey couldn't make out anything familiar, just these tall strange buildings bouncing sunlight between their glass windows and brick. None of this shit was up, he thought. Then his eye hit Terminal Tower, fifty-two stories tall, something his thoughts could grab hold of as a landmark. He was in Cleveland, for sure, and it felt, strangely enough, great to be back in the city after so long.

# 13

## 39 YEARS, 3 MONTHS, 6 DAYS

*HE CLEARLY DIDN'T WANT TO BE THERE. HIS STEPS STOPPED SHORT AT* the door, where for a moment he nervously swung his gaze around the courtroom on the thirteenth floor of the Justice Center. When Ed Vernon's feet finally inched forward, they moved in a reluctant shuffle, as if he was being reeled in on the end of an invisible rope. Each step seemed a battle, like he might turn and bolt for the elevator.

Every eye turned. The hard church pews in the gallery were filled with a dozen twenty-something law students. County bailiffs leaned against the wood-paneled walls. In the middle of the courtroom, two large conference tables had been placed together, an arrangement that looked more appropriate for corporate negotiations than legal jousts. The attorneys looked up from their encyclopedia-wide binders, each filled with court transcripts and police reports snapped out on typewriters well before most of the people in the room could drink alcohol or vote or even walk. Ed crossed the room and settled into the witness stand.

He appeared squeezed dry, whittled down at fifty-three and shivering inside a large winter coat. His eyes, distorted behind thick glasses, moved all around the courtroom—everywhere but the attorney's table, where a seated figure fixed him with a laser stare. It had been nearly four decades since Ed had last seen Rickey Jackson. The circumstances had been almost identical. But the skinny teen Ed once knew was gone. Instead, here was a fifty-seven-year-old man, his frame under the orange jumper still cut slim from hours in the prison yard, features pinched into a no-tell poker face, manacled hands calmly before him like a principal ready to hear excuses from a wayward pupil.

Behind that stare, even as Ed Vernon settled into the witness stand, Rickey was still waiting for Ed Vernon to appear. The scrawny paperboy—that was the image locked into his brain; the witness had his right hand up and was already parroting back the oath when Rickey realized this twisted little man was actually the boy he'd been waiting to see for thirty-nine years, three months, and six days.

From my seat in the gallery, I was surfing one surreal jolt of recognition after another. This case had existed so long for me on paper. In the reported details of these men's lives. Childhood addresses. The memories of family members. Prison records. Even the tilt of their handwriting. But this was the first time I'd laid eyes on either one, and somehow both made the jump from my notebooks to real life with little alteration. Rickey—sullen and serious; Ed—spooked and squirrelly. And stacked between them were four decades of emotions now being aired in a courtroom.

The months of waiting had loaded this moment with the pregnant anticipation of a championship heavyweight bout. Ed was here to convince the court he lied in 1975 when his testimony sent Rickey, Kwame, and Wiley to prison. Judge Richard McMonagle presided over the hearing, the man who needed to be convinced. With thirty-six years on the bench, the Republican had the distinction of the longest judicial tenure in county history. A schoolboy part down the middle of his hair offered no softening touch when paired with the flat, expressionless face, a screen of judicial circumspection that was a genetic inheritance as much as a part of the job. McMonagle's father had been a Cuyahoga County judge for thirty years. His brother and cousin also served on the bench. Soon, McMonagle's son would campaign for his own seat. And whatever decision McMonagle made on Rickey's motion would likely be one of the last of his legal career. He was retiring at the end of the year.

We were at a point in the judicial process where the legal system was going to look at itself in the mirror. But the typical language of the courtroom didn't seem adequate. The legal system's machinery is all about scaling down human drama, shrink-wrapping pain and violence and conflict into names on a docket and case law references. In this courtroom what was being fought over seemed grander, and freighted with more weight than brittle legalese and procedure could fully express. The confrontation here seemed to spill out of the courtroom, breaching the walls of the Justice Center, into the city beyond. From my seat, I saw this as a showdown between Cleveland's past and present, the current shiny rebranded metropolitan image called to the mat by the legacy of racial disparity, police violence, and injustice.

In a very typical Cleveland way, the hearing was almost scratched before it started.

On Sunday night thick white flakes began dropping from the sky. By Monday morning the city was wrapped in a whiteout blizzard. The big windows in the thirteenth-floor hallway of the Justice Center normally peered out on an eastern stretch of the city kissing the lakeshore—city hall, the convention center, the erector-set skeletons of new construction. But on the morning of November 17, the view was swallowed by the surprise lake-effect storm. Snow fled past the windows like sand rushing through an hourglass. I stood watching, realizing the ice-snagged roadways might keep people from attending the hearing, especially anyone looking for a good excuse to stay away.

I arrived early. I had slept badly the night before in a friend's spare bedroom, so I was floating on an edgy rush of caffeine and nerves. The first people to join me in the room were law students only a few years younger than myself. They soon were joined by more, and quickly the entire side of the gallery behind the defense table was filled with two dozen OIP interns. Brian Howe—average sized, with dark hair and a neatly trimmed beard running along his jaw from ear to ear—soon appeared, taking his place at the attorney's table. I introduced myself. We chatted briefly—he had other stuff on his mind, obviously. "Just so you know," Howe told me before I left him, "it's not admissible in court, but Ed did pass a polygraph test."

More spectators also arrived, more than the usual courtroom business attracted. There were law professors and other courtroom watchers in attendance. Reporters from the local news stations and the *Plain Dealer*. Terry Gilbert came with his law partner Jacqueline Greene. The attorneys were still representing Kwame and Wiley, and a few months after Rickey's motion hit the court, Gilbert had submitted a similar request on behalf of the Bridgemans. Those motions would also live or die by the outcome of today's hearing. As we chatted before the session started, a few attorneys from the prosecutor's office brushed past us heading for the courtroom. Spying Gilbert, one of the lawyers turned to her colleague. "The vultures have already showed up," she said, loud enough to be heard. "Can you believe that?" Gilbert grumbled to me.

I grabbed a seat on the right-hand side of the gallery, close enough to hear and for my digital recorder to cleanly gobble up the voices from the witness stand. Before the start, I made a trip to the restroom, and as I returned to the hallway I spotted a small man at the windows staring at the moving curtains of snow. Without ever having seen him before, I knew it was Ed Vernon. Alone at the glass, he appeared to be locking eyes with something terrible out there, and for the first time I wondered if this man had the internal fortitude left to do what would be asked of him here. He was joined at the window by a thin man in a flashy pin-striped suit with matching tie and pocket square—Pastor Singleton. Together they bent their heads over a Bible.

Karen Smith was the opener, a warm-up for the testimony everyone was waiting anxiously to hear. Now middle-aged and flashing a pacific, easy smile, she patiently answered Brian Howe's questions, as he steered her through May 19, 1975, when she had walked into the Robinsons' store.

"Were either of the men that you saw as you approached the store Rickey Jackson?" Howe asked.

"No."

"Were either of them Ronnie Bridgeman?"

"No."

"Were either of them Wiley Bridgeman?"

"No."

What happened after Smith entered the store and the white money order salesmen left? he asked.

"Probably within a few seconds we heard what I thought was like firecrackers, and we all turned to the door," the witness said. "And when we turned to the door you could see him, he was kind of, his profile was in the window, and you could see that they had thrown something, something was thrown and he was pressed against the glass. And I believe Mrs. Robinson at that time, as she started going to the door she said, 'Oh, my God, they are shooting.' And when she said that, I immediately felt the need to hide, run. It was a very small store. So I went to, like, the storeroom and just waited, just stood there."

Smith also recounted her own day at the police station. She too was shown a lineup, and the girl recognized Rickey and Wiley from the neighborhood. But she told the police she did not see the same men she had brushed by before the murder.

"What was their response to that?" Howe asked.

"They just started talking to me about the importance of me telling the truth and asked me how would I feel if I didn't identify the people who had done this. I think they asked me questions about my mom, and it came out that my mom caught the bus and how would I feel if she was robbed and had been murdered or attacked by somebody and someone not identifying or telling the truth about them."

"So what was your response to that?"

"My response was while it would be horrible that that happened to my mom," Smith answered calmly, "that she would not want me to lie."

Howe also asked about how the detectives treated the teenager after she failed to identify the suspects.

"I felt like they had little regard for me," she replied. "I felt like I clearly wasn't a favorite or preferred person. At that time Ed Vernon was also there, and I really don't remember what his conversation was but I remember them offering him something to drink and something from the snack machine, and I was not offered that. So I felt that there was preferential treatment towards him and not me."

Ed's turn came after the lunch break. The man on the witness stand appeared small, reduced, in part because he was layered in a heavy over-coat and neat argyle sweater. Big deep sighs escaped his chest like steam out of a radiator. He had a habit of cocking his head to the side when asked a question, eyelids down to slits behind his glasses, suspiciously rolling whatever was said around in his mind, looking for the trap. And the traps would come. But first, Brian Howe began his examination of the witness by asking Ed to recount his day on May 19, 1975. Slowly, the witness told the court he'd been at school until regular classes let out. He then boarded the school bus with the rest of the neighborhood children. As the bus neared Ed's stop on Cedar Avenue, he and the other riders heard gunshots as the vehicle crossed Stokes Boulevard.

"So you hear the shots," Howe reiterated. "What are the other schoolchildren doing at this point, do you remember?"

"Everybody was looking," the witness answered calmly. "Everybody heard it and we stopped talking and looked."

"Did you personally look out the bus at that time?"

"Yes, I did."

"What did you see?"

"Nothing."

Howe moved to highlight the importance of the point here. "Were you ever on the city bus at all that day?"

"No."

"From the bus did you see the victim in this case, Mr. Franks, being beaten?"

"No."

"Did you ever see him get shot?"

"No."

At the defense table, Rickey's manacled hands were pressed palm to palm, his fingers aimed at the ceiling as if in prayer, eyes shuttered, nodding thankfully as the questioning continued. Ed recounted getting off the bus with the rest of the kids. The group then ran up to the store to see what the commotion was about.

"Had you ever seen a dead body before?" Howe asked.

"No."

"What were you feeling?"

"I don't know," Ed said, his head hanging low. "Just scared, because I had never seen anything like that before."

"Did you see anyone running away from the scene?"

"No."

"As you approached the store did you see anyone with a pipe or a stick?"

"No."

"Did you see anyone take anything off of the body that was lying on the ground?"

"No."

"Did you see any green car?"

"No."

But as Ed and the other children walked back home, one of the boys—Tommy Hall, according to Ed—mentioned he knew who probably did it: Bitsy, Buddy, and Rickey. So when Ed returned to the crime scene about an hour later, he volunteered when the police asked if anyone had information. He was just doing what he thought was right, the witness emphasized. He was only trying to help. Ed explained that his family knew he was telling tall tales and it had gotten him in trouble before.

"My mother knew me. She knew I was lying," Ed told the court.

"She told me when I go down to the lineup, all I had to do was not pick out anyone, and they'll let them go."

And that's what he did, Ed explained, when Cleveland PD detectives asked him to point out the assailants who had robbed the store. He recognized the faces from the neighborhood, the faces that went with the names he'd mentioned to police. But he didn't make the identifications. The detectives then took the twelve-year-old into a back room. "They were pretty mad, the detectives," Ed said from the stand before falling into a long pause. When he lifted his head again, his face was wet. "At that point, they began calling me names. They began to push stuff around." His fist smacked down on the witness box's railing. "Beating on the table, the detective said, 'You lied! You know that's perjury! Your mother and father can go to jail.' So I began to cry.

"I'm just sitting there, crying," Ed repeated, his voice shaved down to a dry whisper. The courtroom was quiet. "He said, 'We'll fix it. We'll fix it.' After that, the police took a statement from me saying I was scared and that's why I didn't pick them out of the lineup. But I wasn't scared. I didn't pick them out because I knew they didn't do it."

"Did you ever tell the prosecutors about threats?" Howe asked. "About the actions of the detective when you were in the room after the lineup?"

"No," Ed said. He then tumbled strangely into the present tense, as if speaking of the events was enough to place him back inside those frightening moments. "I am twelve years old. I don't know nothing about going to a prosecutor and talking to them about anything."

"Did you ever tell any of the defense attorneys?"

"No. I didn't tell anybody."

"Why not?"

"How would I know how to go and approach somebody about something that I don't even understand myself? I am twelve."

Ed told the court that before the trials prosecutors had given him copies of his previous testimony. He was told to study the statements so his story remained consistent.

"Were you worried about saying different things at different trials?" Howe asked.

"I am just all confused anyway, so it didn't matter because when they gave me those transcripts to go over I didn't remember all that stuff," he said. "Every time I went to a different trial it was quite a difference." The witness fell silent again. "I can remember just the emotional stress and the pressure that they put on me," Ed replied. "I just couldn't . . . I couldn't take it."

"Did you ever actually see Rickey Jackson involved in the shooting that day?"

"No." The tears were choking his voice now. "I didn't. No."

"Did you ever see Ronnie Bridgeman involved at all that day?"

"No."

"Did you ever see Wiley Bridgeman involved in the crime that day?"

"No," Ed said, his head swinging from side to side.

"Did you ever see any of the three of them at the scene?"

"No."

"Did you ever see a green getaway car?"

"No."

"How did you feel about testifying to something that you knew was not true?"

"I felt really bad, guilty about what I was lying about," he said, the words pushing through his sobs. "I was carrying all of that."

"Are you scared today?"

"No."

"How do you feel seeing him?" Howe asked, waving his arm at his client.

Ed tilted his head. He thought. "I feel . . . I feel really good about seeing him. I feel really good about seeing him."


"Where," Assistant Prosecutor Mary McGrath started off her cross-examination of Ed, condescension dripping off her words, "do we begin?"

The snow had let up by early afternoon; fresh white layered the city's nooks and crannies outside the thirteenth-floor windows. Veteran prosecutor McGrath, a small woman with short brown hair, flicked her bespectacled eyes between the witness and the notes and binders she'd brought to the podium. The strategy behind her cross-examination was clear with the first few questions. McGrath would use Ed's previous testimony to hammer apart his new account.

McGrath began by asking the witness to read from the 1975 court transcripts; she directed Ed to Charles Loper's statements about seeing the boy walking toward the store right before bullets started flying. "So to sum it up, Mr. Vernon," the prosecutor said. "Mr. Loper, who lives attached to the store, testified in 1975 that he saw you get off at the bus stop that is on Fairhill near the store. Why would he make that up?"

Ed seemed to sense the question was coming. "I don't know," he shrugged. "At that time, Mr. Loper was a chronic drinker. He was an alcoholic. So I don't know."

"But he testified that he saw you get off at the bus stop and walk toward the house and you greeted each other?"

"No," Ed said, throwing steel behind the word.

"That's a lie?"

"That's a lie."

McGrath's next series of moves were subtle, and sent me scribbling furiously into my legal pad. The attorney pointed out that on the day of the murder, detectives already had a breakdown of how the crime was committed—how many assailants there had been; how the victim had been beaten, shot, and splashed with a liquid. The police hadn't yet interviewed Anna Robinson, she was still in surgery. So where did police get those details? Ed had to be the source, she argued. "Who knew this information, other than you and Mrs. Robinson, to give the police this information?"

This was bullshit, I knew. In the gallery, I began furiously scratching names into my notebook—Karen Smith, the florist across the street, the motorist who was driving nearby as the robbery happened. They were all interviewed by police on the day of the crime—that's where the details came from. Not Ed. Obviously McGrath knew this. But she was trying to shake the witness, and it was starting to work.

"No," he said, his voice diving into an exasperated whine. "No. I would have never knew anything if I am on the bus with all the rest of the kids. How would I know to give that information?"

"Because you were there," McGrath shot back.

"No, I was not there."

"You saw liquid thrown in his face?"

"You can smile and laugh at me all yo—" Ed snapped.

McGrath cut him off. "No. I am not laughing at all."

"I wasn't there."

The attorney skillfully laid another set of rhetorical booby traps for Ed as she walked him through the lineup again. The witness and attorney tussled over whether he lied to police in his lineup. "Did you recognize Rickey and Ronnie?" she asked.

"I didn't identify them."

"That's not what I asked you."

"I didn't identify them," Ed shouted in a frustrated wheeze.

"Did you recognize them as someone you know?"

"I didn't identify them."

"You knew them? Can we agree to that much? You knew them?"

"They asked me did I see anybody in the lineup that I know, and I said no."

"But that wasn't true," the attorney said. "They asked you if you saw anyone in the lineup that you knew, and you knew these guys from the neighborhood."

Ed broke. "You sound just like these prosecutors and these detectives did back then. You are trying to trip me up with questions, you know, and get me to say things that are not true.

"I am saying it was a lineup," he continued, exasperated. "I was supposed to identify the person that was involved in the crime. Okay? I am not stupid, okay? I understand you are supposed to ask me questions, but I am tired of you trying to make me look like I am stupid,

I am senile, I am crazy, you know. To *know* somebody and to *identify* somebody is two different things."

McGrath pivoted to another tactic; she accused Ed of conveniently waiting for all the detectives involved to die off before coming forward with his new story.

"No!" he barked. "I didn't even know none of these people were dead. It wasn't like I kept tabs on people. Man, who sits around and thinks about stuff like that? Only thing I thought about was telling the truth.

"You don't know how much pain and suffering I have been going through throughout these years. You and nobody else knows. You can ask a thousand questions and it is still not going to free me from the pain and the hurt and the lies that I had to live."

Ed continued, "I don't trust nobody to this day. I don't trust in relationships. This thing has been emotional, it has severed ties in my relationships with my kids' mothers, with my family, with people. I don't trust people because I don't trust, I don't believe them. I don't believe them. I don't believe them."

The hearing was called for the day. McMonagle ordered the testimony to continue Tuesday. I passed another night in Cleveland, using happy-hour drinks to calm my nerves, anxious thoughts running over Ed's testimony, concerns over whether the prosecutor had roughed up his credibility in the eyes of the judge.

The next morning I was at court, red-eyed and twitchy, at 8:30 A.M. sharp, for round two. McGrath was back on the offensive. Ed Vernon slumped in the witness chair. "You testified that the police were feeding you this information. So does that mean that they were saying, 'Ed, here is what happened, I would like you to state that back to me and I will write it down in the report'?"

"What they did was, after I told them that I was a witness, that I saw who did it, they begin to give me information, and they were typing stuff up."

"Can you give us an example of how they would give you information, Ed?"

"They asked me, 'When you saw what happened, did you see who it was? Did you see somebody standing out in front of the store? Was it two males standing out in front of the store?' This is the kind of stuff that they were giving me."

"So they were asking you leading questions?" the attorney asked. "With information contained in the questions?"

"Yes."

The state's case wrapped with one more piece of evidence, a would-be courtroom stunner that flopped in a spectacular, sickening fashion. It would have been funny, if it weren't so infuriating. In her cross-examination of Ed, McGrath introduced a sworn affidavit written by a retired Cleveland police sergeant now living in Arizona, Joseph Paskvan. In the document, the officer claimed to be one of the uniformed cops at the Cut-Rate after the murder asking the crowd for information. Paskvan said Ed approached him and his partner and named Rickey Jackson, Ronnie Bridgeman, and Wiley Bridgeman as the assailants.

Hearing this in the gallery, I started squirming in my seat again. The sequence laid out in the police documents, at the trials, and as well in Ed's new testimony seemed to clearly establish the boy never told the uniformed officers the names of the assailants at the scene. He only said he *had* information, not *what* the information was. All the other accounts agreed on this. All these accounts also were in accord on how Ed didn't know the full names of the Bridgeman brothers. He only knew their nicknames. Yet here was a retired Cleveland police officer claiming, under oath in a written affidavit, that Ed had approached the uniformed officers on the day of the crime with all three full names. In the best light, Paskvan's memory was faulty; put a more critical spin on the situation, and you see an officer possibly lying in court to bolster a prosecution.

Later, I looked Paskvan up. Between 1973 and 1985, he was involved in nine shootings, three of them fatal. All the victims in these shootings were minorities.[1] In the final shooting in 1985, Paskvan killed a twenty-three-year-old Hispanic man because he believed the deceased was waving a rifle. It turned out to be a BB gun. As with the eight previous shootings, Paskvan was cleared of any wrongdoing, but the officer became a headache for the department. More than nine thousand Clevelanders signed a petition asking for his termination; city council members began calling Paskvan the "exterminator" due to his track record; and the officer's own police chief later referred to Paskvan as a "menace" and fought to keep the officer stranded on desk duty.[2] And here he was in 2014, sticking up for the department, right or wrong.

Pointing out the gaping holes in Paskvan's affidavit was Brian Howe's first order of business when he stepped back to the podium. Howe then worked through the other points McGrath had tried to wrench from the witness, carefully patching up the damage while emphasizing the central point.

"Did you see Rickey Jackson shoot anyone at all on that day?" he asked Ed.

"No."

"Did you see Ronnie Bridgeman shoot anyone that day?"

"No."

"Did you see anyone beat Mr. Franks?"

"No."

"Did you see anyone steal his briefcase?"

"No."

"Did you see anyone throw a cup in his face?"

"No."

"Did you see anyone escaping in a green car?"

"No."

"No further questions," Howe said.

By the end of his testimony, Ed could barely keep his head up. "Oh, Jesus," he moaned. "I am tired."

After Ed's testimony, I shot out of my seat. Ed was in the hallway, slowly drifting toward the elevators. I caught up with him and introduced myself, putting my hand out before he had an opportunity to fully string together who I was. Whatever apprehension he may have had about speaking with me was buried under weariness from his grueling two-day appearance in court.

"Honestly, I just wanted to say thank you for doing this," I said.

Ed's eyes ducked mine, hanging on the hallway carpet. "I just want them to be free."

The state called Tommy Hall next. Now fifty-three and bulky in a tracksuit, Ed Vernon's former neighborhood friend clearly had little patience for being in a courtroom. He'd only turned up after being subpoenaed.

The witness had apparently been called by the state to shoot down another of Ed's assertions: that Hall himself had told Ed on the day of the crime it was Rickey, Buddy, and Bitsy behind the robbery. Hall claimed in the courtroom he'd said no such thing. "Why would I say that?" he testified. "I didn't see nothing."

But Hall also rolled a grenade into the state's case as well. Diving back into his recollections of the day of the murder, Hall told the court he was on the bus and heard the shots but didn't see the crime. After being let off the bus, he and the rest of the neighborhood kids made for the store. Among the kids on the bus that day: Ed Vernon. The witness bolstered Vernon's own testimony on that point. Hall left the stand with both sides unsatisfied with the information he'd offered.

By late morning on the second day of the hearing there was one final witness scheduled to speak: Rickey Jackson. Brian Howe announced his name in the courtroom, and the defendant slowly rose from the table, the links of his arm and leg shackles ringing gently with his steps. "State your name for the record," Howe asked his client.

"Rickey Jackson," he said, with a voice that resounded strongly through the courtroom, a voice belonging to a man not answering queries but finally demanding answers.

"Mr. Jackson, on May 19, 1975, did you shoot Harold Franks?"

"No, I did not," Rickey said, his words calm but full of resolve.

"Did you throw anything in Harold Franks's face?"

"No, I did not."

"Did you steal anything from Mr. Franks?"

"No, I did not."

"Did you shoot Anna Robinson on May 19, 1975?"

"No, sir, I did not."

"You were put on trial, convicted in this case back in 1975. And this was a capital case. Do you remember what your original sentence was?"

"Death by electricity."

"Did the prosecutor and your lawyer ever talk about a deal before the trial happened back then?"

"Yes, they did. I was to plead guilty to committing this crime and I wouldn't be sent to death row."

"Did you take that deal?"

"No, sir, I did not."

"Why not?"

"Because," Rickey said, a sudden flare of emotion cracking his voice, "I am innocent."

Howe gave his client a moment to collect himself. "How did you feel as you were being sentenced?"

"It was a traumatic experience," Rickey said, wiping tears out of his eyes. "My life was just . . . my life was being taken from me with no reason."

When the state began its cross-examination, the questioning was handed off to another prosecutor, Saleh Awadallah. Here, the office was planning to leverage a surprise piece of evidence. In 2010, Rickey made an appearance in front of the parole board—his fifth—where the committee noted in a report that the "offender takes responsibility for his actions and does show good insight into his offense." Wasn't this an admission of guilt, Awadallah asked the witness.

"I felt a lot of empathy for Mr. Franks and his family about what happened," Rickey explained. "The way he was murdered, nobody should have to die like that. And I have always felt empathy towards him and his family because, like him, I am a victim, too."

He continued: "I always expressed remorse about what happened in the way that he died whenever I go to the parole board, and for some reason they wanted to misconstrue that as an admission of guilt on my part. I just wanted them to understand that I wasn't taking the situation lightly."

Rickey went on, his words bobbing on the occasional wave of emotion. "I felt empathy for that man and his family. I had to sit in court while his wife and two sons sat there. I felt that. I felt her pain because I was being made a victim, too."

Awadallah continued to batter Rickey on how his comments before the parole board could only have been an admission of guilt. Rickey remained polite and firm, never taking the bait to become frustrated or angry. "I spent thirty-nine years of my life paying for something I didn't do," he explained. "The Franks family has no closure. The people that did this are still out there."

Howe took one last opportunity to counter the state's insinuations. "You were asked a number of questions about these parole statements from 2010 and 2013," the attorney said. "But back in 1975, when you were under the threat of being executed, did you ever think that maybe they might spare your life if you admitted that you were guilty?"

"Honestly, the thought never crossed my mind about having my life spared, because I was in the right and I felt like the truth would come to light." Rickey paused. "So I stood my ground."


"What happens now?" I asked Howe as the courtroom cleared for lunch.

"Well, we'll come back here and both sides will give final arguments. After that, the judge will take everything under advisement and issue a ruling in a few weeks."

"So it's not like Rickey will be walking free today?" I said, only half serious.

"No," Howe said with a smile. "Nothing like that."

The hearing was set to reconvene again at 2:30 P.M. I stayed inside the courtroom for a few moments, picking out a text message to Kwame, then walked the hallways of the Justice Center. The building's busy-hive atmosphere had cooled into a slower lunch-hour rhythm. The morning dockets had been called, and the rooms were empty. Down below in the lobby atrium, heel clicks and occasional shouts bounced off the stone walls and glass windows. Lawyers casually chatted or eyeballed paperwork. The metal detectors at the entrances spit out infrequent beeps and pings. The feeling inside the building was that business was done, disputes had been settled, decisions already made.

I was worried, although I couldn't reason out why. For two days I'd sat in the courtroom. Listened to each witness. Caught every comment. In my mind, Ed's reversal rang true. And his account was backed up by other testimony. But I was still uneasy. The Cleveland stories I knew, the ones I had grown up reading, even the stories I'd written myself, they all ended with disappointment: your best shot scuttled, the final opening blocked, the full effort falling short. The law was a complicated mechanism; right and wrong, blame and accountability, injury and redress were all fed into one end of a convoluted process and came out the other bent beyond recognition. It was so clear—these men were innocent, they had to be released and their records wiped clean. But the simplest truth seemed the most vulnerable to distortion.

By 2:30 P.M., Rickey's attorneys were back inside the courtroom. The gallery was nearly empty now. Most of the OIP interns were already heading back to Cincinnati. The curious onlookers had melted off elsewhere. Only an attorney from Terry Gilbert's law firm sat with me in my row as we all watched the clock inch past the start time. Ten minutes later, six attorneys from the prosecutor's office walked in together. Bringing up the rear was the prosecutor himself, Tim McGinty, gripping a coffee mug. The county's top law enforcement official walked up to the bench to speak privately with Judge McMonagle.

"All right," the judge announced once the prosecutor had returned to the table. "What's your pleasure, counsel?"

"Your Honor, Tim McGinty on behalf of the State of Ohio," the white-haired former judge announced in an all-business tone. "We are waiving final argument on the issue. The State, in light of the evidence produced by the defense at this hearing, and the total recantation by the key witness, hereby withdraws its motion in opposition for a new trial. The State concedes the obvious. It is no longer in a position to retry the case," he continued. By dropping the opposition to Rickey's petition for a new trial, and publicly acknowledging the state could no longer try the case, McGinty was pressing the appropriate legal button to acknowledge the defendant's innocence. Rickey's face dropped into his hands. "We in doing so fully recognize that the result will be the eventual release of Mr. Jackson and eventually the other codefendant. If the Court does grant their motion to which we no longer oppose, we will move for a dismissal today."

"Thank you," McMonagle said. "No objections?" he asked Howe. "No objections," the young attorney shot back.

"So based on the comments by Mr. McGinty, withdrawing the motion, I will grant that motion for a new trial." The judge turned to Rickey. "Mr. Jackson, we are going to get you back here on Friday just to make sure we get the paperwork done and order your release."

"Thank you, sir." Rickey struggled to speak, staccato sobs jumping from his chest. "Thank you, everybody."

"Mr. McGinty," the judge said, "you made the right choice."

The jagged cries were all I could hear. The moment felt cut off from what had come before or what would follow later. An unreal quality soaked in at the edges, as if this was all a mistake. It was Rickey's tears that validated what we had all just heard. The institutional carpet under my shoes, the jaundiced lighting from the fixtures—it all looked the same. Yet it felt like we'd been picked up and set down in an entirely different place.

The attorneys and OIP staffers formed a tight circle around Rickey's chair. I elbowed up to the front, looking directly into his eyes. "Thank you for coming," Rickey told me.

"Absolutely," I said, failing to find anything more meaningful to say. "Can you believe this?"

"I can't," I said. "I can't believe this."

"Thank you," he told his attorneys. "Everybody did a great job. I'm in shock. I can't believe this," he repeated. "I can't believe this is over."

"Do you want to call someone?" an OIP staff member asked. The woman explained this might be his only chance for some time to personally share the news.

"I can't even think right now," Rickey responded, swinging his head. Then from memory he recited a number. The OIP staffer dialed on her iPhone and held it to Rickey's ear.

"Hello?" he said. "Who is this? . . . This is Rickey . . . Hey, it's over, man . . .

"It's over, bro. I'm coming home . . . Friday . . . Friday, man . . . Friday. I don't know what time, but be here to get me, please . . . I've got to go . . . I'll talk to you Friday . . . let everybody know . . . I love you. Bye."

I recognized the tiny voice shouting through the phone static on the other end. It was Kwame.

Rickey glanced around the courtroom, his face crumbling in exhaustion. "I just want to go lay down. I didn't believe this was going to be over."

# 14

## NOT YOUR TOWN ANYMORE

Cleveland, November 21, 2014

KWAME HE COULDN'T BE SURE ABOUT, BUT RICKEY REMEMBERED THE last time he saw Wiley. Hard to forget. Lucasville, 1980. He was working as a porter, scooting up and down the range on errands. A guy he knew mentioned his friend had just been transferred to the block from isolation, one of the guys from his case, Wiley. "That's my brother," Rickey excitedly replied.

Behind the bars of his cell, Wiley seemed the same. The two talked easily for a few minutes. But the reunion was short-lived. Something changed, a switch flipped in Wiley. He began mumbling strange words. Rickey failed to understand what he was saying. Then Wiley started screaming, bashing his fists into the wall, overturning the bed. By the time the guards got the cell open, Wiley had smashed the sink into pieces. Rickey, bewildered and unnerved, stepped back from his friend's blunt rage. Wiley seemed to want to tear the whole place down brick by brick.

That memory and many more were skating the edges of his mind now as he waited in a holding cell at the Justice Center for his release. Wiley and Kwame. His mother. Cleveland. To keep himself straight, he tried to focus on sunlight. Rickey knew it was out there waiting for him. Not midday glare squeezing through the mesh wiring of a window, or what rubbed the tops of the high prison walls, setting the metal rings of wire on fire. Clean full light out of a fat sun in the blue sky.

Before that, however, Rickey had to get through everything sitting between him and those first free rays: the elevator ride down thirteen stories to the sheriff's intake office; the paperwork and waiting; waiting and paperwork; the push through the heavy glass door into a hallway slick with overhead industrial light and dancing with cell phone flashes; the forty or so television cameras and as many reporters from around the world waiting to capture his first words as a free man; then down the hallway, into the Justice Center atrium, over the chipped marble flooring, past lines waiting for the elevators and the suited men and women at the snack bar and the metal detectors, to the revolving doors leading to the outside world.

He didn't know about any of that yet. He was just waiting and thinking, and as he passed the time, wearing the stiff new outfit from Walmart, the jailhouse walls began talking at him.

I was supposed to be on a flight back to Miami on Wednesday morning, but I'd skipped it. I wasn't going to miss Rickey's release.

I was staying with my friend in Tremont, a trendy neighborhood just west of downtown popular with recent transplants to the city. The houses are all two-story structures slotted shoulder to shoulder on tiny lots, modest dwellings for the Slavic and German immigrants who filled this neighborhood in the early twentieth century and worked in the factories and refineries just down the hill. The steel mills and chemical factories were still there, and as I was getting ready in the quiet house I looked out the window past my friend's small backyard to the industrial acres below. Rooster tails of steam and exhaust rose from vents and smokestacks, the ice in the air deepening the discharge into bold mushroom clouds. Church bells clanged, old-world religion in the air. My phone peeped. Kwame and LaShawn were here to pick me up.

We had an hour to make the five-minute drive to the Justice

Center for the 9:00 A.M. hearing, but Kwame was working the pedal with a heavy foot. He blasted his Ford through a red light at an empty intersection in Tremont. LaShawn turned to me in the backseat, flashing a nervous smile. Neither Kwame nor his wife had slept much in the three days since he'd gotten Rickey's call. He was going on fumes, but news from yesterday had redoubled the excitement: Wiley had been brought to Cleveland from the Allen Correctional Institute in Lima on Judge McMonagle's order. He could also be released within a few hours.

We pulled into a parking space behind the old courthouse. Kwame, a black knit hat perched on his head, buttoned up his dark peacoat. "Let's go make history," he announced. Down in his coat pocket he had a surprise for Rickey.

McMonagle's courtroom was already full of a dozen TV cameramen setting up their tripods in the jury box. The media buildup around the case was intense. The news peg—the longest wrongful conviction to end in exoneration in U.S. history—drew a lot interest. Over the last two days, both Kwame and I had given interviews with local TV, and the requests kept coming. Now I noticed the familiar faces of local correspondents entering the court. Many were looking in our direction, and soon camera lenses were angling our way.

We stepped back into the hallway to wait. I recognized more outside the chambers. These were harder to place, mostly middle-aged men, black and white, chatting with one another. When OIP interns and attorneys arrived and warmly greeted the men, I realized these were exonerees, guys who, like Rickey, Kwame, and Wiley, had been wrongfully convicted and later freed by OIP. Clarence Elkins. Dean Gillispie. Each time a new exoneree won release, the others came to show support, a kind of welcoming party to the outside. "When he gets out, it's going to be like he's getting off a spaceship," Gillispie told the nodding group.

As LaShawn spoke with the exonerees, Kwame—a man who so seamlessly mixed with people—stepped away, turning to the wall. His face bunched up with tears. No one seemed to notice these private, heavy moments he took for himself. For years Kwame had held his story as a secret. Today was the first occasion when he could publicly acknowledge who he was and what had happened to him, his debut among others bound by the same misfortune.

We sat in the first row of the gallery. Every chair was filled. LaShawn squeezed her husband's hand and leaned toward him. "This is the longest nine o'clock I've ever had to wait for," she whispered. Kwame nodded. "It's like waiting for a roller coaster to start," he said.

When Rickey was led into the courtroom, the orange jailhouse jumper was gone. He was wearing pressed dress slacks, a white collared shirt peeking out from the V-neck of a zip-up sweater printed with an argyle pattern. Camera flashes lit up the lenses of the new glasses perched on his nose. He smiled for the media, perfect white teeth blazing in the glare, and raised his right hand to where Kwame, LaShawn, and I sat. "That's beautiful," Kwame whispered.

Judge McMonagle appeared a few moments after the hour, sweeping to his seat and quickly calling the room to order. "The case will be dismissed. Mr. Jackson, you are going to be free to go," the judge announced, his voice steady and drained of affect or histrionics. "Life is filled with small victories, and this is a big one. Know who your friends are, because everyone is going to want a piece of you. You better trust the people you know you can trust. So I wish you good luck."

Rickey thanked the judge. Then it was over. The hearing lasted less than three minutes. Rickey started moving toward the gallery, but the sheriff's deputies nudged him in back to the side door. He still had to be processed out. Kwame and LaShawn were on their feet and in their coats, moving to the hallway. Wiley's court appearance was set to begin downstairs. But a swirl of news cameras netted the couple before they could stop. Voices implored Kwame to talk about how he was feeling.

"I fought this fight for these guys for years, and this happened. I could go die tomorrow, and I'd be fine. Because they made it, they made it through that fight and they're still standing." His features twitched with feeling for a moment. "They owe it to perseverance. You look up perseverance, you'll find strength and integrity. That's what happened today. We didn't win. We just recaptured what was ours."

Emotion rushed into his face, and he excused himself. But the cameras followed, chasing Kwame and LaShawn down the hallway like paparazzi hounding a star.

"Ed Norton," Kwame said. We all laughed, everyone in the group eyeing me, thinking about the comparison. "Ed Norton can play Kyle in the movie," Kwame repeated.

"Who's playing you, then?" I asked.

"Who you think?" he scoffed. "Denzel." That broke everyone up again. Kwame was in full performance mode, killing with stories and jokes. He seemed to be partly trying to defuse his jitters. In a moment, Wiley was going to walk into the courtroom and it would be the first time the brothers had seen one another since their time on death row.

"Wiley suffered the most," LaShawn would later tell me, and it was impossible not to concur. Twenty-one and proud at the time of his arrest. The dazzling hero in the eyes of friends and family. Prison did more than strip away the layers of that personality. The pressure of incarceration also worked loose the mental issues that had been lying in wait. A 2014 mental health assessment noted Wiley had spent nearly half of his time in prison in mental health units, where he was diagnosed with depression and schizophrenia on multiple occasions. He was hospitalized for harming himself, and regularly refused his mandated medication. He fought with guards, slapped a prison psychiatrist, and had squandered his brief parole arguing with his parole officer. Words continued to be Wiley's safe harbor, love poetry addressed to an old girlfriend his main outlet. His lines showed a mind still burning a higher grade of intellectual fuel but unable to move forward.

He also never seemed to be able to get away from Lucasville, Ohio's most brutal lockup. After Kwame and Rickey were transferred to other prisons in the mid-1980s, the tensions tied to overpopulation and racial divides continued boiling behind the prison's high security walls.

Wiley was dealt out to other facilities over the years, including mental health units across the state. But invariably he was shipped back inside Lucasville, courtside for the ill will poisoning the facility. He was there on Easter Sunday, 1993, when 450 prisoners began tearing apart L Block. Nine inmates were killed by their fellow prisoners; eight guards were taken hostage. One was killed as the standoff stretched past a week and the Ohio National Guard mobilized outside. After ten days, the rioters surrendered. The violence caused more than $40 million in damage. Wiley was there, caught somewhere in the madness. It wasn't something he talked about.

Wiley stepped into the courtroom in a navy-blue suit Terry Gilbert had been able to get him. He was a few inches shorter than Kwame, rounder in the gut. His beard and hair were both running toward unruly and sprouted out in snow-white tufts. He waved to Kwame. I looked at the youngest Bridgeman brother. Fresh tears were running down his face. But his features glowed with pride.

"That's my big brother."


Rickey was waiting in an upstairs holding cell after the hearing. To pass the time, his eyes grazed the walls, chiseled with the usual jailhouse graffiti. Names. Dates. Swastikas. *Go fuck yourself. Back again, how stupid.* Then Rickey's eye hooked on something familiar: *144 RIP.*

One-four-four. The random jail graffiti corresponded with the first three digits of his prison number, the ID he'd been given four decades back. His identity, quite literally, as he'd come to know it. The number. Not me. 144061, rest in peace. Not me. The number's dead and gone. I'm here now.


A small army of television crews had landed in town. More and more outlets—ABC, NBC, CBS, CNN—began running headlines referring to THE LONGEST WRONGFUL CONVICTION IN U.S. HISTORY. I felt a slow-burning frustration every time I read the line.

There was a self-congratulatory tone throughout the coverage: look, America, we fixed an old mistake, everyone should be happy. "Tonight, two men in Cleveland, Ohio, are walking free for the first time since 1975, a nearly forty-year nightmare, locked away solely on the testimony of a child," Brian Williams announced later that evening on *NBC Nightly News*. Right, I remember thinking, that's a simplified way of looking at it.

The thirty-second soundbite version being promoted here was that a boy lied, innocent men were sent to prison, and now they had been cleared. That view, however, ignored all the critical context of Cleveland racial politics, not to mention the direct role police detectives allegedly played in forcing Ed to falsely testify. Without those pieces, the Jackson-Bridgeman case existed in a vacuum, a onetime piece of tragic luck; but within the frame of Cleveland's history, the wrongful conviction felt chained to so much more than what a boy saw or didn't see. The breezy television spots edited out the most crucial elements.

Kwame was having a similar reaction to the media interest wrapping around the case. A few days before Rickey and Wiley were released, I asked him if he felt the way the newspapers were tying a bow on the exoneration was wrong. It seemed to overlook the culpable parties, I said. Kwame answered that he forced himself never to forget about who was involved, from the police to the prosecutors to the Arthur Avenue neighbors who let them down to the city itself.

"It's not my town anymore, and that's what I'll tell Rickey and Wiley out here: it's not your town anymore." The way Kwame saw it, he was the advance man for Rickey and Wiley; he'd been out here, lived through the damage you couldn't mend and the changes you couldn't undo, suffered through the emotional bends triggered by life beyond prison. He was there to guide them through that new world. "And I'm still getting caught up," he told me. "So you can imagine, Buddy and Rickey, they're just coming out the door."

The revolving door pushed Rickey Jackson out into a bitter wall of icy lake breeze. Gray clouds capped the city—not the sunshine he'd expected, but it was up there somewhere. Rickey took a deep breath and started walking. He didn't have a direction or destination. One foot just followed the other. His attorneys filed behind on the sidewalk, camera crews and photographers chased along. Images of the procession bobbed in the dead dark glass of empty storefronts as they moved down Ontario Street and onto Public Square.

Kwame waited in the sheriff's office hallway for Wiley. When he appeared, the brothers embraced for the first time in years. Kwame took his brother's head in his hands like a child's, looking him deep in the eyes, then rested his forehead against Wiley's own.

A half-hour later the three childhood friends from Arthur Avenue all met again in the lobby bar of the Renaissance Hotel on Public Square, a cold walk away from the Justice Center. The crowd of friends and lawyers clapped as the three men embraced, arms around each other's shoulders and heads bent in a huddle. They stood there, pooling four decades of grief, oblivious for a few moments to the happy noise in the room. When the three heads straightened up, LaShawn stepped forward, wrapping Wiley in a hug before turning to Rickey. "Hey there, brother," she said.

OIP had arranged a group lunch with the exonerees and their supporters. Rickey chose Red Lobster. "Honestly, it was just the first thing that popped into my head," he told me later. Twenty OIP students, past exonerees, Mark Godsey, and Brian Howe were all clustered around the long table. Whole appetizer menus were polished off. Ricky, Kwame, and Wiley all bulldozed through the Admiral's Feast. Toasts were hoisted. Someone ordered a glass of champagne for Rickey. "Tastes like manna from heaven," he announced. Awkward pauses hung in the air occasionally between the three friends, but mostly they bantered and joked as if they were back driving through Cleveland in Wiley's Sebring. "I don't think Wiley's stopped smiling," LaShawn kidded her brother-in-law from across the table. I said my goodbyes after lunch.

Later Kwame fished his surprise for Rickey out of his coat pocket.

His hands held a small digital camera. As he powered it on, Kwame explained that before Rickey's mother died, Kwame went to visit her in an East Side high-rise where she lived out her last years—ironically, just down the hall from Anna Robinson. Before leaving, Kwame wanted to take a photo of Rickey's mother, hopefully to show him one day. "You're lucky I'm an idiot with technology," he told Rickey. He accidentally had the camera set on video, not snapshot. Instead of a picture of Essie Mae, Kwame had captured a short video, just a few seconds of the elderly woman setting her hips for a picture. But for Rickey those brief moments were recovered time.

That night—after the celebrations, the interviews with big media outlets, the words that didn't quite come and the silences they struggled to fill—Cleveland's three native sons hopped in Kwame's car and drove the streets until late into the night. They didn't get out, just rolled past old neighborhoods, including Arthur Avenue, now dead quiet, wrapped in darkness broken only here and there by streetlights.

# Epilogue
## COMEBACK

*The city must never be confused with the words that describe it.*
**--Italo Calvino**

*I WAS THERE WHEN RICKEY'S DOG WAS KILLED.*

It was a bright spring morning, Northeast Ohio just shaking free of the winter. The kitchen at Rickey's house forty minutes east of downtown was washed with sunlight. Rickey's fiancée, Rissa, was busy at the counter, chatting with me as I sat with her five-year-old son while he gobbled up a plate of waffles.

Rickey was outside with the dog, Kush. I'd watched him sprout from a yapping pup to a beefy pit who roamed Rickey's eight acres with an intense protective strut. I instinctively froze whenever I spotted him. Rickey loved the dog, though. Before we got down to an interview, he'd wanted to let Kush out.

When the front door cracked open, I swung around. "A car just hit Kush," Rickey said, his voice small and restrained. His eyes were red.

We all—Rickey, Rissa, the little boy, and I—bolted outside, up a driveway twisting through a lawn shadowed by towering elms.[1] Cars flowed both ways along the rural country road above, each swerving out of the way of the panting, bleeding dog lying on the asphalt. The driver hadn't stopped. Rickey wrapped the dog in a blanket, loaded him into his Lincoln Navigator, and hurried to the animal hospital.

Kush didn't make it.

I returned a few days later for our interview. Rickey and I sat on his screened back porch, the view looking out on the deep woods wrapping the house on all sides. We talked for hours, an intense one-on-one drilling deep into his childhood. When we touched on his relationship with his mother—all those unresolved feelings—tears were back in his eyes.

"There was a period of my life where I thought my mother didn't love me," he told me. "When she passed away, I started analyzing stuff. She did the best with what she had. I wish I could have had more time with her. I just wish I could have sat down with her, had that dialogue. And you know I never got to. I just wanted her to know—shit, I appreciated her."

Later the screen door clicked open, and Rissa walked in.

"He's making me cry, baby," Rickey said, wiping his face.

"Aw," she cooed protectively, sitting next to him on the couch. "Want me to beat him up?"

I started packing up my notebooks and recorder. Rickey apologized about canceling the other day. "Yeah, man, sorry about Kush."

"No need to apologize," I told him. "Seriously. If I had been in your place, I'd have been a mess. I'm sorry about Kush."

"Thanks," Rickey said, his eyes pinned to the corner of the room as if he was studying a sign.

"But you know, in a way, I'm kind of glad it happened," he said. "Glad that I could feel that way about something. Does that make sense? Be that upset about something. After what they did to me. They took so much away from me, you worry you won't be able to feel certain things again. That those parts don't work. I feel bad for the animal. But I'm happy that I could feel something deeply like that. That I was still able."

Optimism was now a big business in town. *The Cleveland Comeback. Believeland.* They inevitably started wrapping catchy names around the feeling, downtown at city hall, in the chamber of commerce mailers, at young professional happy hours. The momentum I'd picked up on in 2014 didn't quit but appeared to have accelerated.

Busted-up buildings suddenly had new boutique tenants in their shop space. New neighborhoods with buzzy names—"Hingetown," "Uptown"—seemed to sprout overnight. Bright murals dazzled street corners. The long-empty banks of the Cuyahoga River downtown were now busy with new restaurants and six-figure condos. With LeBron back at the helm, the Cleveland Cavaliers were selling out every night, filling the sidewalks downtown with thousands of people on game days. The city hosted the 2016 Republican National Convention. *Forbes* magazine, which only a few years earlier had labeled Cleveland "America's Most Miserable City," flip-flopped, crowning the town "America's Hottest City Right Now." Even Cleveland's forgotten soul singers the Ponderosa Twins Plus One enjoyed a moment of resurgence when Kanye West recycled their hit, "Bound," for his own single "Bound 2."

The optimism was unmistakable, more so because Clevelanders seemed so happy to embrace it, to celebrate the change working through the city. You began seeing this T-shirt everywhere, a clothing company's motto that suddenly became so ubiquitous it read as an epigraph for a town grabbing hold of its potential: CLEVELAND AGAINST THE WORLD. The energy, the new buildings, the enthusiasm—it all seemed to suggest that after years of free fall and black-eye headlines, the town wouldn't be left for dead as a ghostly relic of the last century. What had started back in 2014 had seemed to bloom. The "Cleveland Against the World" mantra itself read like a boiled-down version of Frederick Jackson Turner's own nineteenth-century enthusiasm for the Midwest.

There were still reasons to question the refurbished new picture of the city. The energy collecting in Cleveland pooled downtown, leaving the neighborhoods sidelined even more. In 2015, Douglas Massey, the sociologist who first detected hypersegregation in his book *American Apartheid*, published a paper examining the 2010 census data. Overall the number of U.S. cities gripped by hypersegregation dropped from thirty-three to twenty-one between 1990 and 2010.[2] Cleveland, however, was among the cities that had failed to pull itself out of hyper-segregation, and the "Believeland" laser focus on downtown and gentrifying areas only indicated that the divide would remain in place.

But nothing undercut the smoke and mirrors of this municipal health more than the death of Tamir Rice.

One day after Rickey Jackson took his first steps outside the Justice Center, on November 22, 2014, a twelve-year-old black Cleveland boy was gunned down by police at a civic center on the West Side. The police had been alerted to a man with a gun at the Cudell Recreation Center. The Cleveland 911 dispatcher neglected to tell the responding officers the gun was probably a toy and the individual a young boy. Officers Timothy Loehmann and Frank Garmback rushed to the scene. Exiting his car, Loehmann fired twice, killing Tamir on a lawn of melting snow.

Grainy security footage of the brutal, insensible death quickly sped around the world, splashing onto cable news programs and social media. The city settled into a tense waiting game as Cuyahoga County Prosecutor Tim McGinty announced his office would determine whether criminal charges were warranted against the officers.

Tamir's death falling within hours of Rickey's release—the two events weren't isolated incidents in my mind but linked. Each spoke to the same story of a police department at odds with the city it serves thanks to long-running impunity. And both were a great shame on the city, searing black eyes that should have chipped away at any enthusiasm over grand openings or sports championships.

The Rice shooting initially felt very familiar—but then swung in an entirely new direction. I had covered enough police shootings to understand the process was of official obfuscation, delay, and erasure. The victim of a police shooting disappeared inside the bureaucratic machinery of the official investigation. Weeks would stretch into months; routine questions about the status would be roadblocked by radio silence and "no comment" from the city. Piles of official equivocation and delays would effectively wipe the victim from the record until most of the city forgot.

Yet here the mechanics seemed to be playing out differently. Officials were forced to confront questions about the Rice case in live press conferences. As the weeks stomped on, Tamir's name didn't fade out but echoed beyond Ohio.

This was because of what was rolling across the country. Black Lives Matter, a hashtag that had suddenly blossomed into a social idea with moral weight, was changing the public discussion. The killing of unarmed black men—Trayvon Martin, Eric Garner, Michael Brown—was now a salient political point; people marched the streets chanting their names. The noise and intensity of the movement had hauled the national spotlight onto long-ignored issues regarding the justice system, activating a vociferous call for reform. The evidence was compelling. Cell-phone camera footage provided unimpeachable witness. Long-term statistics limned recidivism rates. Municipal and state budgets attested to the millions lost on failed law enforcement strategies.

The Rice investigation was not immune to this charged atmosphere. As the months passed, I became more hopeful that such an ugly moment of police violence would end with a just resolution. Criminal charges would be filed, I felt; the officers responsible would be held accountable. I ended up in intense debates—sometimes shouting matches—with friends and colleagues who said I was naïve, stupid, or complicit. But I truly believed.

The energy on the national stage only partly fueled my new optimism. My own recent experience was the second factor. I had been there when Rickey Jackson learned his nightmare was over. Those brief minutes inside the stuffy courtroom were profound in a way I was still struggling to understand. But my main takeaway was that the justice system had corrected its own horrific misstep. Yes, it took nearly four decades. But inside the high drama of those final moments in the courtroom in November, there was an official acknowledgment of a past wrong. Prosecutor Tim McGinty, the man now weighing the decision whether or not to charge Tamir's killers, had spoken words to the court I kept returning to: "The State concedes the obvious." So much of the court system was about denying the obvious. This was new.

The Brelo verdict should have been a check on my new optimism. In May 2015, Cleveland patrolman Michael Brelo went on trial for his part in the 2012 deaths of Timothy Russell and Malissa Williams. Brelo's own role was undeniable. But after the state presented its evidence in Brelo's manslaughter trial, Judge John P. O'Donnell determined prosecutors had not proven that any of the officer's bullets had killed Russell or Williams.

What was really remarkable about the judge's written opinion, however, was how it acknowledged but ultimately dismissed the longstanding outrage coiling around the case—the same energy building around the Rice decision. Seventy years of racial tension—Luna Park's "Jim Crow Days"; Bruce Klunder's death; Hough and Glenville; Carl Stokes's frustrations; White Art's police-approved drug sales—hung at the margins of O'Donnell's decision.

"Some say the volatile relationship between police and the community is rooted in our country's original sin. Whether it is or not, that sin won't be expiated and the hostility between the police and people won't be extirpated by a verdict in a single criminal lawsuit," the judge wrote.[3]

"I will not sacrifice him to a public frustrated by historical mistreatment at the hands of other officers."

On paper, Rickey, Kwame, and Wiley each quickly became millionaires.

After the Cuyahoga County prosecutor's decision to drop the fight against the exonerations, the three were officially cleared in the weeks following the events in November 2014. Ohio is one of the states that provides financial compensation for wrongful imprisonment. Because, as McGinty had said, the state conceded the obvious, the financial claims moved smoothly through the Ohio court of claims. Rickey would eventually receive $2.65 million from the state. Kwame and Wiley took home $2 million and $2.4 million, respectively. Rickey purchased his house on the eastern edge of Cleveland; Wiley, Kwame, and

LaShawn all moved together into a house just north of Akron. The money freed them from their past ordeal while sealing their futures up in relative comfort. They purchased big cars and put pool tables into their finished basements.

But even though the state conceded the obvious, the city did not.

In July 2015, the three exonerees filed a federal civil rights lawsuit against the department and the deceased officers involved in their arrest, including Eugene Terpay, John Staimpel, and James T. Farmer. The legal complaint alleged that poor training and mismanagement on the part of the city directly led to the wrongful arrests and prosecutions. The city, however, fired back in court against the three. Lawyers for the city even began to question whether the three men were actually innocent of the 1975 murder.

The city had set the stage for an extended legal siege in federal court—years of filings, depositions, and courtroom arguments. But Kwame, Rickey, and Wiley wanted to proceed. It wasn't so much about more money; seven-figure sums could only do so much to alter the texture of their remaining days. Rather, the federal lawsuit became about extracting a price from the police and city for what had happened—if that meant money, so be it; more importantly, it would mean a full account of who was responsible for what.

In Rickey's mind, until that moment, this would never truly be over. "It's the longest wrongful conviction in history, so it should be the biggest money settlement," he explained to me one afternoon. "I just want my money and then never have to deal with the city again. Never have to go answer questions again. Never tell my story again. But until this is done, I feel like they still have a hold on me."

And yet what the courts offered seemed paltry sized up against the immensity of the loss. What was taken could not be returned. And as with the Brelo case and the Tamir Rice shooting, the names of a few officers were standing in for a far deeper breakdown of the criminal justice process.

Kwame also understood that the justice offered by the courts paled compared to what was true justice demanded.

"It makes you question not just the system but everything," he told me one day at his house. "Again, my thing is accountability. It's not just saying, 'We're sorry,' or giving somebody some money for compensation. You've got to go back and hold that judge or prosecutor accountable. All the way up the ladder. It's on everybody. Because for me, it goes way further than the cops they keep wanting to put it on.

"Look at the Brelo thing," he continued. "They cleared all them other cops, and then they put it on one guy. And then they let him go, so now no one stands accountable. How can that be? When there are two people dead with 137 Cleveland police bullets in them?"

He shook his round head, peering back into his own back lawn, where Wiley was slowly walking the hedges, admiring the swirling colors of the flower beds.

"This was something that was instilled in me from my mom," Kwame told me. "Accountability. Way back from when I burned down Mr. Wittick's car. If I did it, I did it. If I didn't, I didn't."


It was always "they." The specifics were swallowed up in the pronoun's wide, indiscriminate arena.

"They tried to kill me, take my life," Rickey told me.

"They fucked me up bad," Wiley said. "I'm a bitter man now."

"They did this to us," Kwame said.

Kwame's own read on the empty consolation of his federal lawsuit hit at a deeper reality. The current structure of the American legal system, besides being ill equipped to handle claims of innocence, also fails to deal with the fallout of exonerations. Justice in its most basic terms is about spotlighting responsibility. This has been a function of the modern state since it emerged after the Middle Ages. In Canada and European countries, a wrongful conviction can trigger an investigation into what went wrong. But the American justice system repeatedly fails to fully analyze its own mistakes and abuses. In wrongful convictions, lawsuits and cash settlements have become common, but the system itself has little inclination to push deeper with a detailed inquisition into how it could break down so catastrophically.

This continues despite the rise of CIUs and wider national attention to the issue. And although police officers are often named in federal lawsuits filed by exonerees, they are indemnified and defended by their departments; they regularly bear no personal cost in the eyes of the court. Prosecutors and judges involved in wrongful convictions are almost never asked to account for the role they played. As far as blame is concerned, it is fixed both too narrowly—on a few officers—and too broadly—on the "system" itself. It was no surprise that when the three men tried to aim blame at the bad actors behind their decades of wrongful incarceration, they were left reaching for an unspecific word, the foggy "they."

These same issues about justice are particularly raw to the touch in foreign countries pulling free from violent periods of civil war or transitioning from authoritarian rule to democratic institutions. From Brazil and South Africa to Rwanda to the former Yugoslavia, each country weighed the question about the best way to come back from what had happened. The thinking traditionally breaks into two schools: Do you drill into the recent past, name names, pin accountability? Or do you move forward? Do you forget? Let go?

One school of thought firmly dug in behind the former is also the intellectual philosophy of the War Crimes Tribunal in The Hague. To march on from an ugly past without prosecuting bad actors only deepens the broad divide between people, the theory holds. Truth is the key to reconciliation, and truth means successfully laying blame. As Richard Goldstone, a South African jurist who worked on both the Rwanda and Yugoslav tribunals, told the journalist Lawrence Weschler,[4] "specific individuals bear the major share of the responsibility, and it is they, not the group as a whole, who need to be held to account, through a fair and meticulously detailed presentation and evaluation of evidence, precisely so that the next time around no one will be able to claim that all Serbs did this, or all Croats or all Hutus."

Here in the States, we don't frame the last seventy years of social upheaval in such stark terms, and certainly our history is not marked by anything close to the mass graves, ethnic cleansings, and authoritarian clampdown experienced elsewhere. But this is a viewpoint stuck firmly in the experience of white Americans. Across the color line, the psychic toll of the twentieth century has been extensive. The push for equality in the 1960s was met with a vicious counterattack—snarling police dogs, bombed churches, assassins' bullets. Redlining and school segregation deepened the social divide. And the correctives—Johnson's War on Poverty and the Warren Court's civil rights rulings—only put down the groundwork for further isolation and repression. For decades, all this has fueled the collective suspicion and grief black Americans feel toward the country's institutions, particularly the criminal justice system. Yes, that suspicion and grief is often applied in broad strokes. But a justice system that fails to hand out blame and punish bad actors only perpetuates broad distrust and distance, rancor and anger, as the war tribunal's proponents argue. If we don't punish a police officer or prosecutor for misdeeds, the whole system becomes bad.

The Black Lives Matter movement drew from this deep-rooted suspicion and broadcast it widely. The speed of social media provided a rapid-fire version of accountability: facts and names were circulated as quickly as a lightning strike. In this, it was a street expression of the same principles driving the world court. We knew the names of the victims; we knew the names of the officers involved; we knew the details.

But the calls for justice on the street were not answered by the system, time and again. The movement may have unleashed new energy, but it ultimately couldn't shake what had stood for decades—the system designed to protect its own. The Tamir Rice decision was a clear signal.

The announcement came in December 2015. It was an icebox Monday afternoon between Christmas and New Year's, a patch of dead static when most people have unplugged or hit the mental snooze button. Prosecutor Tim McGinty called a press conference, described the situation a "perfect storm of human error," and announced his office would not pursue criminal charges against the officers involved. Winter rain began dashing Cleveland. Small protests broke out that night, but the feeling was more of exhaustion than outrage. Tamir's death ended as so many other Cleveland stories did, with weak words of equivocation, familiar bitterness, and a new grievance to enter on a long rolling list. The exonerations were steps toward optimism. The Rice decision yanked me back to familiar ground.

*Beautiful* was a word that came easily and often off Kwame's lips. He found a kind of music in it, stretching the syllables out in a singsong delivery. After spending so much time with him over the years, hearing him reach for the word time and again, I realized it wasn't just a quirk of personality. He meant it. That a man who had been forced to see so much damage and ruin and hate still had an eye for beauty was a lesson.

*Beautiful* was also the only word I could think of on a Saturday afternoon in June 2017. Rickey and Rissa's wedding day. The ceremony and reception were held at the Great Lakes Science Center, right on the lip of the lake downtown. Guests were pouring into the seats on the second floor; R&B murmured from the speakers. Rickey—in an aqua-green vest and tux—stood with his groomsmen, waiting for his bride to walk down the aisle.

It was a bright day. The floor-to-ceiling windows behind the altar where the vows would be exchanged looked directly out onto the Cleveland skyline. The lake spread at our backs. The view I had in the audience put Rickey on a straight line with the municipal buildings where the main plot twists in his life had unfolded. Directly ahead stood the old courthouse, its battered stone dull in the sunlight. Behind loomed the Justice Center, where the case had ended. And then there was Rickey, smiling and unbowed, waiting to take his next step. From my angle he stood taller than either building.

# Acknowledgments

This book was written over a three-year period. Countless people helped turn a jumble of fragmented ideas and uncharted feelings into the final story.

Although I take a (justified) shot at the city of Cleveland's lackadaisical public records response in the book, the city's records department did provide me with valuable documentation—until they stopped responding to my requests. Regardless, I am grateful for the material I got. The staff at the Cuyahoga County Clerk of Courts was incredibly helpful in tracking down old documentation, as were the folks at the Cleveland Public Library, which has done a wonderful job collecting the odds and ends of municipal business.

True conviction is in short supply out there. The men and women grinding through the courthouses and prison visiting rooms on behalf of the wrongfully convicted have this in abundance.

Every bad cop in Cleveland may curse his name, but Terry Gilbert's relentless fight and dedication to his values have made the city a better place. Mark Godsey has created a truly beautiful and dedicated machine at the Ohio Innocence Project, a place where an attorney like Carrie Wood can have a huge impact. Brian Howe and Jacqueline Greene, both tenacious advocates of the law, were also incredibly helpful in walking me through the legal terrain related to the case. Elizabeth Wang from Loevy & Loevy also deserves thanks.

This book came about because of my journalism career, and on that front, there are many people to thank. Lute Harmon Sr. at Great Lakes Publishing gave me my first job when I had no business inside a newsroom. Michael D. Roberts taught me to see Cleveland—and any city—not as simply a place but a grand Faulknerian stage. From Pete Kotz I learned that journalism was a righteous big stick you could swing at the bad guys—and that there are bad guys out there worth taking on. I found my writing voice and developed empathy and heart on the page thanks to Erich Burnett, the *Cleveland Scene* editor who guided me through "What the Boy Saw." At *Miami New Times*, Chuck Strouse and Deirdra Funcheon encouraged me to follow my instincts, no matter how weird or unconventional. Fred Barbash at *The Washington Post* believed in me enough to pluck me out of the alt-weekly underground. Vince Grzegorek, besides being one of my closest friends, was the propulsive editorial engine behind *Good Kids, Bad City*. A true son of Cleveland, he also kept my bullshit in check.

I've been lucky enough to work alongside many talented reporters, both friends and professional mentors. These include Nate Rau, Ken Whitehouse, Brantley Hargrove, Joe Tone, Michael E. Miller, Terry McCoy, Emily Codik, Tim Elfrink, Allie Conti, Liz Tracy, Francisco Alvarado, Sam Allard, Eric Sandy, Henry Gomez, Rachel Dissell, Andrew Tobias, Eric Heisig, and Peter Pattakos, to name an outstanding few.

This book's backstory is a long tale in its own right, full of ups and downs, probably best heard over a beer or many. Like the best kind of cornerman, David Patterson, my agent at the Stuart Krichevsky Literary Agency, was supportive even when the match looked grim. The late PJ Horoszko took a chance on this project when others would not, and it's my great sadness I will never be able to properly thank him. Anna deVries picked up this manuscript and brought insight, patience, and expertise to the work. The rest of the staff at Picador have been amazing walking me through the process.

My mother and father have put up with me for three decades, and they deserve all available medals for that. But they've also given me the two best gifts parents can—a sense of right and wrong, and the idea that we're supposed to use our time here making the world better than we found it. My brother Evan has also been a great supporter and friend.

My wife Kim supported me on all fronts as I was writing this book—spiritually, emotionally, and financially. Unfailingly kind and generous, she pulled me up and kept me going, made me want to be better and work harder. Every word here is dedicated to her.

I also must thank Ed Vernon—for both sharing his decades of agony, and also finding the courage to confront a past wrong in such a high-pressure setting.

Finally, Kwame, Wiley, and Rickey: I've learned more from each of you than I can put into words right now, lessons I know will stick with me till the end. Whatever part I played in this story has been the great honor of my life. Thank you.

# Notes

## PROLOGUE: BUSTED PAVEMENT

1. Samuel R. Gross and Michael Shaffer, "Exonerations in the United States, 1989–2012," National Registry of Exonerations, University of Michigan Law School, June 2012.

2. Norris, Robert J. *Exonerated: A History of the Innocence Movement* (New York: New York University Press, 2017).

3. Allison D. Redlich, James R. Acker, Robert J. Norris, and Catherine L. Bonventre, editors, *Examining Wrongful Convictions: Stepping Back, Moving Forward* (Durham, N.C.: Carolina Academic Press, 2014), 226.

4. Philip Wiley Porter, *Cleveland: Confused City on a Seesaw* (Columbus: Ohio State University Press, 1976), 16.

5. Rich Exner, "2010 census population numbers show Cleveland below 400,000; Northeast Ohio down 2.2 percent," Cleveland.com, March 9, 2011, http://www.cleveland.com/datacentral/index.ssf/2011/03/2010_census_figures_for_ohio_s.html.

6. Rich Exner, "Cleveland's poverty is second among big cities; gap between rich and poor grows nationally," Cleveland.com, September 28, 2010, http://www.cleveland.com/datacentral/index.ssf/2010/09/clevelands_poverty_is_second_a.html.

7. Rich Exner, "Child poverty: ranking every Ohio city, county—Census Snapshot," Cleveland.com, December 21, 2017, http://www.cleveland.com/datacentral/index.ssf/2017/12/ranking_every_ohio_city_county_3.html.

8. Leah Goldman, "The 25 Most Dangerous Cities in America," *Business Insider*, May 23, 2011, http://www.businessinsider.com/most-dangerous-cities-2011-5.

9. Kurt Badenhausen, "America's Most Miserable Cities," *Forbes*, February 18, 2010, https://www.forbes.com/2010/02/11/americas-most-miserable-cities-business -beltway-miserable-cities.html#48916eb54ca0; Adam Ferrise, "French government warns citizens to avoid Cleveland Heights, Lakewood, Euclid," Cleveland .com, November 14, 2013, http://www.cleveland.com/metro/index.ssf/2013/11 /french_government_warns_citize.html.

10. Peter Krouse, "Frank Russo, Jimmy Dimora got fake palm tree, tiki hut as bribe, new federal charges say," Cleveland.com, March 28, 2011, http://www.cleveland .com/countyincrisis/index.ssf/2011/03/money_manager_charles_randazzo .html.

11. Rachel Dissell, "The Cuyahoga County corruption case: a who's who," *Plain Dealer*, September 15, 2010, http://www.cleveland.com/countyincrisis/index.ssf /2010/09/the_cuyahoga_county_corruption.html.

12. Amanda Garrett and John Caniglia, "Bill Mason's office went after hundreds of people with little or no evidence," *Plain Dealer*, November 21, 2010, http://www .cleveland.com/rule-29/index.ssf/2010/11/bill_masons_office_went_after.html.

13. "Facing the foreclosure crisis in greater Cleveland: What happened and how communities are responding," Federal Reserve Bank of Cleveland, June 2010.

14. Mark Naymik, "Group begins counting every abandoned property in Cleveland by walking every street in the city," Cleveland.com, June 11, 2015, http://www .cleveland.com/naymik/index.ssf/2015/06/group_begins_counting_every_ab .html#incart_river.

15. Patrick O'Donnell, "Cleveland schools have highest ranking in years, but still earn mostly F grades on state report cards," *Plain Dealer*, September 14, 2017, http:// www.cleveland.com/metro/index.ssf/2017/09/cleveland_schools_have_highest _ranking_in_years_but_still_earn_mostly_f_grades_on_state_report_cards.html; Sally Holland, "Cleveland tries to turn around troubled school system," CNN, April 19, 2011, http://www.cnn.com/2011/US/04/19/cleveland.schools/index .html.

16. Sam Dillon, "Large Urban-Suburban Gap Seen in Graduation Rates," *The New York Times*, April 22, 2009, https://www.nytimes.com/2009/04/22/education /22dropout.html.

17. Stephanie Chen, "11 bodies, one house of horrors: Why Cleveland women were 'invisible,'" CNN, October 26, 2010, http://www.cnn.com/2010/CRIME/10 /26/cleveland.sowell.victims.one.year/index.html.

18. Gabriel Baird, "Six-month suspension for officers who mistook body for deer," *Plain Dealer*, May 25, 2010, http://blog.cleveland.com/metro/2010/05/six-month _suspension_for_offic.html.

19. Jon C. Teaford, *Cities of the Heartland: The Rise and Fall of the Industrial Midwest* (Bloomington: Indiana University Press, 1993), 113.

20. Frederick Jackson Turner, *The Frontier in American History* (Tucson: University of Arizona Press, 1986), 153–54.

## 1. A SPARK PLUS A SPARK PLUS A SPARK

1. Kwame Ajamu, interview by author, March 23, 2016.

2. Louis H. Masotti and Jerome R. Corsi, *Shoot-out in Cleveland: Black Militants and the Police, July 23, 1968* (Washington, D.C.: U.S. Government Printing Office, 1969), 50. The account of the Glenville shooting is pulled from this exhaustive report.

3. Kenneth L. Kusmer, *A Ghetto Takes Shape: Black Cleveland, 1870–1930* (Chicago: University of Illinois Press, 1978), 5.

4. Carol Poh Miller and Robert A. Wheeler, *Cleveland: A Concise History, 1796–1996* (Bloomington: Indiana University Press, 1997), 17.

5. James Harrison Kennedy, *A History of the City of Cleveland: Its Settlement, Rise and Progress, 1796–1896* (Cleveland: Imperial Press, 1896), 102.

6. Kusmer, *A Ghetto Takes Shape*, 5.

7. Kusmer, *A Ghetto Takes Shape*, 9.

8. *Cleveland Leader*, March 7, 1865.

9. Kusmer, *A Ghetto Takes Shape*, 38.

10. Quoted in Estelle Zannes, *Checkmate in Cleveland: The Rhetoric of Confrontation During the Stokes Years* (Cleveland: Case Western Reserve University Press, 1972), 6.

11. Leonard N. Moore, *Carl B. Stokes and the Rise of Black Political Power* (Chicago: University of Illinois Press, 2002), 18–21.

12. Daniel R. Kerr, *Derelict Paradise: Homelessness and Urban Development in Cleveland, Ohio* (Boston: University of Massachusetts Press, 2011), 145–166.

13. Moore, *Carl B. Stokes and the Rise of Black Political Power*, 33.

14. Cleveland Citizens Committee on Hough Disturbances, Testimony of August 22–25, 1966.

15. Kwame Ajamu, interview by author, February 6, 2016; Wiley Bridgeman, interview by author, September 14, 2016.

16. Moore, *Carl B. Stokes and the Rise of Black Political Power*, 20.

17. Carl B. Stokes, *Promises of Power: A Political Autobiography* (New York: Simon and Schuster, 1973), 52.
18. Stokes, *Promises of Power*, 47.
19. John Skow, "The Question in the Ghetto: Can Cleveland Escape Burning?" *Saturday Evening Post*, July 29, 1967.
20. "Cleveland Little Hoover Commission," Public Administration Service, November 7, 1966.
21. Louis H. Masotti and Jerome R. Corsi, *Shoot-out in Cleveland: Black Militants and the Police, July 23, 1968* (Washington D.C.: U.S. Government Printing Office, 1969), 73–74.
22. Stokes, *Promises of Power*, 146.
23. Masotti and Corsi, *Shoot-out in Cleveland*, xiii.
24. "Cleveland Police: What's on Their Mind," *Plain Dealer*, September 30, 1968.

## 2. THAT PARTICULAR DAY

1. Kwame Ajamu, interview by author, October 18, 2016.
2. Kwame Ajamu, Wiley Bridgeman, and Rickey Jackson, interview by author, March 7, 2016; Anthony Singleton and Ed Vernon, interview by author, November 17, 2016.
3. James Neff, *Mobbed Up: Jackie Presser's High-Wire Life in the Teamsters, the Mafia, and the FBI* (New York: Atlantic Monthly Press, 1989), 241–265; John Petkovic, "The Cleveland Mafia: Death of a Don Ignites Bomb City, USA," *Plain Dealer*, May 26, 2016, http://www.cleveland.com/entertainment/index.ssf/2016/05/the_cleveland_mafia_death_of_a.html.
4. Daniel R. Kerr, *Derelict Paradise: Homelessness and Urban Development in Cleveland, Ohio* (Boston: University of Massachusetts Press, 2011), 188.
5. Karen Smith, interview by author, fall 2010; *State of Ohio v. Ronnie Bridgeman*, Court of Common Pleas, Cuyahoga County, 1975; *State of Ohio v. Rickey Jackson*, Court of Common Pleas, Cuyahoga County, 1975.

## 3. BLACK AND BLUE

1. Kwame Ajamu, Wiley Bridgeman, and Rickey Jackson, interview by author, March 7, 2016.
2. Harry Jaffe and Tom Sherwood, *Dream City: Race, Power, and the Decline of Washington. D.C.* (New York: Simon & Schuster, 1994), 64.
3. Lyndon B. Johnson, *Public Papers of the Presidents of the United States: Lyndon B. Johnson, 1968–1969* (Washington: U.S. Government Printing Office, 1965), 59.

4. Elizabeth Hinton, *From the War on Poverty to the War on Crime: The Making of Mass Incarceration in America* (Cambridge: Harvard University Press, 2016), 31.

5. Ibid.

6. Estelle Zannes, *Checkmate in Cleveland: The Rhetoric of Confrontation During the Stokes Years* (Cleveland: Case Western Reserve University Press, 1972), 152.

7. Roldo Bartimole, "Cleveland cops want 50 new machine guns, 170 carbines for growing exotic arsenal," *Point of View*, October, 1971.

8. Quoted in Estelle Zannes, *Checkmate in Cleveland: The Rhetoric of Confrontation During the Stokes Years* (Cleveland: Case Western Reserve University Press, 1972), 146.

9. "Black police sergeant counters FOP head's 'wipeout' statement," *Call and Post*, January 10, 1970.

10. Roldo Bartimole, "Cleveland Cops' White-Hot Racism," *Point of View*, January 27, 1970.

11. Ronald Turner Deposition, 57, June 13, 2016.

12. William Tell Deposition, 161, 187, October 23, 2016.

13. Arthur X, "Policeman Tells All," *Call and Post*, August 30, 1975.

14. Arthur X, "Police Brutality a Reality," *Call and Post*, September 13, 1975.

15. Maxine L. Lynch, "Gun-Happy or Fair? Leisman Either Liked or Hated as Policeman," *Plain Dealer*, February 23, 1980; Susan Q. Stranahan, "M14 Was Not Police Issue, Trial Is Told," *Plain Dealer*, October 14, 1972.

16. "Policemen to Answer Rape Charges Today," *Plain Dealer*, February 19, 1972.

17. James Nelson Coleman, "Victims Outraged by Shock Probation," *Call and Post*, December 23, 1972.

18. Richard Klein, *Cleveland Mayor Ralph J. Perk: Strong Leadership During Troubled Times* (Cleveland: MSL Academic Endeavors, 2013), 51.

19. Daniel R. Kerr, *Derelict Paradise: Homelessness and Urban Development in Cleveland, Ohio* (Boston: University of Massachusetts Press, 2011), 189.

20. Todd Swanstrom, *The Crisis of Growth Politics: Cleveland, Kucinich, and the Challenge of Urban Populism* (Philadelphia: Temple University Press, 1985), 108–115.

21. "City Police Tied to Burglary Ring," *Plain Dealer*, March 7, 1974; "Cheat Spot Payoff Alleged," *Plain Dealer*, March 8, 1974; "Police Drinking After Bar Hours," *Plain Dealer*, March 9, 1974; "Police Shut Eyes to Prostitution," *Plain Dealer*, March 10, 1974.

22. "2 Patrolmen Cite Police Vice," *Plain Dealer*, March 11, 1974.

23. Joseph L. Wagner, "Perk picks clergy for police probe," *Plain Dealer*, March 15, 1974.

24. Leslie Kay, "Grand Jury Blasts Police Laxity," *Plain Dealer*, May 31, 1974.
25. Robert H. Holden, "Do Police Give Money's Worth?," *Plain Dealer*, May 19, 1975; W. Joseph Campbell, "Homicide Rate Here Matches U.S. Spiral," *Plain Dealer*, October 30, 1974.
26. Holden, "Do Police Give Money's Worth?"
27. Robert G. McGruder and Karl R. Burkhardt, "Lack of Control Jeopardized Police, Injured Two Hostages, Witnesses Say," *Plain Dealer*, June 2, 1974.

*4. X-RAY EYES*

1. Wiley Bridgeman, interview by author, June 29, 2016; *State of Ohio v. Wiley Bridgeman*, Court of Common Pleas, Cuyahoga County, 1975.
2. "'Odd Couple' of jurisprudence impress their peers," *Palm Beach Post*, September 22, 1985.
3. Tom Feran, "Daniel R. McCarthy, lawyer oversaw Cleveland schools desegregation," *Plain Dealer*, October 21, 2011.
4. *State of Ohio v. Rickey Jackson*, Court of Common Pleas, Cuyahoga County, 1975.
5. Leslie Kay, "20-Year-Old Guilty in Robbery-Slaying," *Plain Dealer*, August 13, 1975; Andrea E. Naversen, "Jackson Guilty in Robbery, Slaying of Salesman," *Plain Dealer*, August 14, 1975.
6. James F. McCarty, "Law & Disorder with Rumpled Suits and Befuddled Ways, Thomas Shaughnessy Has Managed to Become the Matlock of Cuyahoga County," *Plain Dealer*, October 23, 1994.
7. *State of Ohio v. Ronnie Bridgeman*, Court of Common Pleas, Cuyahoga County, 1975.
8. "17-Year-Old Guilty of Murder, Could Get Death Penalty," *Plain Dealer*, September 28, 1975.

*5. WE YET EXIST*

1. "Report of the Joint Finance Subcommittee on the Southern Ohio Correctional Facility at Lucasville," Ohio General Assembly, July 28, 1976.
2. John Perotti, "Lucasville: A Brief History," *Prison Legal News*, December 1993, https://www.prisonlegalnews.org/news/1993/dec/15/lucasville-a-brief-history/.
3. John Perotti, "Lucasville: A Brief History"; Staughton Lynd, *Lucasville: The Untold Story of a Prison Uprising* (Oakland: PM Press, 2011), 15–21, 214.
4. "48 on Lucasville Death Row React Quietly," *Plain Dealer*, July 3, 1976.
5. "Death Row Inmates Stage Hunger Strike," *Call and Post*, August 21, 1976.
6. W. James Van Vliet, "Murder Conviction Here Is Set Aside," *Plain Dealer*, April 21, 1977.

7. *State of Ohio v. Wiley Bridgeman,* Court of Common Pleas, Cuyahoga County, 1977.

8. "Verdict Confirmed, Man to Get Chair," *Plain Dealer,* February 17, 1978.

9. "Bridgeman Claims Innocence, Says He Doesn't Want to Die," *Call and Post,* February 29, 1978.

10. Richard G. Zimmerman, "Ohio's Death Law Tested by 2 Cases Before High Court," *Plain Dealer,* January 18, 1978.

11. Victor L. Streib, *The Fairer Death: Executing Women in Ohio* (Athens: Ohio University Press, 2006), 60–65.

12. Richard G. Zimmerman, "Ohio Killers Win Reprieves in High Court," *Plain Dealer,* July 4, 1978.

## 6. MENS REA

1. Anthony Singleton and Ed Vernon, interview by author, April 28, 2016; Anthony Singleton and Ed Vernon, interview by author, November 17, 2016.

2. Bob Becker and Madeline Drexler, "Popular Poison: Cocaine Deadlier, Demand Up," *Plain Dealer,* July 3, 1086.

3. Tom Andrzejewski, "Sleeping Giant Is Shaken by Drug Scene in America," *Plain Dealer,* September 1, 1986.

4. Jim Parker, "Feds Join Probe Here of Violent Jamaican Drug Gangs," *Plain Dealer,* September 13, 1987; Eric Stringfellow, "Detroit Trio Ran Ohio Drug Ring," *Plain Dealer,* April 5, 1990.

5. Eric Harrison, "Cleveland Scandal: Did Cocaine Sting Fuel Drug Sales?" *Los Angeles Times,* June 14, 1989, http://articles.latimes.com/1989-06-14/news/mn-2039 _1_police-cars-drug-dealer-biggest-cocaine-bust.

## 7. ALHAMDULILLAH

1. Kwame Ajamu, interview by author, February 6, 2016.

2. Terry Gilbert, interview by author, August 22, 2016.

3. Karen Farkas, "Case resulting from slaying is built on DNA tests," *Plain Dealer,* January 27, 1991.

4. Robert J. Norris, *Exonerated: A History of the Innocence Movement* (New York: New York University Press, 2017), 44–47.

## 8. THE MALES ARE FROM THE NEIGHBORHOOD

1. Kyle Swenson, "Shots in the Dark," *Cleveland Scene,* June 29, 2011, https://www .clevescene.com/cleveland/shots-in-the-dark/Content?oid=2655374.

2. Douglass S. Massey and Nancy A. Denton, *American Apartheid: Segregation and the Making of the Underclass* (Cambridge: Harvard University Press, 1993), 77.

## 9. WHAT THE BOY SAW

1. *Herrera v. Collins*, 506 U.S. 390 (1993).
2. *Kansas v. Marsh*, 278 Kan. 520 (2006).
3. Samuel R. Gross and Michael Shaffer, "Exonerations in the United States, 1989–2012," National Registry of Exonerations, University of Michigan Law School, June 2012.
4. Allison D. Redlich, James R. Acker, Robert J. Norris, and Catherine L. Bonventre, editors, *Examining Wrongful Convictions: Stepping Back, Moving Forward* (Durham, N.C.: Carolina Academic Press, 2014), 22.
5. Eric Heisig, "Cleveland Ordered to Pay $13.2 Million Judgment for Police Officer in Wrongful Conviction Suit," Cleveland.com, October 13, 2016, http://www.cleveland.com/court-justice/index.ssf/2016/10/cleveland_ordered_to_pay_132_m_1.html.
6. Martin Kuz, "The Unluckiest Man on Death Row," *Cleveland Scene*, November 22, 2001, https://www.clevescene.com/cleveland/unluckiest-man-on-death-row/Content?oid=1478288.
7. Vince Grzegorek, "Call It Even," *Cleveland Scene*, July 6, 2011, https://www.clevescene.com/cleveland/call-it-even/Content?oid=2668451.
8. C. Ronald Huff and Martin Killias, editors, *Wrongful Convictions & Miscarriages of Justice: Causes and Remedies in North American and European Criminal Justice Systems* (New York: Routledge, 2013), 46–50.
9. Ivan Tanksley, interview by author, spring 2011.
10. Valerie Abernathy, interview by author, spring 2011.
11. Lynn Garrett, interview by author, spring 2011.
12. William J. Stuntz, *The Collapse of American Criminal Justice* (Cambridge, Mass.: Belknap Press, 2011), 224–230.
13. Stuntz, *The Collapse of American Criminal Justice*, 256.
14. Stuntz, *The Collapse of American Criminal Justice*, 193.
15. James Q. Whiteman, *The Origins of Reasonable Doubt: Theological Roots of the Criminal Trial* (New Haven: Yale University Press, 2008), 56.

## 10. SUPER FLOP

1. Michelle Alexander, *The New Jim Crow: Mass Incarceration in the Age of Colorblindness* (New York: The New Press, 2012), 60.

2. Brandon L. Garrett, *Convicting the Innocent: Where Criminal Prosecutions Go Wrong* (Cambridge: Harvard University Press, 2011), 195–200.

3. Garrett, *Convicting the Innocent*, 200–202.

4. *In re Davis*, 130 S. Ct. 1, 3 (2009).

5. Rickey Jackson, interview by author, April 26, 2016.

6. Robert J. Norris, *Exonerated: A History of the Innocence Movement* (New York: New York University Press, 2017), 15–17.

7. Quoted in Norris, *Exonerated*, 27.

8. Quoted in Norris, *Exonerated*, 54.

9. Quoted in Norris, *Exonerated*, 2–3.

10. Garrett, *Convicting the Innocent*, 204.

11. Garrett, *Convicting the Innocent*, 217.

12. Norris, *Exonerated*, 103.

13. Jacob Baynham, "The Correction," *Cincinnati*, November 2010.

14. Carrie Wood, interview by author, December 11, 2016.

15. Scott Crowley, interview by author, March 4, 2017.

## 11. HYPERTENSION

1. Anthony Singleton, interview by author, April 21, 2016.

2. Sierra Merida, interview by author, January 5, 2017.

## 12. WE CAN FIX THIS

1. "52 places to go in 2015," *The New York Times*, December 21, 2015, https://www
.nytimes.com/interactive/2015/01/11/travel/52-places-to-go-in-2015.html.

2. "Justice Department, Federal and State Partners Secure Record $7 Billion Global Settlement with Citigroup for Misleading Investors About Securities Containing Toxic Mortgages," U.S. Department of Justice, July 14, 2014, https://www.justice
.gov/opa/pr/justice-department-federal-and-state-partners-secure-record-7-billion
-global-settlement.

3. Rich Exner, "Cleveland population loss slows; find latest census estimates for every U.S. city, county and state," Cleveland.com, May 19, 2016, https://www.cleveland
.com/datacentral/index.ssf/2016/05/cleveland_population_slows_fin.html; Patrick O'Donnell, "Cleveland school district planning to cut $21 million from school budgets next year as enrollment slide continues," *Plain Dealer*, February 26, 2014, https://www.cleveland.com/metro/index.ssf/2014/02/cleveland_school_district
_plan_1.html; Rich Exner, "Decade after being declared nation's poorest big city, 1-in-3 Clevelanders remain in poverty," Cleveland.com, September 18, 2014,

https://www.cleveland.com/datacentral/index.ssf/2014/09/decade_after_being
_declared_na.html.

4. Ron Rutti, "Cleveland fire truck freed from unsteady street," *Plain Dealer*, March 29, 2014, https://www.cleveland.com/metro/index.ssf/2014/03/cleveland _fire_truck_freed_fro.html.

5. "Prosecutor's Summary," Ohio Bureau of Criminal Identification and Investigation, February 3, 2013, http://www.ohioattorneygeneral.gov/Files/Briefing -Room/News-Releases/Cleveland-Officer-Involved-Shooting-Investigation /General-Reports/Prosecutor-s-Summary-2-4-2013.aspx.

6. "Exonerations in 2014," The National Registry of Exonerations, January 27, 2015.

7. Ibid.

8. Denise Grollmus, "Trial and Error," *Cleveland Scene*, May 24, 2006.

9. Ibid.

10. Kim Schneider, "Most Interesting People 2013: Tim McGinty," *Cleveland Magazine*, December 17, 2012, https://clevelandmagazine.com/in-the-cle/people /articles/most-interesting-people-2013-tim-mcginty.

11. Brandon L. Garrett, *Convicting the Innocent: Where Criminal Prosecutions Go Wrong* (Cambridge: Harvard University Press, 2011), 48–49.

12. Ronald Huff and Martin Killias, editors, *Wrongful Convictions & Miscarriages of Justice: Causes and Remedies in North American and European Criminal Justice Systems* (New York: Routledge, 2013), 97.

## *13. 39 YEARS, 3 MONTHS, 6 DAYS*

1. *Paskvan v. City of Cleveland*, 70 F. 1272 (6th Cir. 1995).

2. John S. Long, "Restricted officer wins case," *Plain Dealer*, December 3, 1988.

## *EPILOGUE: COMEBACK*

1. Rickey Jackson, interview by author, 2016.

2. Tanvi Misra, "America Has Half as Many Hypersegregated Metros as It Did in 1970," *City Lab*, May 21, 2015, https://www.citylab.com/equity/2015/05/america -has-half-as-many-hypersegregated-metros-as-it-did-in-1970/393743.

3. *State of Ohio v. Michael Brelo* (Cuyahoga County Court of Common Pleas, May 23, 2015).

4. Lawrence Weschler, *Vermeer in Bosnia* (New York: Vintage Books, 2005), 23–24.

# Index

# About the Author

KYLE SWENSON is a reporter for *The Washington Post*. A finalist for the Livingston Award for Young Journalists, he is also the recipient of the Society of Professional Journalists' Sigma Delta Chi Award for Feature Reporting. His work has appeared in *The Village Voice*, *The New Republic*, and *Longreads*. A graduate of Kenyon College, he currently lives in Washington, D.C.